BARRY SCRAPYARD

THE PRESERVATION MIRACLE

Alan Warren

BARRY SCRAPYARD

THE PRESERVATION MIRACLE

DAVID & CHARLES

(Previous page) In October 1981 former Somerset & Dorset 2-8-0 No 13809 passes through Edale and heads for Manchester with the *Wyvern Express*. (*Graham Wignall*)

Some of the material in this book first appeared in *Rescued From Barry*, but that material has been completely revised and updated.

British Library Cataloguing in Publication Data

Warren, Alan, *1953–*
 Barry scrapyard : the preservation miracle.
 – Rev. and updated
 1. Woodham, Brothers 2. Locomotives –
Wales – Barry (South Glamorgan)
 I. Title II. Warren, Alan, *1953–*
Rescued from Barry
 625.2′61′0941 TJ603.4.G7

ISBN 0-7173-9209-3

Typeset by Typesetters (Birmingham) Ltd,
Smethwick, West Midlands
and printed in Great Britain
by Butler & Tanner, Frome and London,
for David & Charles
Brunel House Newton Abbot Devon

CONTENTS

FOREWORD

Enough has been written about railways, tracing their history from the early horse-drawn lines to the latest and most modern developments, to fill several rooms of book shelves as any visitor to the Clinker, Garnett and Transport Trust Collections at Brunel University can testify. Despite this, I have felt for a long time that there was a large gap waiting to be filled, namely the history of the preservation of the artefacts and relics of those railways so otherwise fully chronicled in railway literature.

The joy of this book is that it takes the first step in filling that gap by linking both the past and the present. Indeed I like to believe that the determination and dedication of the early railway pioneers is reflected by the resilience of the preservationists today. Certainly this can be no truer than of those involved in the operation which became widely known as 'Barry Rescue'.

As someone actively involved at the sharp end of railway preservation, I can fully appreciate the daunting task which faced so many of the purchasers of the rusting hulks collecting at Dai Woodham's scrapyard at Barry. The fact that they not only raised the funds to acquire and transport so many locomotives but also succeeded in breathing life – or at least steam – back into them is a tribute in itself. There were plenty of those, supposedly in the know, who said it couldn't be done. Certainly there were cases where I thought that rescue was impossible and I am delighted that for many of them I have been proved wrong.

The fact that the author has himself been active in railway preservation for many years no doubt assisted in the sympathetic account of the activities of the various groups, as well as in his extensive research into the history of individual locomotives. My hope is that your interest will be so aroused by the pages that follow that you will go and visit at least one of the rescued engines – with this book in your hand for reference, of course! Offer your encouragement, support, etc., but most of all express your appreciation. A little can go a long way. It may be that it will be your interest thus shown which will provide the necessary impetus to start, continue or complete restoration or merely to maintain an engine in its pristine condition. If Alan Warren's work sparks off only one such initiative, he will indeed have done a service for us all.

In the last century Britain pioneered the development of railways throughout the world as I was forcibly reminded by recent visits to the excellent Dutch Railway Museum in Utrecht and the Smithsonian in Washington. I believe that we continue to lead the way in railway preservation and this book provides some useful lessons from which we can all benefit.

In the meantime I commend this book to you as an authoritative record of a story that continues to exercise its fascination over all those who have been excited by a whiff of steam.

DAVID MORGAN
Chairman, Association of
Railway Preservation Societies

A general view of Woodham's yard in November 1968 while at its peak. Only one locomotive had left by this date and there was no sign of the mass exodus to come . . . (*Steve Worrall collection*)

After less than sixteen months on the scraplines 0-6-0T No 47298 is already showing signs of neglect as rust begins to eat away at its platework. Standing silently at Barry in November 1968 this Jinty had to wait another six years for rescue. (*Steve Worrall collection*)

INTRODUCTION

At last it is all over. The fate of every one of the Barry locomotives has now been determined, thus bringing to an end an episode unique to the railway preservation movement that has lasted for almost 20 years following the departure of ex-LMS 4F 0-6-0 No 43924 to the Keighley and Worth Valley Railway in September 1968.

During those 20 years much has been written about Barry and the frequently heated controversy it aroused as to whether there was any need to preserve yet more Bulleid Pacifics or Stanier Black Fives. Most of these arguments have little relevance now although of course it could be many years before some of the locomotives rescued during the latter stages of Barry's existence are returned to steam. In fact it is almost certain that a few groups or individuals will find the task of restoring a 90 ton hulk of scrap metal too much for their sometimes inadequate financial and physical resources. Should this unfortunate situation ever occur, what will happen to the engine concerned? Hopefully someone else will step in with the necessary cash and facilities to continue the task of rebuilding but it is not beyond the bounds of possibility that one of the ex-Barry locomotives could be sold for scrap for the second time to pay off creditors or satisfy the demands of a worried bank manager. At least let us hope that any engine which suffers this indignity is not cut up indiscriminately but carefully dismantled instead so that its major components such as boiler, wheels, cylinder castings etc can be used to restore a more fortunate member of the same class. I personally hope this predicament will never arise but no one involved in railway preservation should become too complacent about the monumental task that lies ahead to rebuild and maintain in service the incredibly large number of steam locomotives currently 'preserved' in this country.

While acknowledging the point this book nevertheless takes a positive attitude to the railway miracle that emanated from the rather unlikely setting of Barry in South Glamorgan. Accordingly it only briefly deals with the origins of the scrapyard and its continued existence over such an unusually long period so as to concentrate more on the 213 locomotives that somehow managed to survive the terrible fate that was met by so many thousands of their contemporaries during the run down of steam traction on British Railways. Consequently the aim has been to give an individual profile of every one of the locomotives that escaped the cutter's torch at this aptly named 'graveyard by the sea.' This has been achieved by splitting each one's story into three main sections. The first provides brief historical details of the particular class involved and any other interesting related facts. It is not intended to be a complete account of the class development as there are many books available which cover this subject in much greater depth. The second section attempts to portray the range of duties carried out by the locomotive concerned. Allocations are quoted together with examples of the sort of workings it would have appeared on, including any special or unusual trains that were recorded in the railway press at the time. Of course, locomotive rosters are extremely complicated affairs and in the space available it is quite impossible to list every route that would have been worked but those quoted should give a reasonable indication of the sort of trains dealt with. The final section tells of the fate that has befallen each locomotive since purchase from Barry. Once again this has been deliberately left brief as most readers will be aware of the latest situation regarding any particular engine by the informative notes and news section of the monthly railway magazines.

The locomotives are listed in the order they left Barry rather than being grouped together into classes. Not only does this add extra interest to the whole story but it will also help illustrate the contrasting popularity of some classes with preservationists – for example 92 other locomotives had already departed from South Wales before the first of the extremely successful BR Standard Class 9F

(*Above*) Spring Gala Weekend on the Severn Valley Railway. GWR 2-6-2T No 4566 hurries its 3-coach rake of 'blood and custard' Mark 1s along the Severn Valley line near Arley on 12 April 1987 while working the Bewdley to Highley shuttle service. (*B. Sharpe*)

Safe! U Class Mogul No 31618 has been set aside from the other locomotives at Barry in November 1968 while its new owners arrange transport to Kent. Restoration of an ex-Barry engine at this time was a comparatively easy task, No 31618 being successfully resteamed in May 1974. (*Steve Worrall collection*)

It is October 1979 and Standard Class 5 4-6-0 No 73082 *Camelot* bids farewell to its scrapyard surroundings of the previous thirteen years. Following a lengthy loading operation which involved removal of the front bogie, Mike Lawrence's low-loader is ready to leave Barry on a three-day journey to the Bluebell Railway where restoration of the locomotive is now under way. (*Steve Worrall*)

(*Opposite, above*) The attractive lines of Maunsell's U class are clearly evident as No 1618 runs round its train at Sheffield Park in May 1979. For a while in 1987 this 2-6-0 ran without its smoke deflectors, altering its overall appearance quite markedly. (*Graham Wignall*)

(*Opposite, below*) The one that started it all. 4F 0-6-0 No 43924 leaves Oakworth on the Keighley and Worth Valley Railway with an Oxenhope bound train during the summer of 1979. Initially restored as LMS No 3924 this engine ran in early British Railways livery from 1976 to 1983. (*David C. Rodgers*)

2-10-0s was purchased! Also listed for the sake of completeness are those engines acquired purely as a source of spares, for although one or two of them have already been dismantled most can still be seen waiting their turn tucked away in a quiet siding somewhere. The sequential listing also serves another purpose for those readers wishing to locate a specific locomotive – by referring to the summary at the rear of the book the order of departure for each engine is given so that its place in the main text can easily be traced.

This revised edition continues where the original book left off in August 1983 and thus completes the Barry story by giving the individual histories of the 53 additional locomotives whose fate had then yet to be decided. At the same time the opportunity has been taken to update the original text to include the numerous transferals from one preservation site to another that several of the ex-Barry locomotives have undergone during the past few years. In one or two instances the 'historical' part of the text has also been re-written to include additional information brought to my attention since the first edition; in most cases this has been due to those kind enthusiasts who took the trouble to write to me and share the results of their researches into the history of their own favourite locomotive.

Hopefully this new edition will stimulate further interest into the phenomenon of Barry and its scrapyard for although the purchase of the last locomotive has seen the end of one chapter it really marks the beginning of a new period in British railway preservation. The contrasting pro-Barry and anti-Barry factions can now stop arguing over the fate of the various locomotives. The fact is that 213 of them, all of which were at one time literally knocking on death's door during their enforced exile in South Wales, have been saved from the melting pots of the steelworks and given a second chance to perform again the duties for which they were originally designed. Our energies should now be directed to ensure that this treasure trove of steam railway heritage, once almost lost, is maintained for future generations to enjoy. With this objective in mind I should state that, like the first edition, a proportion of the royalties from this book will be used towards the restoration of one of the Barry survivors.

ALAN WARREN
Sawston
Cambridge

In the Beginning

The 1955 British Railways Modernisation Plan is a convenient point at which to begin an outline of the circumstances leading up to the incredible chain of events behind the Barry story. In an attempt to solve the problem of post-war operating inefficiencies and the discontent of its workforce with an increasingly dirty and out of date working environment BR proposed the replacement of more than 16,000 steam locomotives with alternative forms of traction. Obviously such a fundamental change in direction was going to take time to implement and at first progress was limited to the replacement of those older steam designs employed on shunting and light branch duties. This was because suitable diesel shunting locomotives and the first generation of diesel multiple units were already available for traffic while a successful fleet of large main line engines had still to be designed and constructed.

By 1958 a re-appraisal by the British Transport Commission of the 1955 plan resulted in the decision to accelerate the disposal of the steam fleet, despite the fact that many of the BR Standard Class 9F 2-10-0s had still to be built. This far-reaching decision soon led to large groups of condemned locomotives arriving at the major BR works for cutting up – frequently the yards at the works concerned could not cope with the storage of such an enormous quantity of engines and consequently dumps of withdrawn locomotives began to appear in adjacent sidings or in one or two cases on nearby closed branch lines. Within a very short time the rate of withdrawals was outstripping the capacity of the main works to dispose of them and finding adequate accommodation for all these engines had become something of a problem for the railway authorities, particularly at Swindon Works where the infamous 'C' shop and its associated 'Dump' were all but bursting at the seams.

Something had to be done urgently and so BR took the unprecedented step of beginning talks with the scrap metal industry, a series of discussions that eventually opened the doors for private contractors to take part in the wholesale destruction of this country's stock of steam locomotives. Perhaps because its needs were most pressing the Western was the first region to commence sales and with one of the greatest ironies imaginable its maiden customer just happened to be a certain Woodham Brothers of Barry Docks. The locomotives concerned in this first sale were four ex-GWR Moguls Nos 5312, 5360, 5392 and 5397, together with solitary 2-6-2T No 3170, the last surviving example of the 3150 class. Following purchase by Woodhams all five engines were removed from Swindon Dump and made ready for their journey to South Wales, the four 2-6-0s travelling down on 25 March 1959 while No 3170 followed a week later. Little could anybody have realised at the time just how significant an effect this seemingly unimportant event was to have on the development of railway preservation in this country.

The origin of Woodham Brothers can be traced back to just after the turn of the century when they traded as a dock porterage concern at Cardiff, transporting stores and similar commodities between the chandler's premises and the large number of ships that were berthed at the docks while loading and unloading their cargoes. Later these operations expanded to the port of Barry, the sort of items handled embracing timber, oil, ropes, lamps and similar merchandise. Subsequently the firm became involved in the road haulage business including the transport, breaking and recovery of scrap materials, an activity that was eventually to lead them into the railway arena during 1957 as dismantlers of wagons made redundant by the 1955 BR Modernisation Plan. Around this time the South Wales steel industry was extremely buoyant with many major developments taking place such as the construction of the new works at Llanwern near Newport as well as the expansion and modernisation of the facilities at Margam near Port Talbot. Like many other firms in the area

(*Opposite, above*) Although not to everyone's taste 4-6-0 No 7819 *Hinton Manor* looks extremely smart in its lined BR black livery while working a midweek service on the Severn Valley Railway near Bewdley in September 1985. (*B. Sharpe*)

(*Opposite, below*) The LMS 8F 2-8-0s were rarely seen this clean during their days in BR ownership but No 48431 still makes a fine sight as it is prepared for another day's work at Haworth on the Keighley and Worth Valley Railway in August 1986. (*David C. Rodgers*)

Having spent most of its time in preservation in Southern Railway green livery, S15 4-6-0 No 841 has now been repainted in black and is seen here leaving Goathland with a train for Pickering on the North Yorkshire Moors Railway on 20 April 1987. (*David C. Rodgers*)

Great Western interloper in Yorkshire. Making a guest appearance on the K and WVR, 2-6-2T No 5572 storms out of Keighley with one of the special trains it handled during their Easter 1987 Enthusiasts Weekend. (*David C. Rodgers*)

The scenic attractions of the Severn Valley Railway are very obvious in this view of *Hinton Manor* crossing the Victoria Bridge at Arley with a late season train in October 1985. (*David C. Rodgers*)

Woodhams could see that substantial profits were to be made from processing scrap metal into the sizes required to fit the pans at the steelworks.

As recounted earlier the first steam locomotives arrived at Barry for processing in 1959 and although the numbers dealt with were comparatively small at this stage, the scale of Woodhams' activities increased considerably between November 1960 and April 1961 with the acquisition of around 40 locomotives from Swindon. Most, but not all, of these engines were broken up soon after arrival on a short siding at the rear of Barry Works but as the number of engines being purchased increased so additional storage was needed and consequently locomotives were stabled on the low-level sidings adjacent to the oil terminal and then on further sidings built on the site of the former West Pond which had been filled in as part of a land reclamation scheme. By early 1964 space was very much at a premium again and so another dump of condemned locomotives was begun in sidings on the higher level adjacent to Barry Works. The procurement of this land was timely for by mid-1964 Woodhams had started to purchase locomotives from the Southern Region, increasing the total number of stored engines by the year end to 110.

1965 proved to be an eventful year for Barry because although 28 locomotives were dismantled in the first six months further cutting virtually ceased from the autumn onwards and the scrapmen concentrated instead on breaking up yet more freight wagons and brake vans. This change of emphasis was partly due to a slight fall in demand for scrap steel but was also due to the practical difficulty of breaking locomotives when compared with the much simpler task of taking wagons apart. Despite this apparent lack of interest Woodhams continued to purchase further locomotives for another three years, many of these being representatives of the modern BR Standard designs. When the official end of steam on BR came in August 1968, the yard contained well in excess of 200 condemned locomotives.

Even at this late stage having been purchased by what was to become probably one of the world's best known scrapyards was not necessarily a guarantee of salvation. Although the dismantling of rolling stock and other railway orientated scrap material kept Woodham's employees occupied for many years, from time to time the supply of wagons would temporarily dry up. On the fortunately few occasions that this did actually happen eight locomotives were put to the torch; two diesels No D600 and D8206 went in 1970, Standard Class 4 No 76080 went next in April 1972 and Collett 2-8-0 No 3817 followed in March 1973. In the summer of 1980 the remaining two diesels, Nos D601 and D6122 were quickly cut up followed by 2-6-2T No 4156 and then finally Standard Class 9 No 92085 in July. Considering the frequent deadlines given by Woodhams as to when the cutting up of unreserved locomotives was to recommence (1984 in particular being taken very seriously by many enthusiasts 'in the know') we must be extremely grateful that it was never necessary to carry the threat out.

In the first edition of this book Dai Woodham wrote about his feelings towards railways and railway preservation in general. He said 'I remember with affection the old railway companies, the Taff Vale and the Barry Railway for instance (by then part of the GWR), both busily bringing coal to what was then a very busy Barry Docks, but the world is changing all the time, not least at Barry. For preservation and the preservationists to survive they must continue to recognise changes and adapt to them whilst still retaining what perhaps I should call the "solidness" of a bygone era. My

No 80151 spent the months after withdrawal stored at both Eastleigh and Salisbury sheds before being delivered to Woodhams in October 1967. Sister locomotive No 80016 also visible in this August 1967 shot at Salisbury was not so lucky, being cut up at Birds of Risca in February of the following year. (*Mike Goodfield*)

A familiar sight throughout the dying years of steam in the 1960s as Hymek diesel-hydraulic No D7074 tows a sad convoy of four withdrawn locomotives past Filton Junction, Bristol, on their way to a South Wales scrapyard. (*Mike Goodfield*)

Although designed for short haul heavy freight traffic in South Wales, 2-8-0T No 5224 does not look out of place at the head of an 8-coach passenger train on the Great Central Railway in Leicestershire. (*Graham Wignall*)

Transferred from the Torbay and Dartmouth Railway the previous year, Standard Class 4 2-6-4T No 80064 heads the 17.00 Sheffield Park to Horsted Keynes near Freshfield Halt on the Bluebell Railway on 22 September 1985. (*Brian Denton*)

N Class 2-6-0 No 31874 enters Alresford cutting on the Mid-Hants Railway with the 14.38 Medstead to Alresford on 26 April 1987. (*David C. Warwick*)

(*Opposite, above*) A season of excursions on the 'North and West' route, to be known as the Welsh Marches Express, was announced in early 1981 with steam haulage over the Shrewsbury to Newport section. On 14 February 1981, No 4930 *Hagley Hall* is obviously going well with the southbound train at Nantyderry, just north of Pontypool Road. (*Graham Wignall*)

(*Opposite, below*) Making its first main line run since restoration ex-S & D 2-8-0 No 13809 passes Dringhouses Yard, York on its way to Sheffield with the return leg of an enthusiasts' special on 2 May 1981. (*Graham Wignall*)

involvement in railway preservation (which was not planned) has been an experience, but it has created many headaches over the years, so much so that I doubt if I would ever do it again . . . It has however provided pleasure for those who I call "genuine" preservationists, and so has probably been worthwhile.' At other times Dai Woodham has been quoted as saying the whole affair was worse than a nightmare. He tells of the problems with theft, telephone calls from the police to his home at all hours of the night followed by the subsequent court appearances. At the same time he has had to cope with frequent quarrelling between railway societies as well as handling the hundreds of letters and phone calls from enthusiasts and the public who wanted to buy engines, look at engines, photograph engines and so on. In fact as a teenager I remember writing to Dai back in 1968 asking for permission to walk around his scrapyard. It took me ages to compile the letter and I then drafted it out in my best handwriting so as to impress. The letter was returned in slightly over a week with just four words written across it – PERMISSION GRANTED. NO PILFERING!

As discussed previously Dai Woodham's decision in 1965 to delay cutting the steam locomotives was made purely for practical reasons and despite what many sentimentalists may think his attitude towards the railway preservation societies did not really come into it. Even so he does confess a respect for what most of them are trying to do, although being a businessman all locomotives have been sold for their equivalent scrap value, not a pound more or a pound less. A price was set and there was no haggling! Whichever way one looks at it the existence of Barry scrapyard has been nothing short of a miracle and surely all railway enthusiasts must agree just how fortunate we have been to have had the opportunity of saving more than 200 locomotives written off by BR as so much scrap metal. A large number of our private railways would be extremely short of motive power if not for Barry – imagine the Mid-Hants Railway for example without its superb collection of ex-Southern steam designs; imagine the Severn Valley Railway without its wide range of ex-GWR and BR locomotives; imagine the BR main line scene without *Leander, City of Wells, Drysllwyn Castle* . . .

In the 1987 New Year's Honours List, Dai Woodham was awarded the MBE. He denies suggestions that it was because of his services to railway preservation and more realistically points at his involvement with the development and creation of jobs in the docks area over a 45 year period. Even so he does admit that the engines aspect may have helped! With a road in Barry also named after him it is unlikely that Dai Woodham's contribution to this town and its 44,000 population will be forgotten for a long while.

Getting the Locomotive out

Most of the early departures from Barry were carried out by rail, this being an obvious choice when so many of the preservation sites concerned had direct rail access with BR, the Great Western Society at Didcot and the Severn Valley Railway at Kidderminster being obvious examples.

Before a move could be arranged however the locomotive had to undergo careful preparation to make sure it was fit to travel. Obviously an engine that had stood for any length of time would have lost the oil from its bearing surfaces and any movement was likely to cause unnecessary but expensive damage, just as a lengthy towing with oil contaminated by dirt and rainwater would normally result in scored journals and hot axleboxes. Following a check over by qualified inspectors from BR the locomotive involved would be shunted out of its gloomy scrapyard surroundings into the adjacent departure sidings to await collection by a BR diesel.

Generally speaking great care was taken in preparing an engine in the manner described for what without doubt was to be its longest journey in many years but even so problems could and did occur. When ex-GWR Castle No 5080 *Defiant*, 2-6-2T No 4160 and 0-6-2T No 5637 were travelling from Barry to the Birmingham Railway Museum at Tyseley during August 1974 the latter engine developed a hot axle box en-route and had to be examined at Gloucester shed. Interestingly the repairs were undertaken by maintenance staff who remembered working on the class during BR days.

All the locomotives to leave Barry by rail either went in their own right as a special train or else

This April 1969 view of just a small part of Woodham's Yard gives an indication of the amazing sight to greet those enthusiasts who made the pilgrimage down to Barry. As can be seen all the non-ferrous items such as whistles, brass safety valve bonnets and the like have been removed but most of the engines are still basically complete. (*Andrew Ingram*)

were coupled into a normal service freight train. In both cases maximum speed was normally limited to around 15mph (although this was exceeded on occasions!) and very often BR would permit one or more persons to ride on the footplate as 'caretaker', a useful provision in that it allowed bearings to be topped up with oil during the very frequent stops made in loops and sidings to allow other trains to pass. Even though the thought of riding on the footplate may sound appealing to most steam enthusiasts, I am not sure the hardy souls who travelled with Standard Class 5 No 73129 on its journey from South Wales to Derby Works in the winter of 1973 would agree with you. The entire trip was made with the engine hauled tender first and one or two of the crew almost succumbed to frostbite during the long journey north!

As time passed BR obviously became more concerned about the practical difficulties of towing derelict locomotives around their system while they were trying to operate a fast commercial service. At the very least hot axleboxes could lead to serious delays on the rail network as a whole, and so from summer 1976 onwards, all removals from Barry were carried out by private road hauliers. The somewhat incongruous sight of an 80 ton steam locomotive balanced precariously on the back of a low loader and travelling at 25 mph along one of our motorways has become a surprisingly common occurrence over the past 12 years or so.

However simple an operation it may seem, the transporting of steam engines by road to all corners of the country calls for a great deal of careful planning and execution. The route taken by these 'abnormal loads' could well cause problems and most hauliers take account of this when calculating

(*Opposite, above*) To mark the 75th Anniversary of the opening of Old Oak Common, British Rail Western Region arranged a series of steam shuttle trains from Paddington to carry passengers to the depot open day on 20 September 1981. Locomotives employed were No 92220 *Evening Star* and No 5051 *Drysllwyn Castle*, running 'pull and push' fashion and the latter engine is seen here alongside an HST at Westbourne Park. (*Graham Wignall*)

(*Opposite, below*) An immaculate *Duke of Gloucester* and equally clean Class 40 No 40106 run round their train at Rothley during Road/Rail 87 weekend on the Great Central Railway. Two generations of main line express motive power both considered redundant by BR. (*Graham Wignall*)

U Class No 31806 is seen working hard near Bishops Sutton with the 10.58 Alresford to Alton on 21 June 1987. (*David C. Warwick*)

Perhaps one of the most widely travelled of all the ex-Barry locomotives, No 34092 *City of Wells* crosses Eskmills viaduct with the return Sellafield Sightseer excursion on 2 May 1987. (*B. Sharpe*)

The Great Western 150th Anniversary celebrations in 1985 produced this impressive display of motive power at the Didcot Railway Centre during May. From right to left 0-6-0PT No 3738, Dukedog No 3217 (from the Bluebell Railway), 4-6-0 No 5051 *Drysllwyn Castle*, 0-6-2T No 6619 (from the NYMR) and 0-6-0PT No 9466 (from the Buckinghamshire Railway Centre) complete the line up. Of all these locomotives, the Dukedog was the only one not to have spent part of its life in exile at Barry. (*Graham Wignall*)

The effects of 10 years exposure to the ravages of sea air and the attention of so called enthusiasts have reduced this unidentified 28XX 2-8-0 to a pathetic looking hulk as it waits its turn for rescue at Barry in July 1975. (*Graham Scott-Lowe*)

Understandably a favourite place for photographers, 2-8-0T No 5239 *Goliath* passes the packed beach at Goodrington Sands with a Paignton to Kingswear train. (*Graham Wignall*)

Standard Class 4 2-6-0 No 76017 impatiently blows off in Ropley Yard on 6 April 1985. Two months later it was named *Hermes* as a tribute to the Royal Navy aircraft carrier which served in the Falklands campaign. (*David C. Rodgers*)

Standard Class 4 4-6-0 No 75069 leaves a crowded Bewdley station with the 12.10 Bridgnorth to Kidderminster service on 13 October 1985. (*David C. Rodgers*)

(*Opposite, above*) Double-headed power on the Keighley and Worth Valley Railway. Standard Class 4 4-6-0 No 75078 and USA 2-8-0 No 5820, known affectionately as *Big Jim*, rattle the foundations of Oakworth station as they pass through on their way to Oxenhope. (*Graham Wignall*)

(*Opposite, below*) Positively gleaming in the early morning sunshine at Loughborough in May 1987, No 6990 *Witherslack Hall* takes water during preparations for the day ahead on the Great Central Railway. (*B. Sharpe*)

their price. The axle weights and wheelbase of the road vehicle used may also be critical as regards bridges etc and the haulier is responsible for notifying the police and county surveyors before setting off, advising them of his exact itinerary. Frequently low bridges also cause difficulties but the journey of Battle of Britain 4-6-2 No 34070 *Manston* from Barry to Kent in May 1983 must have been unique in this respect – routed via the Dartford Tunnel this Pacific's appearance in the Tunnel itself was a strange sight to behold, clearing the massive air vents by just a few inches. Obviously good homework by the haulier concerned paid off here; a small mistake and the headlines in the following day's newspapers about a steam locomotive getting stuck in the Dartford Tunnel would have been only too predictable!

Clearly such slow moving loads, often taking 2 or 3 days to complete their journeys, could cause inevitable delays to other road users; the movement of West Country No 34105 *Swanage* to the Mid-Hants Railway at Easter 1978 led to a large tailback to Bank Holiday traffic on the A33, while Standard 9F No 92240's delivery to the Bluebell Railway blocked Cuckfield High Street for almost half a hour. Not exactly the best way to promote the cause of railway preservation to the general public! Although many different private hauliers have been involved in moving the Barry locomotives perhaps the best known of them all is Mike Lawrence of Burnham-on-Sea in Somerset. There can be few preservation sites left in Britain that have not yet been graced with a visit from one of his low loaders.

The removal of so many locomotives from the yard since 1968 has frequently provided some delightful stories, many of which will probably become part of the folk lore surrounding Barry. Perhaps one of the most well known relates to West Country No 34027 *Taw Valley* which was initially dragged from the scrapyard in March 1980, one of its pony wheels seizing up in protest. After efforts to load it on the transporter failed, No 34027 was eventually pushed on by a Class 08 shunter enabling it to leave Woodhams for the first time. A short while after setting off from Barry tyre friction on the low loader meant that the journey had to be abandoned and the convoy returned with the Pacific being winched back on to the sidings at Barry. Thus *Taw Valley* earned the dubious distinction of being the last locomotive to enter Woodhams scrapyard as well as being the only one to have entered it twice. Eventually a substitute low loader man enough for the job was located and the engine finally left on its way north some three weeks later. Another tale concerns the problem faced by the new owners of LMS 0-6-0 No 44123 when told by Woodhams that it would be several months before their locomotive could be shunted out of the scraplines in the normal way. Refusing to be defeated they obtained some heavy duty traversing jacks and with the help of a lot of muscle power a 10 feet 'sideways shunt' was effected, allowing the engine to leave for its temporary home on the Mid-Hants Railway at the end of 1981. Even when your locomotive had left the scrapyard there was no guarantee that your troubles were over – the hauliers transporting Black Five 4-6-0 No 45163 to Hull in January 1987 met blizzard conditions on the way and were forced to abandon the engine in the Corley Service Area on the M6 motorway until the weather improved.

With transport costs often running into several thousand pounds many groups have approached private industry to seek sponsorship of the move from Barry. These appeals have met with varying degrees of success but some of the major sponsors have included the Midland Bank, Wiggins Teape, Agfa Gevaert, Laminated Profiles of Alton and many other equally generous organisations. One of the more recent departures from Barry was paid for by Beatties, the well known London based toy and model company – in agreeing to pay for the £2000 low loader move from South Wales to Lancashire, 9F No 92207 was suitably adorned with large advertisement hoardings throughout its long journey and as part of the sponsorship agreement these remained attached to the locomotive for twelve months. The award for the wittiest piece of sponsorship must go to Tate & Lyle who paid for the removal of Merchant Navy No 35010 *Blue Star*; the banner affixed to the locomotive simply read 'Tate & Lyle Cane Sugar – More Power To Your Engine'! Nevertheless the amount of private money put into railway preservation in this way must have reached a significant total by now and the importance of this should not be underestimated.

Dai Woodham looks pleased as he receives yet another cheque! Brian Cooke hands over all his worldly possessions for Standard Class 4 No 75014. On the right is fellow shareholder, Bert Hitchen, no stranger to Dai's office, for Bert had already purchased No 34027 *Taw Valley*. On the left is Tony Bainbridge who, with his group, had previously bought Class 9F No 92134. The date is 30 December 1980. (*Brian Cooke*)

The Rush to Buy

During the mid-1960s it was becoming obvious to most enthusiasts that Woodham's premises at Barry was no ordinary scrapyard. Almost every month the journals of several respected organisations such as the Stephenson Locomotive Society and the Railway Correspondence and Travel Society included comprehensive lists of the ever growing collection of steam locomotives being assembled in the Barry Docks area. However, perhaps the prize for understatement should go to the February 1966 issue of *The Railway Magazine* whose Locomotive Notes section confidently stated that 'the many withdrawn engines at Barry look as if they will be in store for a long time, as the facilities for their disposal have been outstripped by the many arrivals there over the last few years'. If only they had known!

One of the many contract conditions entered into between the private scrapyards and British

The attractive lines of the BR Standard Class 4 2-6-4T design are clearly shown as No 80079 leaves Highley for Bewdley on 6 September 1980. (*David C. Rodgers*)

Two ex-Barry locomotives returned to the GW main line in the summer of 1985. No 5051 *Drysllwyn Castle* and No 4930 *Hagley Hall* pass Whiteball with the Great Western Limited special from Bristol to Plymouth on 7 July 1985. (*David C. Rodgers*)

(*Opposite, above*) Complete with brass bell mounted above the front buffer beam Ivatt 2-6-0 No 46521 works a special train on the Severn Valley Railway on 12 September 1981. (*Brian Denton*)

(*Opposite, below*) The impassioned plea painted on the smokebox door of No 48305 has at last been answered following its unloading at Quorn on the GCR in December 1985. Many years of hard work lie ahead before this once proud locomotive will run again. (*Graham Wignall*)

Smartened up for its long journey from Barry to Lancashire and complete with placard advertising the name of the organisation which sponsored the cost of its movement from South Wales, No 92207 *Morning Star* is ready to be unloaded at its new home on the East Lancashire Railway on 29 October 1986. (*Richard Fox*)

Railways provided that a locomotive purchased for scrap could not be resold for anything other than that. This was primarily to stop less scrupulous dealers buying an engine at scrap value and then selling it on at a highly inflated price to a private railway or preservation society. Accordingly before any of the occupants of Barry could be purchased for preservation, Woodham Brothers had to obtain special dispensation from BR to allow the sale to go ahead. This strange situation existed for a short while but the requirement appears to have been allowed to lapse as time passed.

A small advertisement in the July 1968 issue of *The Railway Magazine* announced the first of countless fund raising schemes that were launched to save the locomotives at Barry. The wording of the advert was quite simple. '43924 for Haworth! The Midland 4F Preservation Society requires £2,500 for the purchase and restoration of this loco for use on the Keighley and Worth Valley Railway, Yorkshire. Donations please to . . . Note: if the fund does not reach the required target, the donations will be forwarded to the K & WVR for purchase of other rolling stock.' Fortunately the doubts expressed in the last sentence were unfounded and following the payment of a £1,000 deposit the proud owners took delivery of their rusty but still largely complete 48 year old locomotive. The movement of this engine from the Docks area caused quite an upheaval at the time owing to its position near the end of one of the long lines of locomotives. Consequently all the engines which were standing in front of it had to be shunted elsewhere into alternative sidings, a situation that was to happen many times again over the ensuing 20 years. By September 1968 everything was ready for No 43924's journey northwards and diesel hauled, it left on the 10th of that month travelling via Hereford on its way to Haworth for restoration. This now historic event was well recorded in the railway press of the time but what is not generally appreciated is that in the same month of No 43924's departure, several steam locomotives were still being delivered to Barry for cutting up, the last arrivals in the yard being Nos 48151, 48305, 61264 (DP 29), 76077, 76079, 76084 and 92212. Most of these had been stored for several months in nearby Cadoxton goods yard before making their ostensibly final journey into Barry Docks during September.

Throughout the life of the yard appeals to save the various locomotives have differed in both their method and manner. Although the vast majority of engines have been purchased as a result of advertisements placed in enthusiast magazines, several have been acquired outright by private individuals while one or two have even been bought for preservation with the help of the Local Authority representing the area in which the locomotive was eventually to be based. For example Standard Class 4 No 75079 was paid for by cash raised from proceeds of the Plymouth Council lottery and in recognition of their gesture the Plym Valley Railway intend to name the engine *City of Plymouth* when restoration is completed. Similarly the purchase of S15 No 30828 was helped with money from Eastleigh Council lottery – when the locomotive returned home in March 1981 it was given a full civic reception attended by several dignitaries including the Mayor and local Member of Parliament!

Many groups trying to buy locomotives soon realised that appealing to the public to send in the odd pound or two as a straight donation with nothing in return was not really the most successful way of accumulating the necessary finance. The Camelot Locomotive Society which was formed in 1974 to buy No 73082 from Barry was quoted a price of £4,500 by Woodhams; the usual trail of sales stands, raffles and appeals was then followed but although steady progress was made it soon became clear that it was not even approaching its target which, thanks to inflation etc, had increased by 1978 to £9,500. It was a case of trying to catch a rising price but only managing to run very hard just to stand still. However the engine was finally purchased, excluding the tender, for £8,100 in 1979 with the aid of loans from the bank and society committee members.

An alternative approach was needed and it soon became very much the vogue to offer part ownership in a particular locomotive by the sale of shares in amounts varying from £25 each up to £1,000 each; these could be purchased either by a single payment or by standing order instalments. Other benefits were also frequently offered including free limited edition prints and tickets on the first train to be hauled by the engine following rebuilding. The basic idea was to ensure that there was not only enough money to pay for the locomotive itself and subsequent transport costs but also sufficient to finance the complete task of restoration. This method appears to have been successful, bank managers in particular feeling much happier to make short term loans when they know a regular monthly income has already been guaranteed by standing order, and many enthusiasts in Britain (and possibly some abroad) can now claim to own part of this country's railway heritage.

As the total number of locomotives in the yard slowly began to reduce, it became clear that there was a need to coordinate the numerous enquiries made by prospective purchasers as to the availability of any particular locomotive for sale and from the late 1970s onwards it became the norm for Dai Woodham to pass on all such enquiries to the Barry Steam Locomotive Action Group, and later Barry Rescue, who maintained a reservation list on the remaining engines. The way this list worked can be simply explained as follows: – the first society or individual to express an interest became the 'main' reservation holder and was entitled to buy as and when it could; a subsequent group who wanted the same engine was added to the list as the 'second' reservation holder. However if another purchaser came along with the ability to buy the locomotive straight away and provided that a reasonable length of time had passed for the original reservation holders to gather together their funds, they were then given a time limit. The 'main' reservation holder could buy at any time during that period while the 'second' was also advised to be ready to purchase as soon as the end of the period was reached, assuming of course that the first was unable to complete the transaction. Should either of the two reservation holders not take up their options then the locomotive would become available for sale again.

Over the years several factors have influenced the amount each potential purchaser would have to find to become an owner of one of the Barry locomotives. Woodham Brothers have always kept a complete breakdown of the amount and different types of metal that each locomotive contained. By applying the current 'going rate' for steel or copper scrap to the weights known a realistic price was calculated and despite the numerous criticisms directed at him Dai Woodham maintains he has never sold an engine for anything more (or less!) than its existing scrap value.

The first few departures from Barry were obtained at what must seem today absolute bargain prices. The example of ex-LMS 0-6-0 No 43924 had already been mentioned while just a short time later *Drysllwyn Castle*, subsequently to become one of the privileged locomotives allowed to work over the BR main line, cost only £3,000. In 1971 it was still even possible to buy a Bulleid Pacific for around the same amount but these halcyon days could not last for ever and the sharp rise in inflation during the early 1970s saw prices climb rapidly, often outstripping many societies' efforts to raise the necessary funds. The introduction of Value Added Tax at 10% in 1973 (subsequently to increase to 15% in 1979) did not help matters either, while the deregulation of scrap metal prices around the same time pushed the costs beyond the reach of many would-be purchasers. In fact, there was a mini boom in locomotive sales from Woodhams just prior to this period and the acquisition of No 30506 by the Urie S15 Preservation Group illustrates the difficulty of the situation quite nicely. They bought their engine for £4,000 on 26 March 1973; just six days later and VAT etc would have increased the price to around £6,600. In fact when they purchased sister locomotive No 30499 in March 1980 it was to cost them slightly less than £10,000 and that did not include the tender which was to add another £3,000 to the overall price.

Not only has Mike Lawrence's familiar low loader been used for removing locomotives from Barry, it has also been involved in the transferring of certain engines from one preservation site to another. Here it is seen taking No 4160 from Tyseley to the Plym Valley Railway in May 1981. (*Jeff Nicholson*)

On an open day at Derby Works in 1973 No 47357 (16440), still in primer after rebuilding, stands on display with No 5690 *Leander*. (*Midland Railway Trust Ltd*)

In 1987, the final year of major purchases from the yard, the going rate (excluding VAT) for a cross section of those locomotives then still available was as follows: 28/38XX with tender – £9,000, 41XX – £6,000, 52XX – £6,500, 66XX – £5,750, 79XX with tender – £9,000, Black 5 or 8F without tender – £8,000, 80XXX – £9,500. Ironically a lessening in demand for scrap metal around this time meant that it was actually cheaper to purchase a locomotive in 1987 than in 1984!

During the negotiation period with Woodhams and even after the cheque had been handed over it rarely proved possible to undertake any serious restoration work in the confines of Barry yard. Most energy was expended in giving the locomotive a quick respectable coat of paint, greasing bearings and the like, removing parts likely to be 'acquired' by other groups, and general tidying up to prevent bits falling off during transit. Some groups even went as far as making up false chimneys, smokebox doors and replacement deflector plates to give the engine a little more dignity on the journey to its new home.

Over the two decades of Barry's existence the rate of removals fluctuated quite markedly, 1977 being particularly unusual in that only one locomotive, No 44422, was extricated from the yard. A listing of the number of departures for each year from 1968 onwards is given below:

1968 – 1	1973 – 18	1978 – 11	1983 – 7
1969 – 2	1974 – 19	1979 – 11	1984 – 10
1970 – 8	1975 – 14	1980 – 8	1985 – 9
1971 – 6	1976 – 8	1981 – 21½	1986 – 14½
1972 – 10	1977 – 1	1982 – 4	1987 – 10
			1988 – 20

TOTAL – 213

(The '½' shown against 1981 and 1986 represents the removal of the boiler and frames respectively of No 30825 during those years.)

Saved from Extinction

The importance of Barry scrapyard to the preservation cause has already been referred to elsewhere in this introduction but perhaps what is not generally realised is just how many different classes of British steam locomotive design would be extinct but for the existence of Barry and the efforts of those enthusiasts dedicated to retaining an important part of our railway history.

The locomotives and classes concerned can be summarised as follows:

Locomotive numbers	Class	Remarks
2885, 3802/3/14/22/45/50 3855/62	'2884'	Collett's 'improved' version of the earlier Churchward heavy freight 2-8-0.
4247/8/53/70/7	'4200'	Churchward's 2-8-0T design for heavy short haul mineral traffic.
5322/9303	'4300'	Churchward's 2-6-0 design of mixed traffic loco for secondary services.
4920/30/6/42/53/79/83 5900/52/67/72	'4900'	Collett's original Hall design as opposed to the later Modified Halls from 6959 onwards.
4110/15/21/41/4/50/60 5164/93/9	'5101'	Collett's development of the '3100' class with increased weight and other detail alterations.
5224/7/39	'5205'	Collett's development of the '4200' class with enlarged cylinder and other detail alterations.
7200/2/29	'7200'	1930s rebuild of the '4200' and '5205' classes.
30499, 30506	'S15'	Urie's design for LSWR mixed traffic duties.
30541	'Q'	Maunsell class 4F 0-6-0
30825/8/30/41/7	'S15'	Maunsell development of Urie 'S15' design.
31618/25/38, 31806	'U'	Maunsell's successful Mogul passenger engine.

31874	'N'	Maunsell mixed traffic design for the SECR.
42968	'5MT'	Stanier taper boiler design for secondary duties.
53808/9	'7F'	Fowler's heavy freight design for the Somerset and Dorset Joint Railway.
71000	'8P'	Riddle's unique express passenger locomotive.
76017/77/9/84	'4MT'	BR Standard design of mixed traffic 2-6-0s.
78018/9/22/59	'2MT'	BR Standard design for light duties.

Although critics of Barry can claim that some of the classes are now over-represented in preservation surely this is better than not having any at all? And who knows, in the future some of the duplicated locomotives may give up a few of their more important components to keep at least one member of the class in active service. Who will complain then?

The Ones That Got Away

Although it serves no real purpose other than to pass the time on a rainy day it is nevertheless still appealing to dwell a moment on the might-have-beens of Barry. For example how much better we would all feel if Woodhams had purchased a few A1s, a handful of Patriots, a couple of Clans, or any one of those many classes now unrepresented in preservation. Unfortunately they all too swiftly met their end at some other scrapyard, often within a day or so of arriving with a one-way ticket at their final destination. Every one of us probably has our own favourite engine that we wish had ended up at Barry but of course this is pure fantasy and in many ways helps us to realise much more the importance of Woodham's scrapyard.

Even so we must not forget that many locomotives *were* put to the torch at Barry, some with almost indecent haste, and although perhaps slightly outside the scope of a book dealing with the locomotives rescued from Woodhams, it is still worth taking a brief look at a few of the more interesting engines that only just missed their chance for survival, 'the ones that got away'.

(*Overleaf*) One of the magnificent sights made possible by the existence of Barry scrapyard. No 5051 *Drysllwyn Castle* and No 4930 *Hagley Hall* pass Horse Cove between Dawlish and Teignmouth with the Great Western Limited special of July 1985. (*Peter J. C. Skelton*)

Locomotive Nos	Remarks
0-6-0PT Nos 1367 & 1368 (scrapped by 1965)	Two of Collett's much photographed dock shunting tanks which saw service at Weymouth Docks and latterly on the former SR Wenford Bridge mineral branch.
2-6-2T No 3170 (scrapped by 1959)	The last survivor of Churchward's 3150 class (built 1907).
0-6-0PT Nos 5407, 5417 & 5422 (scrapped by 1965)	The only three of this 25 strong class of auto-fitted tanks to arrive at Woodhams. None of the class have been preserved.
2-6-2T No 6115 (scrapped by 1965)	Originally built for the London outer suburban services this was the only one of the class to be broken up in Woodham's yard.
0-6-0PT No 6406 (scrapped by 1961)	The only one of this large class to arrive at Barry. The three preserved examples were all purchased direct from BR.
0-6-0PT No 9499 (scrapped by 1965)	Built in 1955 and withdrawn in 1959 this engine had seen only slightly more than four years service with BR. (16 other members of this modern design met their end at Woodhams.)
4-6-2 Nos 34045 & 34094 (scrapped by 1965)	Two unfortunate Bulleid Pacifics that just did not survive long enough to be rescued.
2-6-4T No 80067 (scrapped by 1965)	The only one of 15 Standard 2-6-4Ts purchased by Woodhams that was actually broken up at Barry.
D600 & D601 (scrapped by 1980)	Two representatives of the original North British Locomotive Co Warship class. Only examples of the Swindon designed Warships still to survive.
D6122 (scrapped by 1980)	One of the unsuccessful North British Type 2 diesel hydraulic locomotives. None of the class now survive.
D8206 (scrapped by 1970)	An unusual purchase by Woodhams, but at least one example of this Class 15 design has been preserved.

It is also worth noting with regret that 10 members of the ex-GWR 45XX/55XX small prairie tanks were scrapped at Barry between 1961 and 1965. Fortunately 13 of their sisters were to survive the cutter's torch there.

Two ex-Barry locos renew their acquaintance on the main line. No 75069 and No 5690 *Leander* stretch their legs through Haresfield with the Swindon–Gloucester–Newport portion of the Red Dragon special train in June 1986. (*Peter J. C. Skelton*)

Tales of Barry

The very existence of Barry and the legend that has grown up around the eleventh hour rescue of its locomotives from the scraplines has given rise to numerous stories and anecdotes over the years. Many of these are humorous and provide a fascinating insight into the motivation behind the actions of the preservationists concerned but one or two have their more serious side and help illustrate the difficulties experienced by both Dai Woodham and the actual individuals charged with the task of rebuilding a near derelict locomotive. This brief collection of 'Tales of Barry' is in no particular order and although space prevents the inclusion of many stories surrounding Woodham's yard some of the more interesting ones have been recounted here. We can be certain that as time passes and as more locomotives are returned to steam, the legend of Barry will continue to grow and more tales unfold.

Hands Off!

In the early years of Barry any society purchasing a locomotive would try to obtain spares for their engine by carefully removing the parts from unreserved members of the same or similar class. Of course Woodhams were normally asked if this stripping could be carried out and permission was nearly always granted; at this stage it was preferable to see valuable spares saved rather than destroyed while the imminent cutting of the remaining engines was being threatened almost every year.

However, by the late 1970s a new phenomenon was being experienced at Barry, the unpleasant one of theft. Although local thieves and souvenir hunters accounted for many items going missing over the years they removed the parts they wanted without generally causing any great damage. But this was a new style of theft and on a much more serious scale – vital parts were now disappearing from the yard almost every weekend with total disregard as to whether the engines were reserved or even bought and paid for by their new owners. Some typical examples include Churchward 2-8-0 No 2807 which had its main driving wheel bearing stolen, an operation that would have involved jacking the locomotive up in full view of everyone. Similarly Standard 2-6-4T No 80150 had the front half of its smokebox cut off and taken along with the smokebox door while Bulleid Pacific No 34072 had the driving wheel springs severed and stolen. Perhaps the worst demonstration of all relates to another Bulleid Pacific which had its boiler washout plugs removed; as this could not be done in the normal way those responsible actually cut out the surrounding area of firebox with an oxy-acetylene torch causing inestimable damage. In addition to these examples there have been numerous thefts of axleboxes, springs and other suspension components which in many cases have caused derailments during shunting operations in the yard.

It is impossible to estimate the exact value of material stolen from Woodhams during the past 20 years but often the thoughtless action of one individual in carelessly removing a part worth just a few hundred pounds resulted in the group who eventually bought the engine receiving a bill approaching ten times as much just to put the damage right. On one occasion Dai Woodham was sent photographs by a preservation group showing other 'enthusiasts' stealing parts from engines; in fact the position got so bad that in 1981 a total ban was placed on weekend working parties in the yard. As a salutary reminder of the seriousness of the situation, the number of people fined and even jailed for thieving from Barry ran well into double figures.

Going Once, Going Twice
Although it has often proved an uphill struggle for many individuals to raise sufficient funds just to buy a locomotive from Barry, there are instances where one or two of the engines achieved the distinction of having been bought twice while still standing on Woodham's premises. In 1979 *Wootton Hall* was paid for by a member of the Quainton Railway Society but he unfortunately failed to agree terms with that society for its accommodation at Quainton Road. So without even having left the yard No 4979 was resold to Woodhams and it was to be another seven years before the Fleetwood Locomotive Centre finally came to *Wootton Hall's* rescue in early 1986.

A slightly different situation existed in regard to the double purchase of ex-GWR 4-6-0 No 6023 *King Edward II*. Long dubbed 'Project Impossible' because of the heavy cannibalisation that the engine had undergone during the previous 15 years, a process that had included having a section of the rear driving wheels torched off, the locomotive was finally purchased by the Barry Steam Locomotive Action Group amidst much scepticism in March 1982. While preparations were made for its removal to the Preston Park base of the Brighton Locomotive Works Project, BSLAG were approached by the Bristol Marketing Board about acquiring an interest in the King. Under the general role of fostering interest and involvement in the City of Bristol's promotional and tourism activities, the City's commercial institutions were being encouraged to support worthwhile local projects; for this particular project of rescuing a steam locomotive, the institution involved was the well known sherry company, Harveys. Following much soul searching and thoughtful negotiations it was agreed that BSLAG would sell No 6023 to Harveys who would take the engine to Bristol Temple Meads station and finance its restoration to full working order. So after having been considered by many enthusiasts as being a complete waste of time and money, *King Edward II* confounded everybody by actually being bought twice!

With Luck on their Side
Although the rebuilding of an ex-Barry locomotive demands a great deal of money, patience and skill, the restorers themselves always hope that a little luck will come their way to make life just that bit easier. This was certainly the case with the 45491 Group during the reconstruction of their Black Five; despite being faced with an incredibly long shopping list of missing parts several important

items came to light in sometimes strange circumstances. Requiring a steam dome cover they were rather pleased to learn that a man living near Peterborough had one in his garage as a souvenir from an unfortunate Stanier 8F that met its end at Cohen's scrapyard in Kettering, while even more welcome news came in 1981 when one group member miraculously traced a pair of Black Five connecting rods to a scrapyard in Lancaster where they had been lying for over 12 years. These once belonged to No 44897, one of the last steam engines withdrawn from Carnforth shed at the end of steam in August 1968; needless to say these rods were quickly purchased for the bargain price of only £100 the pair, a saving of many thousand pounds when compared with the cost of having a new pair cast and machined. Even the acquisition of their tender contained an element of luck for the 45491 Group; at the time of purchase of the engine in July 1981 they had to forgo buying a tender in order to pay for the road transportation up to Blackpool but in January the following year they went back to Woodhams to buy the only Stanier tender then left available for sale. This was a green liveried example from ex-LMS Jubilee No 45699 *Galatea* and as luck would have it the tyres were less than ¼″ worn from new, once again saving a good deal of money.

A similar tale of good fortune concerns Churchward 2-8-0 No 2857 on the Severn Valley Railway. Purchased by the 2857 Society in May 1974 this locomotive was resteamed in the autumn of 1979 and worked its first passenger train over the SVR early the following summer. However, luck was soon to run out, for bulged superheater flue tubes and a cracked cylinder block led to the engine being withdrawn almost immediately. It was a relatively simple task to renew the flue tubes but a cracked cylinder block was a much more serious matter; fortunately when Briton Ferry Steelworks at Neath in South Wales was being demolished a spare brand new cylinder block was amazingly found among a stack of redundant material. Following machining it was soon fitted on to No 2857 and the locomotive successfully entered service for the second time in August 1985, taking part in the GW150 celebrations just a few weeks later.

Whoops!

Despite the fact that railway accidents resulting in serious damage or even loss of life are thankfully very rare, at least three of the ex-Barry locomotives can claim to have been involved in just such unfortunate happenings.

The first incident concerned Somerset and Dorset 2-8-0 No 89 (later BR No 53809) back in November 1929 when it was four years old. At the head of the 3.25pm Evercreech Junction to Bath goods the footplate crew were overcome by fumes when passing through the notorious restricted bore of Combe Down Tunnel and the train ran away out of control, eventually crashing at over 50mph in Bath goods yard. Regrettably three railwaymen were killed and two others injured in the wreckage; as for the 2-8-0 itself, No 89 was sent to Derby Works for repair and soon returned to work again hauling heavy freight traffic over the Mendips.

The second accident involved LMS Crab No 2765 in February 1937 while it was working an overnight express freight from Manchester to London St Pancras. Travelling at speed it became derailed just outside West Hampstead station, tearing up the track for some distance with its train of box vans piled up in complete disarray behind it. Fortunately the engine embedded itself in the earth and remained upright ensuring there were no casualties but it still took the breakdown crane from Kentish Town a long while to clear up the mess!

The third mishap befell Standard Class 4 2-6-0 No 76017 in September 1954 after having been in traffic just fifteen months. Put in charge of the heavy 7 am Banbury to Southampton fast goods it ran away while travelling downhill near Whitchurch; passing right through a sand drag it was spectacularly derailed and fell down the embankment wedging itself in a group of trees. Eastleigh and Salisbury breakdown gangs attended the clearing operations and reopened the line the following day but the locomotive itself was not recovered until two weeks later. During restoration of the engine on the railway a slightly twisted pony truck, a boiler that did not fit quite right in the frames and a cracked chimney with a liner insert fitted, remained as testimony to 76017's adventure.

If At First You Don't Succeed . . .

As the only ex-LNER locomotive ever to have been bought by Dai Woodham, B1 4-6-0 No 61264 has always held a fascination for those who have followed the story of Barry scrapyard. Spending most of its working life based at Parkeston Quay in Essex, this B1 ended its days ignominiously as a stationary boiler at Colwick near Nottingham, having been renumbered 29 in the BR Departmental series. It was then subsequently intended to convert the engine into a snowplough at Derby Works but when this scheme was abandoned it was put on the tender list and sold off for scrap instead.

The Thompson B1 Locomotive Society took an interest in the remains of this engine during 1975 and obtained expert opinion as to its overall mechanical condition and in particular the state of the boiler and firebox. Considering that all the non-ferrous parts and cab fittings had been 'removed' the locomotive was accepted to be a restorable proposition. Thus reassured the society took out a loan and purchased the engine soon afterwards, moving it to Loughborough on the Great Central Railway during the summer of 1976. Shortly after delivery society members began the long task of restoration, concentrating at first on the tender but soon turning their attention to the boiler; they were already aware that this was lagged with blue asbestos but as the GCR's other B1, No 61306, was also due for a boiler overhaul at the same time it made sense to have the deadly material removed by specialists from both locomotives simultaneously.

On completion of this work it was realised something serious was wrong. While inspecting the two stripped boilers it was noticed that the one belonging to No 61264 appeared to have several additional steel plates on its boiler and firebox casing. When descaling operations were begun the rust was almost ¼" thick and the copper inner firebox was wafer thin. Obviously work was stopped immediately and advice sought from an ex-BR boiler expert from Crewe; his report totally stunned the society. Estimated repairs deemed necessary included a new copper firebox, new tubeplate, the steel firebox casing to be cropped above the existing rivetted seams with new side plates required and the majority of the firebox stays needed replacing. The report concluded that without the availability of the long disappeared specialised facilities of a BR works, the boiler was beyond repair.

The society's committee clearly had an interesting decision to make. Did they pack it all in there and then and sell the locomotive to the highest bidder for scrap or did they investigate the possibility of having a new boiler and firebox built from scratch? Fortunately they chose the latter course and soon began to ask for quotations from engineering firms who might be interested in carrying out the work. Initial estimates varied between £50,000 and £100,000, quite a daunting sum for the society.

However, before it became necessary to raise this amount, fate stepped in to lend a hand. By the early 1980s welding techniques had developed to such an extent that it was now considered possible to repair the boiler after all and the work was accordingly given to Resco Railways of Woolwich, the boiler itself being delivered to their workshops in August 1984. As if they had not already suffered enough, the society were distressed to learn that during 1985 Resco was to close down their railway repair operations and an alternative would have to be found. Luckily this did not take too long and in December 1985 the boiler made the long journey down to Devon to undergo repair at the Gunnislake base of Roger Pridham.

So after having experienced both the elation of saving their locomotive from the scrapman and then the despair of having to consider scrapping the engine, the Thompson B1 Locomotive Society can at last look forward to the day No 61264 steams again; a wonderful demonstration of the resilience and perseverance of those involved in railway preservation.

With fellow ex-Barry resident No 76017 *Hermes* standing out of use in the shed yard, No 31806 heads away from Ropley with an afternoon train for Alton in August 1987. (*Mike Frackiewicz*)

No 5239 *Goliath* makes light work of its 7-coach train, complete with Devon Belle observation car, as it crosses Broadsands viaduct en route from Kingswear to Paignton in July 1987. (*Peter J. C. Skelton*)

Danger! – Blue Asbestos

During the summer of 1980 a letter was circularised by the Association of Railway Preservation Societies to all relevant private railways and steam centres in Britain. Issued by Major P. M. Olver, Inspecting Officer of Railways at the Department of Transport, it read 'It is essential that before a locomotive leaves Barry either by road or rail, the blue asbestos should be removed from the boiler and firebox cladding or alternatively sealed to the satisfaction of the local Environmental Health Officer at Barry and this Department's Inspector . . .' Advice could be obtained from the Department but generally any locomotive lagged with blue asbestos HAD to be dealt with. Whether the lagging was taken off on site at Barry or elsewhere depended largely on what the Railway Inspectorate felt; a locomotive not stripped on site had to be completely sealed during transit. Interestingly not all the engines at Barry carried asbestos boiler insulation although it was present on the cylinders of most of them.

The numerous societies and individuals attempting to purchase a locomotive already had enough problems of their own without the added worry and expense of now having to remove blue asbestos. Nevertheless the fibres from this material could cause serious illness and it was a problem that would not go away. Thus the Standard Nine Locomotive Company Ltd, who had only just paid for 9F No 92134, found themselves to be the first group to have the stripping of their engine carried out under DOT guidelines at Barry. The locomotive was clothed in mattressed asbestos cladding all round the boiler, firebox and cylinders, and the material could easily be seen protruding from the gaps in the rust eaten metal boiler sheeting. A specialist firm was called in and at a cost in excess of £1,000 a team of men wearing protective clothing and masks carefully removed the well damped material, sealing it into bags for subsequent disposal at an authorised tip.

In the case of Black Five No 45491 purchased the following summer, the blue asbestos lagging was not removed at Barry as the metal boiler cladding was deemed to be in good enough condition for the whole boiler and firebox to be cocooned in plastic sheeting and the asbestos soaked with water to prevent particles escaping into the air during transport northwards. Within one week of arrival at its restoration site near Blackpool the blue asbestos was removed by specialist contractors.

The problem of this deadly material is of course still being experienced by British Rail who are obliged to sell all condemned rolling stock containing blue asbestos to the one or two approved scrap metal contractors with the appropriate equipment for its safe disposal. How many prospective purchasers were put off from buying a Barry locomotive because of the blue asbestos inconvenience is unknown but in reality the expense of removal formed only a small proportion of the total cost of acquisition, transport and restoration. Thankfully not too many societies had to concern themselves with the matter anyway for when the problem of blue asbestos was first realised Dai Woodham had to pay to have it removed from all those engines where the boiler cladding was missing or had fallen away to expose the material to the atmosphere. Only on those where the cladding was secure was the insulation left for the new owner to dispose of.

A Tender Problem

All of the tender locomotives purchased by Woodham Bros arrived at Barry with their tenders still attached but it was not long before many of these became separated and consequently either dispersed around the yard or sold off individually. One of the main reasons for this was the acquisition by Briton Ferry Steelworks of several ex-Bulleid and ex-BR Standard tenders for conversion into ingot carriers, a process which involved the removal and scrapping of the tank. This immediately left many locomotives 'tender-less' but in those early days any group buying an engine thus denuded were permitted to purchase a substitute tender from one of the unreserved locomotives. During the early 1970s it was also common for groups to acquire a second tender as a spare, assuming of course they had sufficient funds to do so, in order to ensure the long term future of their engine.

Within a very short time it became clear that there were not going to be enough tenders at Barry to go around so an alternative supply had to be found. One or two societies chose to build a brand new tender from scratch and in the case of the owners of No 73082 *Camelot* and No 34059 *Sir Archibald Sinclair* they were able to obtain suitable original chassis and wheelsets by travelling to Briton Ferry and purchasing the by now redundant ingot carriers; for the new coal and water tank they placed an order with Shipyard Services Ltd of Brightlingsea, an engineering firm who in 1982 had built a 5250 gallon tender to go with Bulleid Pacific No 34027 *Taw Valley*. Several other firms have also been approached by locomotive owning groups seeking a new tender; Procor UK of Wakefield, better known as builders of freight rolling stock, completed a new tender body for Standard 2-6-0 No 78022 on the Keighley and Worth Valley Railway during March 1983 at a cost of £4,000, while a private workshop in Derby was given the job of constructing a new tank for GWR 4-6-0 No 4936 *Kinlet Hall*.

Many societies could not afford the expense of building a new tender so had to look elsewhere for inspiration. Although BR scrapped their steam locomotive fleet very quickly they fortunately transferred a large number of tenders into departmental stock as water or sludge carriers or even snowploughs. This has provided a useful source for a few groups although invariably these tenders require considerable work to return them to their original condition. Even so the Erlestoke Manor Fund thought it preferable to buy a Collett 3000 gallon tender of 1944 from BR at Plymouth where it had been used as water carrier for a steam crane rather than try to restore the 70 year old tender which had been bought with their locomotive from Barry. In the mid 1980s it was not unusual for tenders to still occasionally appear on BR sales lists while at the same time several societies who initially bought more than one tender from Barry have made their spare available for sale. In the years ahead there is no doubt that many more locomotive owners will have to consider the option of completely replacing their existing tenders but at least the expertise built up by several engineering firms in the last decade should guarantee that this does not become too much of a problem.

The Locomotive Restorers

It has often been said that buying a locomotive from Barry was the easy part but for many societies the initial optimism must have soon faded when the enormity of the task that lay ahead was truly appreciated. Not only did the problems of acquiring missing parts and the technical knowledge to put them all together have to be sorted out but the question of how it was all going to be paid for remained the biggest hurdle for many of the ex-Barry locomotive owning groups to overcome.

Human nature being what it is, a challenge appeals to most people and those involved in the restoration of steam locomotives are no exception. When confronted with a derelict hulk of scrap metal with many of the bits missing, they do not have a lot of choice! The section of the book that follows sets out to describe, with the help of some of the locomotive groups concerned, the sheer hard work involved, together with an indication of the excitements, the disappointments, the expense and the elation of seeing the newly restored engine at work for the first time. All railway enthusiasts who enjoy the sight of a steam locomotive at work owe a great deal to these individuals who give up so much of their spare time and money in pursuit of their hobby.

The Port Line Locomotive Project – An Exercise in Co-operation
by Bill Trite, Chairman

The restoration of Merchant Navy Pacific No 35027 *Port Line* has been all but completed in just under five years since the engine left Barry scrapyard.Such a rate of progress for so large a locomotive has far exceeded even the most optimistic early forecasts of the owners, the Port Line Locomotive Project; indeed, the first edition of *Rescued From Barry* set the anticipated date of No 35027's return to steam not at five but at a minimum of seven years away – and that was at the project's own insistence! Leaving aside this deliberate tendency to play down expectations during what turned out to be a long-distance sprint to reconstruction, *Port Line's* dramatic resurgence is without doubt one of the most remarkable of the Barry stories and a permanent tribute to the skill and determination of a dedicated group of like-minded people.

The scheme to save *Port Line* began in a way now recognised as the classic Barry rescue story – an individual's nostalgic desire to see returned to its former glory the locomotive which created the most memorable impressions on a young mind in the late fifties and early sixties. Thus it was that in the last days of 1980 the project's subsequent chairman Bill Trite set out to bring together a small group of people to finance the purchase and relocation of *Port Line*, and thereafter to organise the engine's reconstruction and operation. At the time it was considered too late in the day to begin yet another loco fund based on donations and a subscription paying society, so an early decision was taken to seek seven individuals each able to contribute £1,500. A capital base of £10,500 was more than sufficient for the primary objectives, with cash in hand for contingencies. The seven would form the initial labour force and set the future course for the project on the basis of an equal shareholding in the locomotive.

And so it turned out, eventually. There were difficulties: – many individuals able to commit significant cash sums to Barry engines had already done so; in addition No 35027 had been 'reserved' by other groups who would be given every opportunity to purchase first. However, the ready involvement of Francis Blake of Barry Rescue brought a vital source of contacts and potential co-owners, such that although the first six months of 1981 proved fruitless, the reverse was true of the second half of that year. Between July and October the group was firmly established. In came William Bath, whose mechanical engineering skills and commercial flair were to prove invaluable to the project over the following years; Andrew Moore, who would take over the general administration of the project with meticulous attention to detail; Andrew Walker, Andrew Johnson, Arthur Hunt and Keith Marshall completed the nucleus of seven. In due course the existing reservations were challenged according to the procedure laid down by Woodham Bros and BSLAG, and after much uncertainty which persisted until the last day of the year, *Port Line* was purchased by the project on 5 January 1982 for £6,500.

If acquisition had not been easy, extrication from Barry and re-siting during 1982 were to be fraught with even worse problems. In effect the entire year was lost. As ill luck would have it, *Port Line* lay boxed-in towards the centre of the longest line of locomotives and tenders remaining at Barry. No shunting of the yard took place that year until October, and then only under some pressure from the project when No 35027 was at last released for collection. In the meantime members of the project had spent months visiting preserved railways in the south and Midlands seeking acceptance for *Port Line* as a long-term resident. After many promising starts and ultimate disappointments an invitation to base the engine at the (then) North Downs Steam Railway restoration site at Higham, North Kent, was accepted. Alas, as soon as *Port Line* was free to move from Barry, it was discovered that no right existed to move such large locomotives into Higham, and that the NDSR's lease of the Higham yard from BR was both unacceptably short and about to be terminated for good. Another seemingly endless round of visits and meetings across the country followed, with no satisfactory result until discussions were opened with the Swindon & Cricklade Railway who were pleased to accept No 35027 with little further ado. The project breathed a sigh of relief and quickly made preparations for collection from Barry and delivery to Blunsdon, near Swindon. Fate, however, had not yet dealt its last card; the transporter due to remove *Port Line* was damaged whilst delivering West Country No 34007 *Wadebridge* to the Plym Valley Railway. While replacement vehicle parts were flown in from the USA, the unfortunate *Wadebridge* was destined to

Safe at last! *Port Line* begins its journey from Barry to Blunsdon in December 1982 – will the signalman set the points for Bridgend or Colwinston?! (*Port Line Locomotive Project*)

After a lot of hard work and the expenditure of a lot of money, *Port Line*'s wheels and frames are carefully reunited at Blunsdon. (*Port Line Locomotive Project*)

remain unloaded for nearly a fortnight. By the time *Port Line* eventually arrived at Blunsdon – in torrential rain – it was nearly Christmas.

Thus it was not until mid-January 1983, two years after the first moves to rescue and restore *Port Line* had been made, that work on the locomotive could commence in earnest. The essential tasks for that year were virtually self-defining and labour-intensive, amounting to the complete dismantling of the engine into its component parts. Despite constant exposure to the elements, a continuous handicap throughout the restoration, on-site work saw the rapid removal of boiler, firebox and cylinder cladding, running plates, brake gear and ashpans. The cab was unbolted, slid backwards and removed. Countless bolts, nuts and fixtures which had rust-welded themselves together succumbed to the oxy-acetylene torch. In May the boiler was lifted from the frames and stored separately nearby. Jacking of frames enabled the bogie and trailing trucks to be freed and removed, the driving wheels to be rolled-out and driving wheel axleboxes released. By the end of September 1983 steam-cleaning of what had become very much just a 'kit of parts' commenced, in preparation either for undercoating or, where corroded, grit-blasting. That month also found the project making its most important missing part acquisition, by purchasing the last remaining Bulleid tender at Barry. It eventually joined its new locomotive at Blunsdon on 20 October. This first-series Merchant Navy tender had spent its entire working life behind sister engine No 35006 *Peninsular & Oriental SN Co*, but while at Barry had been acquired separately for use with rebuilt Battle of Britain No 34053 *Sir Keith Park*. It was to cost the project £9,000 (half as much again as the engine!) but still represented a clear financial advantage over the cost of manufacture from new, and of course with the added bonus of authenticity. The extra cost burden was partially offset by the addition of two new owners: Chris Hinton and Nigel Ewens.

In addition to the tender, various other important missing parts had by now been obtained, including most of three sets of motion with coupling rods and a connecting rod, the 3-part weighshaft assembly, lubricators, reverser, steam generator, buffers, smokebox door, vacuum ejector, clack boxes and snifting valves. In the face of severely mounting pressure on limited financial resources a turning point was reached at a celebrated meeting at Camden Town Hall on 17 December 1983. Here the decision was taken by the then owners to expand the ownership base of *Port Line* by offering for sale an initial block of 180 shares in the locomotive at £250 each. Success of the scheme was considered essential if the rate of progress achieved to that point was to be maintained. The plan contained three key elements: actual part ownership of No 35027, the option of low instalment payments over 50 months, and guaranteed access to the locomotive and its footplate at all reasonable times. An advertisement was accordingly prepared for insertion in the steam press in March 1984.

Response to the project's offer took even its originators by surprise. Within six months 120 shares had been taken up and virtually all the remainder during the rest of the year. This ownership extension provided not only the financial basis upon which most of the major engineering tasks were completed during the next 2½ years, but also a steady stream of essential on-site workers who have been moulded into an extremely effective team. Off-site specialist tasks were steadily completed: re-profiling of wheels, machining of journals and crank pins, white metalling and machining of axleboxes, re-bushing of valve gear, manufacture of new motion pins, refurbishment of the reverser and a vast amount of casting and machining of new parts. At Blunsdon grit-blasting of frames and boiler (where necessary) was followed by extensive welding of the cab sub-frame, smokebox, tender and other items. Re-wheeling of frames, springing of driving wheels and re-positioning of bogie and trailing trucks was complete by the end of 1985, to be followed by reassembly of pistons, piston valve slide bars and all motion including coupling and connecting rods. Lubrication runs, atomiser and sanding pipes and steam brake pipes were re-positioned, with steam brake cylinders and brake gear refurbished and reinstated. Two Davies and Metcalf Monitor injectors were acquired and fitted, along with backhead fittings and manifold. Other purchases included two connecting rods, safety valves, brass window frames, electric conduit, lamps, manifold valves, axlebox oilboxes and covers, a replacement chimney (the original was cracked) and seemingly miles of copper piping.

The project has received little in the way of sponsorship, with one exception in the form of the Swindon based Austin Rover Young People's Training School. The latter has manufactured various fittings and refurbished others, but most notably has completely replated *Port Line's* cab and running plate. One of the last tasks they dealt with was the manufacture of boiler and firebox cladding.

Well before *Port Line's* near-completion it became clear that the project's resources could absorb a second locomotive, ideally an unrebuilt light Pacific to complement the Merchant Navy. Thus eventually there arrived at Blunsdon, again after some reservation system difficulties, Battle of Britain 4-6-2 No 34072 *257 Squadron*. Work has commenced on this engine after an initial period of storage, with a share issue launched successfully under the administration of Simon Troy.

To finance necessary boiler work and various remaining tasks on *Port Line* prior to resteaming, a final block of shares in the locomotive was released in early 1987. The response, as before, although almost expected this time, was remarkable despite the absence of easy instalment facilities. It is perhaps a measure of the progress made and a recognition of the project's ability to match its words with deeds that the issue was very rapidly subscribed, leaving in total nearly 300 people with a direct interest in either or both of *Port Line* and *257 Squadron*. In addition to the vital flow of finance from share purchase by all involved, at the core of the project's success has lain its workforce. Many of the 300 have frequently given of their time and effort, and from them has evolved a regular working team remarkable for its members' diverse occupations and backgrounds, and for the way in which various skills and individual strengths have been used in a complementary way to the benefit of the whole project. Some, like Andrew Scott and Brian Hains, have come from the Swindon area, while others have hailed from much further afield – Mike Price from Folkestone, Geoff Reber from Woking, Geoff Belcher from Fleet, John Thornton from Middlesex, Dave Shepherd from South London, John Miller from Yeovil and Frank Mead from Salisbury. In addition to those previously mentioned, all have contributed time, effort and money to the maximum possible in a joint undertaking that is now a permanent tribute to the endeavours of each.

As for the future, the project, its locomotives and support vehicles are destined to move to the Swanage Railway with the successful conclusion of negotiations towards this end. Ultimately this railway will provide a line over 10 miles in length, which can justify the operation of so large a locomotive as the Merchant Navy. Furthermore the planned link with the BR system at Wareham offers the future opportunity of working over approved routes on the national system – one reason why *Port Line's* restoration has been to the highest possible mechanical standards.

Members of the Port Line Locomotive Project are sometimes asked to try to account for its relative success; that at least has the merit of highlighting some important lessons for the future of this project and perhaps others. Firstly, the project has demonstrated, at least to its own satisfaction, that nothing compares with a personal, measurable stake in an enterprise to encourage and promote individual effort and commitment. In other words, the more owners with a significant shareholding, the more willing workers. Secondly, the climate within the organisation is openly encouraging towards individual expression of opinion and takes care to recognise and use the particular skills that different individuals have to offer. This is an important component in an *esprit de corps* that is second to none among preservation groups. Thirdly, there is a completely free flow of information within the organisation that is unconfined to a few individuals 'in the know'. Fourthly, by good luck or judgement – or perhaps as a result of the factors already mentioned – the project seems to have found the right blend of skills and resources: engineering, commercial, organisational, administrative, promotional and, of course, elbow grease. After thousands of hours of work and the expenditure of approximately £100,000, the result is there for all to see.

(*Overleaf*) The kit of parts is slowly put together again at Blunsdon and *Port Line* begins to recapture some of its former pride. This stage in a locomotive's restoration must be heart-warming indeed for those involved. (*A. Scott*)

No 6990 Witherslack Hall – *The People and the Project*
by Dave Fletcher of the *Witherslack Hall* Society

The 1960s were the traumatic years for the majority of railway enthusiasts as they saw their beloved steam engines being hauled away to the scrapyards and mile after mile of track closed and torn up. Most of these enthusiasts did no more than bemoan the fact, whilst some at least made an effort to preserve something of the past resulting in a proliferation of schemes and proposals, very much reminiscent of the railway manias of the 19th century. The seeds of the preservation movement were being sown. Many failed to germinate, some wilted after only a short while, others took root and flourished. The acorn from which the *Witherslack* oak grew was sown by a group of members of the then embryonic Shackerstone Railway Society, later to become the Market Bosworth Light Railway, with a proposal to preserve one of the locomotives then at Barry. In the process of launching the scheme, one of their number was invited to speak to the Lutterworth Railway Society and succeeded in generating so much interest that the Society agreed to join forces with the group to raise funds. Two of the Lutterworth Railway Society members, Alan Green and Ron Cobb, were elected to the committee to represent their interests and a closer look was taken at the selection of machines then available at Barry. After much deliberation and debate, it seemed to the group that one of the ex-Great Western Hall Class locomotives offered the best prospects for restoration. Originally forming itself as The Hall Society, the various contenders were whittled down until eventually No 6990 *Witherslack Hall* appeared at the top of the list. The added bonus to the Lutterworth based group was the fact that No 6990 had actually run through their now demolished ex-Great Central Railway station during the Exchange Trials of 1948 when operating services between Marylebone and Manchester, and indeed was the sole survivor of those trials. Having made their choice and renaming the society as the Witherslack Hall Locomotive Society, the prospective restorers set about the task of raising in excess of £3,000 for the purchase price – no small sum in those days.

The beginning of fund raising efforts saw the society's stand at various traction engine rallies, backed up by the usual charity fund raising efforts through jumble sales, raffles, whist drives etc, and an appeal was also launched in the railway enthusiast press inviting subscriptions for shares in the locomotive and for new members. However the funds came in at an agonisingly slow pace, teaching the society at an early stage that a generous response from enthusiasts was not to be relied upon! With a membership of just over 100, the idea was floated of pledging a monthly donation for additional shares and thankfully the response to this began to make a real assault on the target figure. With renewed confidence, a few gallons of primer were taken to Barry to give the engine a protective coat of paint, although perhaps the real concern was that it would rust away before sufficient funds could be raised, for now the group also faced the problem that the escalating price of scrap steel meant that the purchase price of the locomotive was going up faster than the funds were coming in. The major turning point came on the weekend that two founder members, Alan Green and Ray Kemp, found themselves in the company of Chris Pratt, a solicitor and Dave Bishop, a bank official, two enthusiasts from nearby Rugby. To this captive audience the story was told, arms twisted and subscriptions extracted, thereby adding two valuable members to the roll. One took over the responsibility of treasurer and the other became membership secretary and general legal adviser. It was not long before the committee found themselves in the office of Dave Bishop's manager to discuss the question of raising a bank loan. There can be little doubt that a major factor influencing the bank's decision to support the society was the regular monthly income being subscribed by its members.

At this, the project burst into life and attention could be focussed upon three problems – preparing the remains for removal, finding a home and moving it there. The original intention had been to move it to Shackerstone for restoration but the policies of that organisation at the time led to second thoughts and following an invitation from the Main Line Steam Trust, plans were made to move to Loughborough, already the home of one ex-Barry locomotive, Bulleid Pacific No 34039 *Boscastle*. On 18 November 1975, the rather badly corroded tender was winched on to a low loader and

The restoration of an ex-Barry locomotive is not a job for the faint hearted, requiring the engine to be dismantled into all its component pieces. Here, *Witherslack Hall* is hardly recognisable as such while undergoing rebuilding inside Loughborough shed during March 1977. (*Dave Fletcher*)

transported to Quorn and Woodhouse station. Before leaving Barry the driver, knowing he had been detailed to collect the locomotive the following week, walked around the hulk eyeing up the problems and in all seriousness enquired if it would be possible to 'start it up' to assist with the loading. With equal seriousness, he received the reply that if he would like to bring a bag of coal with him, he was welcome to give it a try! Some twenty-seven years after she had last visited the town, No 6990 returned to Loughborough on 27 November 1975, her copper chimney cap rising proudly above the traffic jam she had caused. Unloading at Quorn was not without incident; first she dropped a bogie wheel into the gap between ramp and trailer bed and then caused considerable damage to the brand new winch which the commendably safety conscious driver had attached in order to lower her down the ramp. Sixty-five tons of locomotive with a mind of its own and no brakes takes some stopping at the best of times!

Subsequently towed to Loughborough, work started almost immediately by stripping off the boiler cladding and asbestos lagging and then, after being shunted into the newly erected locomotive shed (a converted aircraft hangar), an all out assault was made on the acres of rust scale that covered everything that was not alternatively smothered in tarry black grease. When pausing from their labours with the chipping hammer, wire brush and scraper, the working party exposed themselves to

With all the activity of a beehive, a busy Sunday morning sees a group of volunteers tackling a varied assortment of tasks at Loughborough in June 1976. (*Dave Fletcher*)

the standard questions from the Sunday afternoon visitors concerning the proposed steaming date, whilst the seemingly incredible number of former drivers who recalled working on Halls in their heyday gave rise to the feeling that the Western Region's rostering clerks must have had some difficulty in fitting them all in! Oddly, nobody seemed to know a former shed fitter whose experience would have been invaluable at this stage. On one occasion, a mere two months after work had commenced, one irate visitor, camera at the ready, was most put out at the state of things, for having heard that she had been rescued he had travelled some distance expecting to photograph her in action. An invitation to don overalls and give a hand towards achieving that objective fell upon stony ground! Every preserved railway goes out of its way to attract and welcome visitors, for without them no scheme could possibly survive but there are occasions when one also welcomes their departure. The Stores Department was now receiving an increasing mound of bits and pieces as the locomotive was being dismantled, and here discipline became essential while enthusiasm had to be curbed if ever the society was going to get everything back together again. Things came to a head one Sunday morning when arriving to find the tender brake gear, pivots, bolts, washers and hangers in an unlabelled pile outside the cabin door after some busy beaver had let his enthusiasm run away with him the previous day!

The human side to these restoration projects is the one aspect that seems to be rarely told, for when all is said and done, they are stories of often only a few dedicated individuals intent on seeing a once proud locomotive steam again. In any form of volunteer work it tends to be overlooked that people do have other commitments in life, not least of which is the need to earn a living, closely followed by obligations to families and home, even to other leisure interests, all of which seriously ration the amount of time a volunteer can justify committing to a long term project. Contrary to popular impression, railway restorers are not a bunch of single-minded individuals who spend their lives in boiler suits and sleeping in cabs and carriages! Of the *Witherslack Hall* 'black hand gang', only one or two had worked in engineering before and none had any of the experience and specialist skills applicable to this particular field. Throughout the long years of rebuilding the team consisted of no more than half a dozen regulars with their occupations ranging from a heavy goods vehicle fitter, a farmer and a civil servant to an accounts clerk, an assembly worker and a school metalwork teacher. Various members joined for a while, made their contributions and left; among their occupations was a plumber, a hospital technician, a car salesman, a delivery driver, a motor cycle mechanic and even a professional pop musician. A number of teenagers showed interest from time to time, proving most invaluable when it came to wriggling into small spaces or tackling some of the mundane cleaning jobs, but as is the way with the young, school examinations and girl friends took their toll. So many times is the question raised over the number of former steam locomotive fitters being recruited to the preservation scene, as though putting a locomotive together and sorting out the problems is a mysterious art known only to those who have spent a lifetime in that environment, but after a few weekends squirming around underneath trying to de-rust some inaccessible corner or trying to free off a corroded component, most of the team began to understand why these old-time fitters kept well clear of the project, and indeed, why most of them maintained that they had been glad to see the back of the things!

A steam locomotive is basically a large but mechanically simple machine and given a good measure of common sense, a few drawings and someone with a reasonable feel for engineering, it does not take all that long to get the feel of it and to dispel some of the mystique and aura that surrounds them. The essential thing is to know when to leave it alone and find out what should be done. Where data is absent or unclear, it is necessary to ask the right questions of the right people, and many a journey was made to Didcot or to Bridgnorth for this purpose and to examine, sketch and photograph the relevant parts of a working locomotive.

Cleaning and painting the lumps of rusty metal that had come from Barry was one thing. Acquiring the missing parts was quite another. Not only was it necessary to realise that a part was needed, but also what it did, how it worked and where it could be obtained. The parts acquisition saga is one that could occupy a chapter all of its own, although certain aspects must forever remain confidential. Suffice it to say that the society will be eternally grateful to those engineering workshop foremen and storemen who turned a blind eye, or who 'accidentally' lost the paperwork. The majority of the straightforward turning, welding and fabrication jobs were carried out in the locomotive shed workshops which, with the passage of time, grew in capability as various machines were acquired (thereby hangs another tale!) and expertise and experience developed. Many small parts were literally made 'in house', for upon retirement from the Civil Service, Dick Hollingsworth took up model engineering and from his back bedroom workshop produced numerous items ranging from a handrail holder and assorted oil boxes to clevis pins and various clamps and fasteners; all to the detriment of progress on his 5″ gauge GWR 0-6-0PT. Although all the brass and copper fittings had been stripped off at Barry, acquiring the non-ferrous components for a Swindon built engine proved to be a relatively simple task, providing that our bank balance permitted. That quirk of history which resulted in so many ex-Great Western designs surviving at Barry to become the subject of restoration schemes, meant that several groups all required the same components. However Swindon's renowned policy of standardisation came to everyone's aid, and it was then a matter of finding out who had the patterns and drawings to enable the rough castings to be machined correctly. By the late 1970s both Didcot and the Severn Valley were well advanced in their researches and facilities, and they willingly gave advice and information. But not all of No 6990's fittings had to be made from scratch; occasionally a telephone call would come out of the blue with the offer of an original component, presumably 'rescued' from some locomotive as it awaited its fate in the scrapping sidings. Gauges and whistles were the most frequent offer, but when the chance came of an injector body and a complete water gauge frame, the society was not slow to react. An early donation was not only a regulator handle assembly but also a heavily tarnished safety valve bonnet, which, although it did not fit a Hall, fitted another locomotive under restoration whose owners just happened to have a Hall bonnet at the back of their store!

Requiring the utmost attention to detail and working in close consultation with the boiler insurance company's inspector, reconditioning the boiler and its fittings proved to be the longest and costliest job. Reconditioned in 1962 and fitted to No 6990 at her last heavy general overhaul at Swindon in the October of that year, it was known that it had done only a relatively low mileage since then, and it was therefore anticipated that the interior of the boiler shell should be in very good condition. Once the tubes had been extracted, a survey of paunches and posteriors amongst the ranks resulted in Alan Green, also acting in his capacity as society Chairman, being selected for duty inside the boiler. Shoehorning him in through the safety valve aperture, the members retired for tea leaving him to shovel out the barrow loads of water scale, which resulted in everything downwind being smothered in a pall of grey dust. When this task was completed internal inspection revealed that indeed everything was in superb condition, with only a small number of wasted stays requiring replacement. The workshop lathe coped with the stays and a touch here and there with the argon welder dealt with the odd patches of corrosion on the exterior. Stunned by the quotation for replacing the 144 small tubes, the society prayed heavily as examination of the 21 large flue tubes commenced. A spirited version of 'The Anvil Chorus' entertained the local residents as the scale was hammered off and following an acid bath to remove the residue, fortune smiled for each tube was in as good condition as the day it left Swindon. Enough remained of the swaged ends to enable new threads to be cut for screwing into the firebox tube plate, and new plain ends were welded on by a contractor approved by the insurance company. Again to conform to insurance company requirements, a 'ticketed' professional boilersmith was called in to fit, expand and bead the tubes into the tube plates and to fit and caulk the new stays. Blanking off plates were made to seal off the various apertures and at last, all was ready for the hydraulic test. With hearts in mouths, the gang peered anxiously at every seam and rivet as the pressure built up, and only at full pressure of one and a half times the working pressure did a few of the stays begin to weep – a problem quickly dealt with by the boilersmith armed with a caulking tool and a heavy hammer. A repeat performance a week later for the benefit of the insurance inspector resulted in clearance to reunite the boiler with the frames.

The 45 ton Ransome and Rapier steam crane recently acquired by the GCR and built, appropriately enough, for the GWR, received its baptism on 16 May 1982 by firstly turning the frames and tender to face south and then providing quite a spectacle for the onlookers as it swung the boiler into the air and lowered it on to the frames. Such was the crowd pressing against the safety barriers that the society Treasurer was contemplating dropping a line to the film manufacturers inviting a donation from the profits they must have made that afternoon! With the boiler and cab back in place, No 6990 began to look more like her old self and hopes ran high for an early return to steam. However, practising pessimists know full well that when one looks like winning, fate steps in to assert itself and in this case not only were the funds exhausted but the availability of two or three key members became seriously affected by changes in employment circumstances – bringing home yet again the lesson that a shortage of either finance or manpower results in a lack of progress. Only as funds became available could orders be placed, for despite the temptation to take a chance for the sake of getting on with the job, the policy of not getting financially overcommitted was maintained. After all, nobody relished the prospect of seeing the Official Receiver standing on the front buffer beam holding an auction.

Little by little, bit by bit, the list of 1001 outstanding jobs was slowly but surely whittled down,

Witherslack Hall begins to look like a proper steam locomotive again as the boiler is very carefully and very slowly lowered into the frames in May 1982. The cab roof stands in the foreground waiting its turn to be reunited with No 6990. (*Graham Wignall*)

ranging from the fiddling little things within the scope of the unskilled to those requiring the attention of the experts. Of the latter, plumbing up the boiler fittings and lubrication and vacuum systems were the major operations. First coerced into joining the project to supervise replating the tender, Dave Holmes was not only an experienced panel beater and welder but had served an apprenticeship as a coppersmith before training as a metalwork teacher. The group could only stand and enjoy the pleasure of watching a craftsman at work as expensive lengths of copper tube were bent to shape with nothing but small offcuts landing up in the scrap box. The final major job of reassembling the motion was taken care of by the Great Central's shed team, whilst the society members got on with lagging the boiler and fitting the cladding.

With the end in sight, now was the time to start thinking about the finishing touches, notably the nameplates and brass trim. Shortly after the boiler had been replaced, a pair of wooden nameplates had been made up by Dave Fletcher to improve the cosmetics, and some amusement was gained at the expense of the Sunday afternoon 'gricers' by rearranging the letters to form various anagrams, then watching the puzzled expressions as various 'Combined Editions' were solemnly searched! Truly, moments of madness keep one sane on jobs like these. Accepting one of several offers to put up the money to have the nameplates made, the order was placed with Roy and Pat Softley of Sheffield who at that time were developing their sideline business in decorative brassware. Such was the excellence of the finished product that they were given the task of producing the splasher

The culminatiuon of many years of hard work is there for all to see as *Witherslack Hall* blasts out of Loughborough on 12 October 1986, its first weekend in service on the GCR. (*Dave Fletcher*)

beading, by no means simple in view of the awkward cross section. Even some of the leading brassfounders of Sheffield had to admit defeat, but perseverance was eventually rewarded and after a considerable amount of hand finishing, satisfactory lengths were produced.

The spring and summer of 1986 saw the light at the end of the tunnel growing bigger and brighter almost daily. The last components had been delivered and fitted, Ron Cobb had the paintwork and lining out well in hand and eventually the day for a long awaited steam test arrived. The honour of lighting the first fire No 6990 had seen for twenty-one years, fell to the society Chairman, but as the pressure rose, so did the number of leaks. Two further tests were necessary before Alen Grice, the GCR's locomotive engineer, pronounced *Witherslack* fit for a trial run down the line. With Alan Green on the regulator and Brian Measures, one of the restoration team who had also qualified as a fireman, plying the shovel, the gang climbed on board. Jets of rust stained water shot out of the injector overflow pipes and clouds of pink steam issued from the cylinder drain cocks giving a colourful start if nothing else, but as they felt her come to life beneath them, the exhilaration experienced by everyone sharing that moment can only be appreciated by those who have known a similar happening. The weeks that followed were devoted to ironing out the teething problems, replacing a number of the original superheater elements that had finally blown, attending to hot bearings and finishing off the minor details in readiness for her appearance at the Great Central Railway's Tenth Anniversary celebrations in the September.

60

One month later, on 8th October, she stood with a colourful headboard and every square inch sparkling in the morning sun, the focus of attention of the Press and television crews on the occasion of her official launch and renaming ceremony. The nameplate was unveiled by David Weston, the famous railway artist and the active President of the society almost from its inception. To scenes of jubilation and much whistle blowing, invited guests boarded the inaugural train for lunch en route to Rothley. For the restoration team, the remainder of that day passed in an euphoric haze, many having to pinch themselves for reassurance that all this was at last really happening!

It is at times like those that the sense of achievement makes everything so worth while, suppressing the memories of far-off dark days when progress appeared so painfully slow that it seemed unlikely that the job would ever be finished. Memories of freezing days of winters past wrestling with some lump of cold metal, of blistering summer days when it was just too hot to move let alone work, of days of despair, days of elation and of week after week of commitment and dedication to the task. And there she is in all her glory – a breathing, living machine. And a tribute to human endeavour.

The Great Western Steam Locomotives Group – One Manor and Four Other Engines to Support
by Steve Worrall

The formation of the Great Western Steam Locomotives Group was something that really started by accident. Yorkshire trout farmer Ken Ryder was visiting the Keighley & Worth Valley Railway and purchased a book listing the locomotives that were still in the scrapyard at Barry.

Until then Ken had surprisingly not even been aware of the existence of the scrapyard and the acquisition of the book sparked off a desire to purchase and restore one of the remaining GWR locos. Contact was made with Dai Woodham and also Francis Blake of Barry Rescue and a visit to the yard subsequently arranged. The scene that greeted Ken at Barry was one of dereliction, corrosion and missing components but he felt that it would still be possible to completely restore 1950 built No 7828 *Odney Manor*. Before proceeding any further Ken wisely decided that he would approach some existing preservation projects for advice. Looking back now eight years later and with *Odney Manor* in full working order some of the 'advice' given at the time makes interesting reading. A self-appointed expert from a well-known railway stated 'You will never get a restoration team together. Anyone with any of the necessary skills is working on other lines and there are no new volunteers left. It is no use getting someone who is BR trained, they only know their own job which is not enough. You will never get an engine out of Barry, all the wheels will be solid.' From another self-appointed expert from a loco owning group came the comment 'The frames are that twisted it will derail itself. It will go up the line like a crab. It has been at Barry too long. The boiler is scrap and will only last ten years.'

After hearing these remarks most people would have abandoned all thoughts of trying to rescue anything else from Barry but Ken Ryder decided to ignore all the advice that he had been given and go ahead. Another visit was made to South Wales and a reservation was placed on *Odney Manor* and also Collett 2-8-0 No 3814. The winter of 1980 was spent planning the formation of a group to restore the two locos and looking at possible locations for a future home. It was at this point in time that the Great Western Steam Locomotives Group came into existence. Negotiations were then entered into with the Gloucestershire Warwickshire Railway which was based at Toddington and was aiming to re-open, in stages, the former GWR mainline between Cheltenham and Stratford-upon-Avon. In March of 1981 Swindon boilersmith Ken Davis met the group at Barry to carry out boiler inspections. He advised the group that No 3814 would require a great deal of work, so the reservation was switched to No 7821 *Ditcheat Manor*. Within two months the purchase price of the two Manors was paid and planning started for the move to the Gloucestershire Warwickshire Railway.

The move from South Wales to Gloucestershire took place in June of that year and within a week of the arrival at Toddington work commenced on dismantling the two Manors. Within a month they

had quickly become a kit of parts, thus allowing the major restoration tasks to commence. Parts removed from the locos needed to be stored securely, so a mess coach and a tool coach from the Worcester breakdown train were purchased. These were to be the first of many support vehicles to be purchased by the group, including a 45 ton steam crane from Old Oak Common. One of the problems of acquiring support vehicles is that they also require restoration and maintenance work which detracts from the loco restoration work itself, and a complete year was spent purely on this task. By now the group's collection of locos had increased to three with the purchase of No 5952 *Cogan Hall*. No 5952 had been reserved by another group but when the reservation was dropped it was decided that the Hall would make a useful addition to the GWSLG fleet and movement to Toddington took place within two days of purchase.

Autumn 1982 saw the group's attention turn to the provision of covered accommodation for the chassis of *Odney Manor*. The locomotive's frames were shotblasted and painted and then a single road shed was built around them using sheets of corrugated iron. Being able to work under cover is one of the most important requirements for the restoration of a steam locomotive as it avoids the cancellation of working parties because of bad weather conditions.

The following year work was again concentrated on the restoration of the group's support vehicles and in particular the steam crane. This resulted in the first successful steaming of the crane in May 1984 and an end to the need for the hire of expensive road cranes for lifting work. At the same time it was decided to launch an appeal to buy a Prairie tank No 5199. With a fully operational crane the major restoration work on *Odney Manor* was able to commence. In November 1984 reassembly work started with the first of the newly machined horn guides being bolted back on the frames and the wheelsets being sent to BREL Swindon for turning and profiling. After examination by BREL it was decided that the driving wheels needed new tyres and these were ordered from BSC Rotherham.

Between March and July of 1985 the GWSLG locomotive fleet increased to five. First by the arrival of No 4936 *Kinlet Hall* from the Peak Railway at Matlock. The engine had been purchased in 1981 by the Kinlet Hall Loco Co Ltd but the slow progress with restoration work at Matlock led the owners to decide to join the GWSLG who had promised to help with the work. Shortly afterwards No 5199 arrived from Barry having been successfully purchased by the GWSLG's 5199 Project. Before leaving the scrapyard it had been necessary to have the loco stripped of blue asbestos by a professional contractor at a cost of £1,500.

To help speed up the restoration of *Odney Manor* it was decided that the tender chassis would be sent to a firm in Shropshire for the fitting of two new tender dragboxes and a new tank. Originally it had been planned that the dragboxes would be fitted to the tender chassis at Toddington. However following the news that unsquare frames had been the cause of hot box trouble on two restored main line locos, it was decided to return the frames to the Shropshire engineering firm which had made the dragboxes. This enabled the frames to be set squarely during rivetting, on a flat base. After the work had been carried out the new tender tank was rivetted to the chassis before its return to Toddington at the beginning of 1986. This then only left a small amount of work to be finished on the tender including the fitting of the brake gear and buffers.

Now the hard work has to begin . . . the purchase of a Barry locomotive is a relatively easy task but it is the many years and thousands of pounds required for restoration that causes the headache. No doubt with this thought in mind, Great Western Steam Locomotives Group volunteers take a break during the loading of No 5199 at Barry in July 1985. (*Quentin McGuinness*)

With the GWSLG having a regular workforce of around 20 people, it has allowed work to take place on two of the Group's engines at the same time. In August 1986, No 5199 was dismantled to allow major restoration work to commence. To the left of the engine can be seen the frames of *Ditcheat Manor* which has already had its boiler removed. (*Quentin McGuinness*)

With a large amount of the tender work being carried out by an outside contractor this of course allowed the group to spend more time working on the boiler and chassis of *Odney Manor* and preparing No 5199 for dismantling. The axleboxes of the Manor were sent to the Severn Valley Railway for metalling and machining. When the driving wheel axleboxes were returned from the SVR No 7828's frames were raised on hydraulic jacks and sleepers until the wheels would clear the cab steps and move under the frames. The driving axleboxes were lifted into the horn guides and secured ready for the frames to be dropped onto the wheels. At this point it was discovered that the axleboxes were too wide! The overall width from the outside of one axlebox to the outside of the other exceeded that between the wheel faces. As a result the axleboxes had to be removed and sent to a firm in Wolverhampton for further machining before they would fit.

The group have had the advantage of help from two former Swindon boilermen and this has greatly assisted with the restoration of *Odney Manor*. Their work has included the fitting and caulking of new steel stays for the firebox but it was decided to contract out some of the last stages of the work to Barlows of Warrington. During the three months that the boiler was at Warrington welding work was carried out to fractures in the firebox and a new set of tubes were fitted. January 1987 saw the boiler returned to Toddington and after the fitting of a new ashpan it was reunited with the frames. This signalled the start of four months intensive work in order to be able to steam the engine for the first time before the start of the summer. Priority was given to completion of the locomotive's main pipework and this was finished in time to light a fire on the morning of 30 May,

To remove or refit the driving wheels of a locomotive when it is in a shed usually means using packing to lift the frames high enough for the wheels to slide underneath. The re-wheeling of *Odney Manor* was protracted by the problems encountered with the axleboxes. (*Quentin McGuinness*)

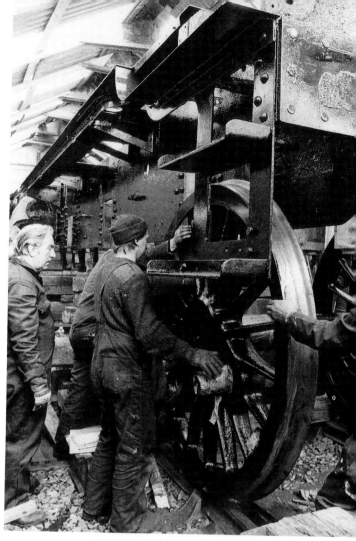

(Far left) There are few-ex-Barry locomotives which have not required the fitting of some new firebox stays and No 7828 *Odney Manor* was no exception. The areas needing new stays are indicated by the chalk markings. (*Quentin McGuiness*)

(Left) This strange looking device is the cylinder boring machine which was used to rebore the cylinders of the Group's two Manors as well as No 5199. (*Quentin McGuiness*)

Covered accommodation is essential for the restoration of a locomotive, even if only of a makeshift nature. To enable work to take place on *Odney Manor* during all types of weather conditions, a small shed was constructed from perspex and corrugated iron. (*Quentin McGuinness*)

the first time for over 22 years. Boiler pressure was allowed to reach 90lbs psi by late afternoon when the fire had to be dropped owing to injector failure.

Steaming a loco is one thing but there can then be quite a long interval before it can actually move under its own power. The summer months of 1987 saw the fitting of pistons, valves and coupling rods as well as the completion of the internal valve gear. A considerable amount of time can be consumed in just carrying out a multitude of those tasks which are not necessarily noticed by the casual observer. Lubrication pipework has to be fitted and many of the fabrications for the boiler cladding can be awkwardly shaped. Eventually all outstanding work was completed and in the Winter of 1987 *Odney Manor* moved under its own power for the first time. This is the moment that makes the years of hard work all worth while. The satisfaction of seeing something that was once a pile of scrap return to life is difficult to beat. Having finished the work the Great Western Steam Locomotives Group will not be sitting back complacently. The first stages of restoring No 5199 have already begun and it is planned to tackle a second tender engine at the same time.

The overall cost of restoring a steam locomotive is not usually known until the final work has been completed. Some machines which left Barry during the early years were returned to steam for under £25,000 as they had not been heavily stripped of parts. The total cost of restoring *Odney Manor*, excluding the original purchase price, was £87,750 and comprised the following:

£11,000	Purchase of second hand parts		£ 250	Insurance inspections
£ 3,000	Machining of second hand parts		£ 2,000	Spring repairs
£25,000	Purchase and machining of new parts		£10,000	Tender frame repairs and new tank
£15,000	Boiler repairs			
£ 3,500	Pipework		£ 1,500	Purchase of nuts and bolts
£12,500	Refurbishing axleboxes and wheelsets including new tyres		£ 2,000	Paint and lagging material
			£ 2,000	Fuels consumed (electricity, coal, oxy-acetylene etc)

In addition to this the group has spent £25,500 on the support vehicles and acquisition of materials for the shed.

For all those who think the restoration of an ex-Barry locomotive is not really that difficult, the accompanying list gives an indication of the incredible number of parts that were missing from 2-6-2T No 5199 when it was purchased from Barry. No other comment is really needed!

8mm Injector	Tank Float Gear	2 Rocking Arms
10mm Injector	Regulator Valve	Sundry Steel Pipework
3 Sight Feed Lubricator	Water Gauge Frame	Sundry Sand Gear Rodding & Lock Gear
Regulator Stuffing Box	6 Cylinder Cocks	3 Cylinder covers
Blower Valve	4 Cylinder Relief Valves	4 Valve Chest covers
Single Cone Ejector Box	Brake Hanger	2 Piston Valves Complete
Steam Fountain	Brake Beams	2 Valve Extension Rods
2 Jay Cocks	4 Buffers	Vacuum Pump Crosshead Bracket
Coal Watering Cock	Front & Rear Couplings	10 Motion Pins
Safety Valve	4 Coupling Rods	2 Driving Wheel Springs
2 Clack boxes	2 Connecting Rods	Set of Superheater Units
2 Live Steam Injector Valves	2 C Arms	Safety Valve Bonnet
Train Heating Valve	4 Slide Bars	Ejector Blower Ring
2 Coldwater Cocks	2 Pony Truck Keeps	Set of Smokebox Steam Pipes
Steam Lance Cock	2 Radial Truck Keeps	Rocking Arm Bracket Covers
Lubricator Warning Cock	2 Gudgeon Pins	Regulator Handle
Boiler Drain Cock	4 Coupling Rod Pins	Coldwater Feed Cock – Rods and Handles
2 Whistle Valves	4 Eccentric Rods	Water Tank Gauge
2 Whistle Bells	4 Eccentric Straps	Tank Lids
Duplex Vacuum Gauge	2 Pistons	Radial Truck Stays
Steam Pressure Gauge	2 Crossheads	Set of Oil Pots and Boxes
Train Heating Gauge	Vacuum Pump	Number and Shed Plates
Five Way Lubricator –	Expansion Link	Firehole Door Castings
– Distributor Valve	2 Radius Rods	

The overhauled boiler from *Odney Manor* is lowered back into the frames in February 1987 after its return from Barlows of Warrington. (*Quentin McGuinness*)

No longer looking like a heap of scrap metal, the interior of *Odney Manor*'s cab resembles that of a newly built locomotive as the cab fittings are put back into place one by one. (*Quentin McGuinness*)

INDIVIDUAL
HISTORIES
OF THE
LOCOMOTIVES
RESCUED
FROM
BARRY

1st: MR 0-6-0 No 43924

BUILT: October 1920
WITHDRAWN: July 1965

ARRIVED BARRY: October 1965
DEPARTED BARRY: September 1968

This very large class of popular 0-6-0 locomotives owes its origin to a design dating back to Midland Railway days in 1911, a total of 197 being built at Derby by that Company. They proved to be so reliable and robust that construction was continued after the Grouping by the London Midland & Scottish Railway which contributed a further 575 to the class between 1924 and 1941. Perhaps surprisingly, all 772 locomotives survived to enter British Railways stock in 1948.

Completed at Derby Works in October 1920, MR No 3924 went new to Wellingborough shed where it worked much of the ironstone and coal traffic down the Midland main line to London, as well as handling more general freight duties in the opposite direction to Leicester, Derby and Nottingham. In March 1930, this '4F' was transferred to the large depot at Saltley on the outskirts of Birmingham before moving on again in July 1937 to Gloucester (Barnwood) where it was to stay for the next twenty five years. Here No 43924 primarily dealt with the goods workings south to Bristol or Bath and north to Evesham, Worcester and Birmingham, the latter journey involving an

ascent of the notorious Lickey Incline. From time to time it also appeared on the occasional local passenger turn as well as helping out with the summer Saturday excursion traffic when all available motive power was pressed into service. In August 1962 it was finally re-allocated to Bristol (Barrow Road), spending its last three years on much the same sort of work.

In 1968, thanks to the persistent efforts of a group of enthusiasts, No 43924 was purchased from Woodham's scrapyard and thus became the first in a long time of locomotives to leave Barry. Initial restoration was quickly completed in 1970 on the Keighley and Worth Valley Railway, where it was painted in post-1928 LMS livery. Subsequently this locomotive has undergone several livery changes and when withdrawn for overhaul in 1987 was wearing mid-1960s BR plain black.

A line up of LMS motive power at Haworth in December 1985 as No 43924 and No 8431 raise steam for a busy day ahead. (David Wilcock)

2nd: SR 2-6-0 No 31618

BUILT: October 1928
WITHDRAWN: January 1964

ARRIVED BARRY: June 1964
DEPARTED BARRY: January 1969

R. E. L. Maunsell was appointed Chief Mechanical Engineer of the South Eastern & Chatham Railway in 1913 and his prototype design for a six-coupled passenger tank was constructed at Ashford four years later as K Class No 790. However, in service these locomotives showed themselves susceptible to violent rolling at speed, eventually leading to the notorious Sevenoaks accident of August 1927. At the time of this accident, an additional 20 K Class tanks were already on order so the decision was made instead to build them as 2-6-0 tender locomotives to Class U.

Thus in October 1928 locomotive No A618 entered service fresh from Brighton Works – had it been turned out as a K Class tank, it would have carried the name *River Hamble*. Operating initially from Guildford, this 2-6-0 was a regular sight on the Reading–Redhill line as well as working between Willesden and Ramsgate with some of the through trains from the north. By the end of World War II it was working out of Salisbury, but this was later followed by brief periods at Reading and Dorchester before coming to Eastleigh during 1954. Here No 31618 spent a good part of its time sub-shedded at Andover to deal with services over the former Midland & South Western Junction line between Cheltenham and Southampton, although as the years passed by it also appeared on an assortment of duties to Portsmouth, Bournemouth, Salisbury and Basingstoke. However, as the Beeching 'axe' began to take effect on many of the ex-Southern routes, it also had the dubious distinction of working one of the last local freight trips over the Meon Valley line between Alton and Fareham in April 1962. Moving on to Basingstoke at the end of 1962, it was finally transferred back to Guildford in March 1963.

Purchased from Woodhams in January 1969, No 31618 was initially taken to a private siding at New Hythe in Kent before going on to the Kent and East Sussex Railway for restoration. In May 1977 it moved to the Bluebell Railway where it has been a consistent performer and a credit to its owners, the Maunsell Locomotive Society.

No 1618 and West Country *Blackmore Vale* doublehead the 1.00 p m Sheffield Park to Horsted Keynes in June 1982. (*Mike Frackiewicz*)

3rd: GWR 2-6-0 No 5322

BUILT:	August 1917	ARRIVED BARRY:	November 1964
WITHDRAWN:	April 1964	DEPARTED BARRY:	March 1969

The Churchward 43XX 2-6-0s were basically a tender version of the earlier 3150 Class 2-6-2 tanks dating back to 1906. They were extremely useful mixed-traffic locomotives and between 1911 and 1932 no fewer than 307 were turned out by Swindon and 35 by outside contractors. They became a common sight over most of the GWR system, but only 241 survived Nationalisation.

No 5322 was constructed at Swindon in August 1917 and, following a short period of running-in, was one of eleven new members of the class sent to France in September 1917 for war service with the Railway Operating Division of the Army. While on the Continent it hauled troop and supply trains from the Channel Ports to the front lines, but returned to England just before cessation of hostilities in April 1919. Resuming service with the GWR, No 5322 worked from quite a selection of depots between then and June 1945 including those at Wolverhampton, Chester, Bristol, Weymouth, Cardiff, Oxley and Didcot, illustrating the general versatility of the locomotive. During the period 1928–44, it had been modified by the addition of a heavy casting behind the buffer beam to reduce

flange wear and was temporarily renumbered 8322. In June 1945, this Mogul was transferred to the sub-shed at Andover for use over the Midland & South Western Junction route between there and Cheltenham. From March 1953, it was based in the London Division staying for periods at Oxford, Didcot and Reading before moving on to Tyseley in the summer of 1959 to help out with the piloting of holiday expresses between Birmingham and Stratford-upon-Avon. When this work was over, it had a few weeks back at Swindon prior to its final move to Pontypool Road in September 1959.

The saying 'Old Soldiers Never Die' has proved true in this case, for in March 1969 this World War I veteran was moved from the scrapyard to a site in Caerphilly for restoration, later going to the headquarters of the Great Western Society centred on the old steam shed at Didcot.

No 5322 stands on display outside the Didcot Railway Centre in July 1981. (*Alan Warren*)

4th: GWR 4-6-0 No 5051 *Drysllwyn Castle*

BUILT:	May 1936	ARRIVED BARRY:	October 1963
WITHDRAWN:	May 1963	DEPARTED BARRY:	February 1970

C. B. Collett succeeded G. J. Churchward as Chief Mechanical Engineer of the GWR on 1 January 1922 and one of his first tasks was to produce a locomotive which could cope with the increased passenger traffic following World War I. The prototype of his new design, No 4073 *Caerphilly Castle*, was based on an enlarged version of the splendid Star 4-6-0s dating back to 1906 and the Castle Class as a whole proved to be so successful that general production continued right up to the early years of Nationalisation in 1950.

No 5051 *Drysllwyn Castle* was one of a batch of 15 built at Swindon Works during 1936 although it only carried this name for a short period, being renamed *Earl Bathurst* in August 1937. It spent the whole of its working life based in South Wales, the majority of this time being at Landore (Swansea) depot from where it regularly headed trains over the main line to Paddington and in later days these included many of the named Welsh expresses such as The Capitals United, The Red Dragon and The South Wales Pullman. Other work in the 1950s saw it traversing the route up to Birmingham and Chester but following the closure of Landore to

steam in June 1961, No 5051 was transferred to Neath for an interval of eighteen months before moving on again, in January 1963, to Llanelly. However, the onset of dieselisation finally caught up with *Earl Bathurst* and it was declared surplus to requirements at the end of May 1963, having amassed an impressive total of 1,316,659 miles in revenue-earning service.

Considered to be in the best condition of all the Castles remaining at Barry, No 5051 was taken by rail to the Great Western Society's depot at Didcot in February 1970. After a complete overhaul it has since worked numerous main line specials over selected BR routes as well as making a guest appearance at the Rocket 150 celebrations held at Rainhill in May 1980. More recently it helped work several of the GWR 150 special anniversary trains during the summer of 1985 but can now be seen back on display at Didcot.

Drysllwyn Castle heads an afternoon Bridgnorth to Bewdley service during its visit to the Severn Valley Railway in the summer of 1986. (*Brian Denton*)

73

5th: WR 4-6-0 No 7827 *Lydham Manor*

BUILT: December 1950
WITHDRAWN: October 1965

ARRIVED BARRY: May 1966
DEPARTED BARRY: June 1970

The Manors were Collett's final 4-6-0 design for the Great Western Railway and were, in effect, a slightly lighter version of his popular Grange Class. This enabled them to work over main and cross-country lines such as the Cambrian, restricted against the use of heavier locomotives where the Granges and 43XX Moguls were barred.

No 7827 is itself not a GWR locomotive for it represents one of the additional 10 Manors built at Swindon in 1950 after Nationalisation. Initially allocated to Chester, it worked all types of traffic down to Wrexham and Shrewsbury as well as across to Barmouth and Pwllheli via Bala Junction. In August 1958 it was transferred to Oswestry and from that date onwards spent the remainder of its working life with BR operating services over the former Cambrian lines, subsequently based at Machynlleth from December 1963 and Shrewsbury from January 1965. During this period it mainly covered local passenger turns to Aberystwyth in addition to frequent appearances on the Cambrian Coast Express. No doubt due to their versatility the Manors were also a very popular choice for special traffic and on several occasions in the early 1960s

Lydham Manor was used on the Festiniog and Talyllyn Railway annual excursions over the Cambrian lines. However, a chance to work that most special of duties came in August 1963 when, double-heading with sister locomotive No 7828, it hauled the Royal Train on the start of its journey between Aberdovey and Barmouth. Right up to October 1965, its last month in service, No 7827 was still working the Cambrian Coast Express and similar main line duties before being consigned to Barry scrapyard along with all the other redundant Manors based at Shrewsbury.

In June 1970 No 7827 was taken by rail to the Dart Valley Railway for restoration, a task completed at Newton Abbot in 1973. Since then *Lydham Manor* has proved to be an extremely valuable asset to the Paignton and Dartmouth Steam Railway.

Lydham Manor emerges from Greenway Tunnel and begins the descent to Kingswear with an afternoon train in August 1986. (*Roger Penny*)

6th: LMS 0-6-0T No 47327

BUILT: July 1926
WITHDRAWN: December 1966

ARRIVED BARRY: January 1968
DEPARTED BARRY: July 1970

The LMS Standard design for a general-purpose 0-6-0T was a direct development by Henry Fowler of the earlier Midland Railway Class 3F tank, dating back to 1899. The newer locomotives were not identical to the older design, having larger tanks, an extended smokebox and other detail differences. A total of 422 was built between 1925 and 1931, and the class was to become a familiar sight throughout the LMS system.

LMS No 16410 was turned out from the North British Locomotive Co Hyde Park works in Glasgow during July 1926 and was to spend its early days working in Scotland, initially based at Motherwell but moving on to Grangemouth in December 1929, Stirling in May 1930 and finally Corkerhill in July 1933. It then ventured south of the border for the first time in October 1934 to the old Midland Railway shed at Cricklewood and while there it acquired the number 7327. By the end of World War II it was working from Willesden and became a common sight on the empty coaching stock trains in and out of Euston, although as a break from this relatively mundane work it made a brief appearance in the Ealing Studios' film *Train*

of Events with the actor Jack Warner on the footplate. In early BR days No 47327, as it had then become, was to be found at Carlisle Upperby where its duties included hauling some of the local goods trains over the former Maryport & Carlisle line, but apart from a brief spell at Derby between September 1960 and January 1962, this 'Jinty' was to spend the remainder of its career from November 1950 onwards working in the Liverpool area, based successively at Brunswick, Bank Hall and Aintree sheds. Around this time diesel shunters gradually began to take over its duties and so in December 1966 this much-travelled locomotive was withdrawn and sold for scrap to Woodhams at Barry.

Following purchase in 1970, No 47327 was taken to Derby Works for initial storage before moving to Butterley where it has now been restored in the green and gold house colours of Ind Coope who have sponsored the locomotive's rebuilding.

A rare shot of No 47327 during its period of storage at Derby Works before moving on to the Midland Railway Trust at Butterley. (*Midland Railway Trust Ltd*)

75

7th: LMS 0-6-0T No 47357

BUILT:	July 1926	ARRIVED BARRY:	November 1967
WITHDRAWN:	December 1966	DEPARTED BARRY:	July 1970

With the exception of the last batch of 15 this entire class of 0-6-0 tanks was built for the LMS by outside contractors. They were extremely adaptable locomotives used for short distance freight and passenger work in addition to the many varied shunting and banking duties, eight of them being transferred to the War Department in 1940 for service overseas.

No 16440, like No 16410, was also built by the North British Locomotive Company in July 1926 but at the Queens Park Works in Glasgow, and it was therefore quite a long journey to its first shed at Devons Road in London. On arrival here it was put to work on some of the local passenger services out of Broad Street together with the usual freight and shunting duties which included trips down to the docks at Poplar. In March 1928 it was transferred to Willesden and frequently appeared on many of the cross-London freights from there to the yards at Feltham, Old Oak Common, Ripple Lane and Temple Mills. Carriage-warming gear was fitted in June 1930, enabling it to perform this task on the numerous rakes of empty coaching stock at Willesden before taking them down to Euston. After 24

years based in the London area, it moved on to Liverpool Edge Hill in April 1950, acquiring the number 47357 shortly thereafter; the work there largely involved trip freights from the main sorting sidings down to the docks, several of these workings taking it over the Mersey Docks & Harbour Board lines. During its time at Edge Hill, No 47357 also acted as station pilot at Lime Street as well as shunting at the numerous depots and yards in the Liverpool area, work on which it remained until withdrawn in December 1966.

After less than three years at Barry No 47357 was taken to Derby Works for rebuilding in July 1970 and on completion was repainted in LMS livery as No 16440. Moved to the Midland Railway Centre at Butterley in 1975 it worked the first public passenger train there in August 1981 but has now temporarily returned to its BR guise as No 47357 in full Crimson Lake express passenger livery.

On its first public working since repainting in BR style crimson lake livery, No 47357 prepares to leave Butterley station in March 1987. (*Midland Railway Trust Ltd*)

8th: GWR 2-6-2T No 4566

BUILT:	October 1924	ARRIVED BARRY:	September 1962
WITHDRAWN:	April 1962	DEPARTED BARRY:	August 1970

This class of small prairie tanks was the very epitome of the Great Western Railway scene, no branch line seeming complete without one. Designed by G. J. Churchward, 175 (including the later 4575 Class modified locomotives) were built between 1906 and 1929, their popularity and flexibility ensuring that they were to be a long-lived class; the first was not withdrawn until 1950, while the last remained in service until 1964.

No 4566 was one of 20 2-6-2Ts built at Swindon during 1924 with outside steampipes and an enlarged bunker. It began work for the GWR based at Newton Abbot, making frequent appearances on the Moretonhampstead and Kingswear branches, but it soon moved to Taunton in July 1927 for use on the Minehead line. After a few years at Swindon and Westbury in the early 1930s it was transferred to Bristol (Bath Road) in November 1935 and spent a lot of its time there working services to Cheddar and Wells, Frome via Radstock and up the Clevedon branch from Yatton. In February 1938 No 4566 returned to Swindon and mainly operated from the sub-sheds at Andover Junction and Chippenham (for the Calne branch). Following

another period at Bristol during the latter years of World War II, it went on to Penzance in November 1946 and regularly took packed trains of holiday-makers through to the popular resort of St Ives from St Erth on the main line, as well as working branch trains to Helston and freight traffic to Hayle harbour. Following dieselisation of these services in September 1961 it was transferred to Plymouth (Laira) but saw little work up to the time of condemnation in April 1962.

Eight years after withdrawal, despite looking slightly the worse for wear, an appeal was launched to bring No 4566 to the Severn Valley Railway in Shropshire, this ambition being achieved in late August 1970 when it was moved to Bewdley in a succession of freight trains. Restoration took a further five years since when it has been a reliable performer for its new owners, looking very much at home with a rake of chocolate-and-cream coaches.

No 4566 earns its keep with a heavy 8-coach Santa Special train on the Severn Valley Railway near Arley in December 1986. (*Peter J. C. Skelton*)

77

9th: S&DJR 2-8-0 No 53808

BUILT:	July 1925	ARRIVED BARRY:	June 1964
WITHDRAWN:	March 1964	DEPARTED BARRY:	October 1970

The former Somerset & Dorset Joint Railway between Bath and Bournemouth was without doubt one of the most loved and most photographed of any British railway, for it possessed a character all of its own. Responsibility for the motive power requirements of the line belonged to the Midland Railway, and in 1914 the first six of this class of 2-8-0s were built at Derby to a design by Sir Henry Fowler, a further five enlarged locomotives being ordered by the LMS after the Grouping.

No 53808 is one of this later batch, turned out from the Darlington Works of Robert Stephenson & Ço in 1925 as S&D No 88 (later LMS Nos 9678 and 13808). It spent the whole of its life based at Bath (Green Park) chiefly working the local freight between there and Evercreech Junction, although throughout the 1950s it was also used on the many summer Saturday holiday expresses to and from the north, taking them on that part of their route between Bath and Bournemouth. The ability of the class to haul these heavy trains unassisted over the steeply-graded northern section of the line made them a popular choice for this work. Only rarely did No 53808 venture up the 'branch' to Glaston-

bury and Highbridge so for almost 40 years it operated over the same stretch of track, a routine broken only by necessary visits to Derby Works for overhaul and repair as well as occasional trips up the Midland line to Westerleigh Yard, north of Mangotsfield. However, in September 1962 it was chosen to haul an Ian Allan enthusiasts' special throughout from Weymouth to Bath, a welcome break indeed, but less than 18 months later it was withdrawn and sold for scrap, despite being the last member of the class to have received a general overhaul.

Purchased by a group of S & D enthusiasts No 53808 was initially taken to Radstock but subsequently moved by rail to the West Somerset Railway in January 1976. Rebuilding largely took place in the goods yard at Washford station but was completed at Minehead, No 53808 making its long awaited public return to steam in August 1987.

No 53808 is prepared at Minehead for the West Somerset Railway Gala Weekend in September 1987 during which it worked a fully loaded 11-coach train to Bishops Lydeard. (*David Wilcock*)

10th: GWR 4-6-0 No 4983 *Albert Hall*

BUILT: January 1931
WITHDRAWN: December 1963

ARRIVED BARRY: June 1964
DEPARTED BARRY: October 1970

The prototype for the Hall Class 4-6-0s, No 4900 *Saint Martin*, was a 1924 Collett rebuild of Churchward's Saint Class No 2925, with 6ft 0in coupled wheels and other detail modifications. Following an extensive period of trials, it showed itself to be a good general-purpose locomotive, able to cope with all types of traffic and as a result production of the class was commenced in 1928 and eventually completed, with some changes, in 1950.

No 4983 *Albert Hall* was built at Swindon in January 1931 and started its career in Wales operating from Goodwick (Fishguard) depot. Like many other members of the Hall class it frequently moved from shed to shed, and during the following thirty-two years No 4983 was re-allocated no less than 21 times, including periods at Plymouth (Laira), Bristol, Weymouth, Oxford, Newton Abbot, Swindon, Newport (Ebbw Junction), Carmarthen, Cardiff, Pontypool Road, Old Oak Common, Duffryn Yard, Neyland and Severn Tunnel Junction! Despite this apparently nomadic existence it did have two relatively settled periods, the first being between April 1939 and March 1950 when it was based at Newton Abbot for general

mixed-traffic duties over the West of England main line, and between January 1952 and June 1958 when it stayed in the Bristol area, working from both St Philip's Marsh and Bath Road sheds in that city. Apart from local services to Taunton, Exeter and Newport, *Albert Hall* frequently travelled deep into Southern territory with the cross-country trains from Cardiff to Southampton, and on one or two occasions in the mid-1950s it worked special excursions up to Wembley in connection with some of the International sporting fixtures held there. After a varied career No 4983 was withdrawn in December 1963 and arrived at Barry six months later.

Removed from the scrap lines in company with 2-6-2T No 4588, No 4983 *Albert Hall* was towed to its new home at the Birmingham Railway Museum at Tyseley, arriving there towards the end of October 1970.

Albert Hall takes water on Lapworth troughs with a down fitted freight on the Leamington to Birmingham line in July 1962. (*M. Mensing*)

11th: GWR 2-6-2T No 4588

BUILT: March 1927
WITHDRAWN: July 1962

ARRIVED BARRY: November 1962
DEPARTED BARRY: October 1970

These attractive little tank engines were an everyday part of the West Country branch line scene and soon proved themselves to be the ideal 'Maids-of-all-Work'. By 1924, 75 members of the class had been built, but from 1927 a slightly modified version was turned out by Swindon, with larger tanks giving an additional 300 gallons' water capacity. These heavier locomotives were known as the 4575 class and could be easily differentiated from the earlier design by having a sloping top to the front end of the water tanks. (See photograph of No 4566 for the earlier design).

No 4588 was built at Swindon in March 1927, going new to Tyseley where it was used on the outer suburban services between Wolverhampton, Birmingham and Leamington, and although the class was not normally associated with this area, it remained there for three years. There then followed periods at Westbury and Bristol (Bath Road) between June 1931 and January 1945 when it became a familiar sight on local passenger and goods work in the Bath, Wells, Radstock and Yatton district, but with World War II drawing to a close, No 4588 moved on to Truro to help out for

several years with traffic on the Falmouth and Newquay lines. At the beginning of 1959, it was transferred to Oswestry, but hardly had time to settle down before moving again to Penzance in March of that year for services on the St Ives and Helston branches. Following a short spell at Taunton between September and November 1961, it went on to Plymouth (Laira) and spent its last few months working on the line to Tavistock and Launceston before withdrawal in 1962.

After thorough examination by a group of enthusiasts from the Dart Valley Railway Association, No 4588 was moved to Totnes in October 1970, but the decision was subsequently made to have the locomotive fully restored at its birthplace of Swindon Works, this being carried out between May and August 1971. Since then it has amassed a considerable mileage on both the Paignton and Dartmouth, and Buckfastleigh and Totnes Steam Railways in Devon.

No 4588 approaches Hood Bridge near Staverton with a Buckfastleigh to Totnes train in August 1987. (*Roger Penny*)

12th: LMR 2-6-0 No 46521

BUILT: February 1953
WITHDRAWN: October 1966

ARRIVED BARRY: March 1967
DEPARTED BARRY: March 1971

H. G. Ivatt, the last Chief Mechanical Engineer of the LMS, produced this modern looking class of locomotives as a replacement for some of the ageing designs which dated back to the pre-Grouping era. Twenty of the class were built by the LMS between 1946 and 1947 and as light passenger tender locomotives they were considered so ahead of their time that construction was continued by BR right up to 1953. In service they earned the reputation for being sprightly hard-working locomotives, economical on fuel and comparatively easy to maintain.

No 46521 illustrates one of the final batch of 25 built at Swindon in 1952/3, which were also fitted with an enclosed cab on the tender to improve conditions on the footplate when running tender-first. Following an initial allocation for one month at Oswestry, No 46521 went to the Central Wales depot of Brecon during March 1953, where it immediately started work on a wide variety of passenger and freight duties up to Llanidloes and Moat Lane on the former Cambrian system, down to Newport on the Brecon & Merthyr line, and across to Hereford via the Midland route. Locomotives of this type came to monopolise the two- or three-coach passenger trains on the mid-Wales line although the steep gradients and sharp curves precluded anything like fast running. In October 1959 No 46521 returned to Oswestry and joined other members of the class there on services to Welshpool, Whitchurch and Llanfyllin, but also occasionally journeyed back to the Brecon area for duty on the lines emanating from Three Cocks Junction. Staying on the Cambrian, this 2-6-0 was finally transferred to Machynlleth in March 1963 and appeared on Pwllheli and Aberystwyth trains.

No 46521 spent only four years on the scrap lines at Barry before being purchased for use on the Severn Valley Railway, where it arrived in March 1971. Successfully steamed in July 1974, it had the distinction of being the first locomotive from Barry to be returned to service on the SVR. During 1975 it temporarily ran in a red livery for scenes in the film *The Seven Per Cent Solution* but has since been repainted in BR green.

Complete with bell mounted on the running plate, No 46521 crosses Oldbury viaduct with a SVR engineering train. (*Graham Wignall*)

81

13th: BR 2-6-4T No 80079

BUILT: March 1954
WITHDRAWN: July 1965

ARRIVED BARRY: January 1966
DEPARTED BARRY: May 1971

The British Railways Standard design of Class 4 2-6-4 tank owes its ancestry to the basically similar locomotives produced for the LMS by Stanier and Fairburn between 1935 and 1948. Although classified as 'mixed traffic', the BR locomotives were more of a fast passenger tank for long-distance outer suburban trains, and their high route availability saw them at various times working over most of this country's railway network.

No 80079 emerged from Brighton Works in March 1954 and went new to Plaistow depot on the ex-London, Tilbury & Southend line, where it worked the intensive commuter traffic between Fenchurch Street, Southend and Shoeburyness. It was while on one of these workings in January 1958 that it collided in thick fog with another train at Dagenham East, and although the tank suffered little damage ten passengers were killed. By now, No 80079 was based at Tilbury and in September 1959 it was recorded heading up the East Coast main line towards Doncaster with A4 Pacific No 60014 *Silver Link* in tow, both going to the Works there for overhaul. When electrification of the LT&S Lines was completed in June 1962, a period

was spent in storage at Old Oak Common before the decision was made to send it to Croes Newydd (Wrexham) depot for use on passenger and freight workings over the Cambrian lines to Welshpool, Aberystwyth and Pwllheli, as well as on the local trains between Wrexham and Chester Northgate. It was also occasionally seen on the Severn Valley line with services down from Shrewsbury, but gradually No 80079 and its sister locomotives were declared redundant, resulting in their being sent to the scrapyard despite having many years of useful life left in them.

Rescue came for No 80079 in May 1971 and after six years of hard work it returned to service on the Severn Valley Railway in the spring of 1977. In May 1980 it took part in the Rocket 150 Cavalcade at Rainhill, while in 1983 it double-headed with fellow SVR locomotive No 43106 on the Welsh Marches Pullman between Newport and Hereford.

No 80079 and No 43106 give a spirited performance on the Welsh Marches Pullman at Ponthir, north of Newport, in February 1983. (*Peter J. C. Skelton*)

82

14th: GWR 4-6-0 No 5900 *Hinderton Hall*

BUILT: March 1931
WITHDRAWN: November 1963

ARRIVED BARRY: June 1964
DEPARTED BARRY: June 1971

General production of the Hall Class was commenced in 1928, with no fewer than 330 locomotives being built over the next 22 years. It was an extremely versatile and reliable class, designed mainly for mixed-traffic duties such as stopping passenger trains, parcels traffic and some of the more important freight workings. However, during the 1950s, when peak summer Saturday traffic stretched motive power resources, they were used indiscriminately with the larger Castles and Counties on hauling 14-coach expresses down to the West Country.

No 5900 *Hinderton Hall* was built at Swindon in March 1931, and after a short period of running-in at Old Oak Common spent the years leading up to Nationalisation operating from quite a variety of sheds including those at Worcester, Hereford, Carmarthen, Swindon, Bristol and Westbury. During March 1953 it was transferred to Tyseley, and apart from performing on local passenger and freight turns, No 5900 assisted some of the heavy expresses over the line between Stratford-upon-Avon and Birmingham as well as often working into South Wales with the through trains from Snow Hill to Cardiff. By the mid-1950s it was based at Wolverhampton (Stafford Road) where it continued at work in the West Midlands, including frequent trips up to Crewe, for a further seven years before returning to Old Oak Common at the end of October 1962. This Hall only stayed here for a few weeks prior to its final allocation at Bristol (St Philip's Marsh) depot from November onwards but the planned elimination of Western Region steam saw No 5900 work out its last twelve months in BR service mainly on freight traffic.

Hinderton Hall was resteamed at the Didcot Railway Centre in early 1976 following an extensive rebuild lasting five years. It then saw use on several main line excursions including the Shakespeare Venturer of March 1979 when it returned to familiar territory at Stratford-upon-Avon. In that same year No 5900 also took part in the 125th Anniversary celebrations of Paddington station but is now back on display at Didcot.

Hinderton Hall and *Burton Agnes Hall* double-head the Great Western Society's Vintage Train near Kings Sutton in May 1976. (*G. R. Hounsell*)

15th: GWR 2-6-2T No 5572

BUILT: February 1929
WITHDRAWN: April 1962

ARRIVED BARRY: September 1962
DEPARTED BARRY: August 1971

Development of the 45XX Class was largely based on the need for a modern locomotive with a light axle loading for branch line work and their construction took place between 1906 and 1929. With a coupled wheel diameter of 4ft 7½in they were capable of speeds up to 60 mph and dealt with a wide range of duties over almost the entire Great Western system.

No 5572, one of the last three small prairie tanks to be built at Swindon, was sent new to Exeter in February 1929 for use on the local stopping services, but by 1933 had moved on to Kidderminster where it chiefly performed on the passenger workings to Shrewsbury over the Severn Valley line. Between September 1935 and August 1953 it was based at Westbury, Bristol (Bath Road) and Taunton sheds but the introduction of a regular interval passenger timetable in the Cardiff Valleys area in September 1953 saw No 5572, along with 14 other members of the class, transferred to Cardiff (Cathays). Here it became the first one to be fitted with apparatus for auto-working and the routes they covered included Bridgend-Cymmer, Porth-Maerdy and Cardiff-Coryton, the latter line servic-

ing the residential areas on the Northern outskirts of Cardiff. The drafting of diesel multiple-units to these trains in February 1958 saw No 5572 re-allocated to Plymouth (Laira) where it became a regular performer on the Plymouth North Road–Tavistock/Launceston branch as well as on the Liskeard–Looe branch from time to time. Just over two years later, in September 1960, it went on to St Blazey where the duties included trips up to Wadebridge from Bodmin Road together with goods and passenger workings on the branch between Par and Newquay, but by April 1961 it had returned to Laira and spent the last 12 months leading up to withdrawal back on the Tavistock line.

Initially taken to Taunton for restoration, No 5572 moved to Didcot and was resteamed in April 1985. Soon after it ran down the main line to Reading to take part in the BR open day there but has also subsequently seen use on the Keighley and Worth Valley and West Somerset Railways.

During its summer 1986 visit to the West Somerset Railway No 5572 prepares to leave Minehead with a special freight train for Williton. (*Tom Clift*)

16th: GWR 0-6-2T No 5643

BUILT: October 1925

WITHDRAWN: July 1963

ARRIVED BARRY: November 1963

DEPARTED BARRY: September 1971

Many of the Welsh railways absorbed by the GWR in 1923 depended upon tank engines, particularly of the 0-6-2T wheel arrangement, to cope with their coal and passenger traffic and so C. B. Collett, Chief Mechanical Engineer at the Grouping, initially took the best of these and modified them to Swindon standards. However, this still left a shortage of suitable locomotives to handle the considerable volume of traffic generated in the valleys, and in 1924 he brought out a more modern version of the traditional 0-6-2T, two hundred of this new design being built over the next four years.

No 5643 emerged from Swindon Works in October 1925 and was allocated initially to Cardiff (Cathays) for just over a year before going to the shed at Coke Ovens (Pontypridd) on the former Taff Vale Railway. From there its main duty was to take the heavy coal trains down to the docks at Cardiff as well as being rostered to some of the local passenger turns. Although spending a month working from Cardiff East Dock during November 1931, No 5643 remained at Coke Ovens until December 1933 when the shed was closed and the entire allocation transferred up the valley to Abercynon. Apart from short periods on loan to Rhymney and Treherbert in the 1940s, it stayed here for the next 28 years handling a variety of duties in the district, mainly over the lines to Aberdare and Merthyr. In June 1961 No 5643 moved to Barry, where in addition to working the remaining steam-hauled freight and passenger services in that area, it also helped with the many summer special excursions to Barry Island. On withdrawal in July 1963 it was only a short journey into Woodham's scrapyard, where it was to remain for the next eight years.

Originally purchased by the now defunct Eastern Valleys Railway Co, No 5643 was delivered to Cwmbran in 1971 but soon travelled north to go on display at Steamtown, Carnforth. From late 1986 onwards, No 5643 has been owned by a few Lakeside Railway Society members and when repairs are complete it will work at Carnforth for a short while before transferring to Haverthwaite.

Cosmetically restored at Steamtown during 1984 it will hopefully not be too long before No 5643 makes a welcome return to service. (*Nigel Harris*)

17th: SR 4-6-2 No 34092 *City of Wells*

BUILT: September 1949
WITHDRAWN: November 1964

ARRIVED BARRY: March 1965
DEPARTED BARRY: October 1971

The Bulleid West Country Pacifics were a light-weight scaled-down version of the earlier Merchant Navy design and intended for use on those secondary routes barred to the heavier locomotives. Despite having a boiler of excellent steaming capacity the class proved expensive to run in terms of both fuel consumption and maintenance costs, and even though the decision was taken in 1957 to rebuild them, 50 remained in their original condition at the end of steam.

No 34092 *City of Wells*, represents one of these unrebuilt locomotives turned out from Brighton Works in September 1949. It was originally named *Wells* in a ceremony held in that city during November 1949, an expensive operation that necessitated track strengthening to permit such a heavy locomotive to pass over the former Somerset & Dorset branch from Glastonbury. First based at Stewarts Lane depot, it spent eleven years hauling boat trains between London Victoria and the Channel Ports including the famous Golden Arrow on which No 34092 became a regular performer. On two occasions in May and July 1956 it was also chosen to haul special trains respectively conveying

President Krushchev of the USSR and King Feisal of Iraq. Perhaps more surprisingly in November 1960 it even managed to work a troop train from the Southern Region right through to Parkeston Quay on the Essex Coast. Following completion of the Kent Coast electrification in May 1961, *City of Wells* was transferred to Salisbury from where it worked both passenger and freight traffic over the main line between Waterloo and Exeter, including Meldon ballast trains.

In 1971 No 34092 became the first Bulleid Pacific to leave Barry, travelling to the Keighley and Worth Valley for repair. Returning to service in April 1980 it has been a consistent performer on BR main line excursions over a large number of routes and in November 1985 became the first Southern Pacific departure from a London terminus since 1967 when it worked a special out of Marylebone. From May 1986 onwards *City of Wells* has been fitted with a Giesl ejector to improve combustion.

City of Wells sparkles in the sunshine as it gets ready to leave Scarborough with the Scarborough Spa Express for York and Leeds in August 1982. (*Alan Warren*)

18th: LMS 4-6-0 No 45690 *Leander*

BUILT: March 1936
WITHDRAWN: March 1964

ARRIVED BARRY: July 1964
DEPARTED BARRY: May 1972

Sir William Stanier's design for a fast passenger locomotive which could operate over most of the LMS system emerged from Crewe in 1934 as an improved taper-boiler version of the earlier Patriot Class. At first, doubts were cast on their steam-raising ability but after various modifications to the design, the Jubilees proved to be very useful locomotives right up to the end of steam, particularly on the former Midland Railway lines out of St Pancras.

LMS No 5690 was built at Crewe Works in early 1936 and began its career working from Crewe running shed on the semi-fast expresses to London and Glasgow, as well as on some of the fast freight duties over the West Coast main line. After nine years on this work, *Leander* was transferred to Bristol (Barrow Road) in September 1947 and found regular employment on the cross-country trains between Bristol, Birmingham, Sheffield and York, although it was frequently 'borrowed' by other depots with the result that it unusually spent a week in January 1957 on the local services between Carlisle and Glasgow! During the latter years of steam operation, diesels began to take over most of *Leander*'s normal duties, and it therefore began to

appear on many special workings to a variety of destinations including Leicester, Marylebone, Southall, Exeter and Bangor at various times between 1962 and 1963! However, by March 1964 it had joined the sad row of withdrawn locomotives on the scrap lines at Barrow Road and was dispatched to Barry soon after.

Following purchase from Woodham's yard No 45690 underwent a six-month overhaul in early 1973 at BR's Derby Works. Since then it has hauled numerous excursions over the main line, based initially at the Dinting Railway Centre for five years but later moving to Steamtown, Carnforth in 1979 and then to the Severn Valley Railway from 1983 onwards. *Leander* took part in the Shildon and Rainhill Cavalcades and has also made guest appearances on the North Yorkshire Moors Railway and at the Midland Railway Centre, Butterley.

A magnificent portrait of *Leander* at work on a Kidderminster to Bridgnorth train in April 1987. (*Peter J. C. Skelton*)

19th: LMS 2-8-0 No 48431

BUILT:	March 1944	ARRIVED BARRY:	August 1964
WITHDRAWN:	May 1964	DEPARTED BARRY:	May 1972

In 1935 the LMS brought out the first of its standard heavy freight locomotives to the design of Sir William Stanier. Sharing a lot in common with his earlier 'Black Five' mixed-traffic 4-6-0s, they became one of the numerically largest classes of locomotive in Britain and their proven reliability and strength saw them adopted by the Government during World War II as the standard freight locomotive for service at home and overseas.

LMS No 8431 was one of eighty 2-8-0s built at Swindon Works in 1944 for temporary use on the GWR. Based at Newton Abbot and Gloucester sheds it was soon put to work on the important wartime freight traffic, and a regular duty of the class was to haul the heavy coal trains between South Wales and Plymouth. The class was transferred away during 1947 and in March of that year this particular locomotive went north to Royston in Yorkshire where it was to stay for just over eight years before returning to GWR territory at Bristol (St Philip's Marsh) in September 1955. Although mainly employed on the heavy goods workings in that area there were also times when it was rostered to the occasional passenger turn, being recorded on

a Weston-super-Mare local in July 1957 and a Bristol to Weymouth excursion in May 1959. The next move was to Old Oak Common at the beginning of 1960, and from there it made trips down the West of England main line as far as Plymouth, in addition to appearing on some of the cross-London freights. In December 1962 No 48431 returned to Bristol for a year, this time based at Barrow Road depot, and although reallocated to Bath (Green Park) in January 1964 it only managed to remain in service for a further five months.

Transported by road to the Keighley & Worth Valley Railway in 1972, No 8431 re-entered traffic in LMS livery during late 1975 and after many years service on the line between Keighley and Oxenhope travelled south in May 1985 to take part in the GWR 150 celebrations held at the Didcot Railway Centre. Following a further repaint during 1986 it has now reverted to BR condition as No 48431.

No 48431 and No 43924 tackle the climb near Haworth with a heavy train in December 1985. (*David Wilcock*)

20th: LMR 2-6-0 No 46447

BUILT: March 1950
WITHDRAWN: December 1966

ARRIVED BARRY: June 1967
DEPARTED BARRY: June 1972

This handsome-looking class of 2-6-0s was designed by H. G. Ivatt with the emphasis on easy maintenance and operation, and accordingly was built with such features as self-cleaning smokeboxes, rocking grates, self-emptying ashpans and outside Walschaerts valve gear. It proved ideal for general light work and branch duties and saw service on all regions of BR except the Southern. After the final batch had been built at Swindon in 1953, the design was altered slightly to incorporate BR standard components and became the 78000 Class, of which 65 were built.

No 46447 was turned out from Crewe Works in March 1950, and with several other members of the class began operating from Workington shed on the Cumberland Coast. Here it replaced the veteran LNWR 'Cauliflower' 0-6-0s on the local services to Keswick and Penrith as well as working up to Carlisle via Maryport. In December 1959 it was transferred to Wigan (Springs Branch) and was used on the stopping passenger trains to Liverpool, Bolton and Rochdale for six months before moving on, in June 1960, for a period of operation on the North Wales coast, being based successively at

Llandudno Junction and Bangor depots. During this time No 46447 became a very familiar sight on the short pick-up goods between Llandudno Junction and Town stations until September 1961 when it moved on again, this time to Nuneaton. There it worked all manner of trains to a variety of destinations including Birmingham, Leicester and Leamington Spa, but by May 1964 had returned to Springs Branch, only to find that diesel multiple-units had taken over most of its passenger duties. Thus the last 2½ years in BR service were fairly quiet mainly dealing with local freight traffic or as a standby for diesel failures.

Following purchase from Barry No 46447 was taken to the Buckinghamshire Railway Centre at Quainton Road during June 1972. After a period of storage in the open it now awaits its turn for rebuilding inside the Ivatt Trust's workshops there.

After 16 years of service to British Railways, No 46447 stands at Barry in 1968, considered to be of no further use . . . (Graham Wignall)

21st: BR 4-6-0 No 75078

BUILT: January 1956
WITHDRAWN: July 1966

ARRIVED BARRY: November 1966
DEPARTED BARRY: June 1972

The Class 4 4-6-0s were perhaps one of the most successful of all the Standard designs produced after Nationalisation. The concept was of a light-weight medium-strength locomotive that had a high route availability enabling it to work over lines barred to the larger Standard Class 5s. In practice, however, the locomotives were used on fairly light long-distance passenger trains over the secondary main lines. All 80 members of the class were built at Swindon between 1951 and 1957 – a further order for ten was cancelled as the onset of dieselisation made their construction uneconomic.

No 75078 was built in January 1956 and arrived at Exmouth Junction shed, near Exeter, towards the end of that month. Its initial work included the local services to Plymouth over the Southern main line via Okehampton, and very occasionally over the attractive coastal section of the GWR main line via Dawlish for crew training purposes. The stay here was short, for only six months later it had moved on to Basingstoke primarily for use on the semi-fasts to Waterloo and Salisbury, although on one occasion in August 1962 it managed to work right through to Wolverhampton with a holiday

relief from Portsmouth Harbour. It was while shedded at Basingstoke that No 75078 acquired the handsome double chimney that all the Southern Region-based examples of the class were to carry. In March 1963 it was re-allocated to Nine Elms in London, and as well as the more usual stopping passenger duties it also dealt with a certain amount of the parcels and other general freight traffic. Its final move in May 1965 was to Eastleigh on the out-skirts of Southampton, where the locomotives worked over quite a large area to Bournemouth, Salisbury, Portsmouth, Reading and Waterloo. After a working life of only ten years No 75078 was withdrawn in July 1966 as surplus to requirements.

On completion of its restoration at Haworth on the Keighley & Worth Valley Railway in 1977, No 75078 has proved to be popular on that line and took part in the shooting of the successful film *Yanks* during 1978.

No 75078 runs round its train at Keighley ready for another trip up the valley to Oxenhope in April 1981. (*Alan Warren*)

22nd: SR 4-6-2 No 34016 *Bodmin*

BUILT: November 1945
WITHDRAWN: June 1964

ARRIVED BARRY: November 1964
DEPARTED BARRY: July 1972

Towards the end of World War II the first of the Bulleid light Pacifics was completed at Brighton Works. Although there was an urgent need for new motive power over most of the Southern system at that time, precedence was given to services in the West Country and West of England main line.

Carrying its original Bulleid-style number, 21C116 emerged from Brighton Works in November 1945 and was named *Bodmin* at a ceremony held in that town during August 1946. Sent new to Exmouth Junction it saw service on such famous trains as the Devon Belle and Atlantic Coast Express as well as on the more humble local passenger workings between Exeter and Plymouth, but it was also recorded in July 1949 as having penetrated deep into Cornwall with a special freight from Exeter Riverside to Truro. *Bodmin* stayed at Exmouth Junction until February 1958 when it was transferred to Ramsgate to work the commuter trains between the Kent coast towns and London. Shortly after rebuilding in April 1958 it was chosen to haul a special all-Pullman train conveying the President of Italy from Dover to Victoria, but on completion of Stage 1 of the Kent coast electrifica-

tion scheme in June 1959, No 34016 became redundant and was re-allocated to Bricklayers Arms where it joined the other Bulleid Pacifics working commuter services via Tonbridge. Completion of Stage 2 in May 1961 saw it move yet again, this time to Eastleigh where it replaced the Lord Nelson 4-6-0s on the boat trains between Southampton Docks and Waterloo in addition to operating local services down to Bournemouth and Weymouth. A cracked inside cylinder led to withdrawal in June 1964, although it was used for testing safety-valves at Eastleigh for a short while.

After an initial period of restoration at Quainton Road No 34016 was transferred to the Mid-Hants Railway in 1976, resteaming taking place some three years later. The standard of work carried out and its subsequent maintenance have been a credit to all concerned.

Carrying a special Royal Wessex headboard *Bodmin* pulls away from Ropley with an Alresford to Alton train in June 1987. (*David Warwick*)

23rd: WR 4-6-0 No 7027 *Thornbury Castle*

BUILT: August 1949
WITHDRAWN: December 1963

ARRIVED BARRY: May 1964
DEPARTED BARRY: August 1972

Despite having produced Britain's first Pacific in 1908, the Great Western Railway preferred to develop the excellent Star class 4-6-0s when it came to designing a new class of express passenger locomotive. Thus when the Castle Class was introduced in 1923 they were the most powerful engines of their type in the country, and throughout their long careers earned the reputation for being exceptionally reliable and economical on coal as well as having the ability for sustained high-speed running.

No 7027 *Thornbury Castle* is not a true Great Western product for it was built at Swindon after Nationalisation, in August 1949. Going initially to the shed at Plymouth (Laira) it quickly moved on to Old Oak Common in January 1951 and worked over most parts of the GWR system with expresses out of Paddington, being recorded on many of the well-known named trains of the time including The Inter-City, The Royal Duchy and The Bristolian, on which it was a frequent performer during the latter part of 1951. Other duties were the Channel Islands boat trains from Weymouth and some of the holiday expresses from the Midlands to Devon and Cornwall, which it worked from Birmingham on-

wards. In May 1960 No 7027 moved to Worcester where the shed staff kept it in fine external condition for working The Cathedrals Express between there and London, and even as late as July 1963 it was still covering many of the Worcester to Paddington trains despite the gradual introduction of the new diesel-hydraulics. Following its last general overhaul at Swindon in August 1963, *Thornbury Castle* was transferred to Reading where it spent the majority of its last three months in BR service either acting as station pilot or in store prior to withdrawal in December of that year.

Although originally purchased by the Birmingham Railway Museum as a source of spare parts for its other Castle locomotives, No 7027 still awaits a final decision to be made on its future role at Tyseley.

Thornbury Castle speeds downhill from Chipping Campden with the 1.15 p m Paddington to Hereford express in May 1963. (*M. Mensing*)

24th: SR 4-6-0 No 30841

BUILT: July 1936
WITHDRAWN: January 1964

ARRIVED BARRY: June 1964
DEPARTED BARRY: September 1972

Along with one or two other pre-Grouping classes, the Urie S15 4-6-0s were selected by R. E. L. Maunsell for further development to help with the Southern Railway's traffic requirements. Initially the class was only increased by 15 locomotives built between 1927 and 1928, but a further batch of ten was added in 1936. It was a particularly handsome group of locomotives which gave long and reliable service, the entire class lasting into the early 1960s.

No 30841 was built at Eastleigh in July 1936 and together with four other members of the class was sent to Hither Green for use on the main line goods trains down to Ashford and Dover via Tonbridge, but shortly after the outbreak of World War II it was transferred to Feltham to help out with the corresponding increase in freight traffic, as well as handling some of the slower-timed passenger workings. By 1950, No 30841 was operating from Exmouth Junction and became a familiar sight on fast freights up the main line to Salisbury, together with one of its depot's shorter-distance duties, the daily goods to Newcourt Sidings on the Exmouth branch. Because of the S15's ability to show a good turn of speed when required, it was also used on

secondary passenger turns, including the services between Templecombe and Salisbury, Axminster to Yeovil Town and Seaton Junction to Exeter. After more than 13 years at Exmouth Junction, No 30841 moved back to Feltham in September 1963 but was withdrawn only four months later.

No 30841 was moved to the East Anglian Railway Museum at Chappel in September 1972 and named *Greene King* in recognition of a local sponsor. Following restoration it took part in the Rail 150 cavalcade at Shildon in 1975 and then hauled two special trains in East Anglia. After a brief spell on the Nene Valley Railway between October 1977 and November 1978 it moved to the North Yorkshire Moors Railway and, with name removed, has recently returned to traffic following a major overhaul.

No 841 departs from Goathland with an afternoon train for Pickering on Easter Sunday 1987. (*Maurice Burns*)

93

25th: GWR 2-6-2T No 5541

BUILT:	August 1928	ARRIVED BARRY:	November 1962
WITHDRAWN:	July 1962	DEPARTED BARRY:	October 1972

The Churchward 45XX prairie tanks were an immediate success when first introduced in 1906, and with the similar 44XX 2-6-2Ts revolutionised branch line working in the West of England. Their exceptional powers of acceleration and general adaptability made them very popular with their crews and they have proved to be an ideal locomotive for this country's private railways.

No 5541 was completed at Swindon Works towards the end of August 1928 and after a period of running-in from Swindon stock shed, went to take up duty from Bristol (Bath Road). There were several other prairie tanks based there for local passenger and freight work, and although No 5541 was more commonly seen in the Radstock and Wells areas, it also worked over the lines to Avonmouth, Portishead, Weston-super-Mare, and the short branch between Yatton and Clevedon. By April 1938 it had moved on to Machynlleth in Central Wales, although for a lot of the time there it was regularly stationed at the sub-sheds of Pwllheli and Portmadoc. For 22 years it worked the pick-up freights and local passenger services along the Cambrian Coast line and frequently appeared on the Pwllheli portion of the Cambrian Coast Express which it took onwards from Dovey Junction. Occasionally it would pilot some of the heavy expresses over the notorious Talerddig Incline but the introduction of BR Standard classes to the area saw No 5541 transferred away in January 1960, initially to Penzance but later to Plymouth (Laira) where it took charge of services on the Launceston line. Although often referred to as a branch, the return journey over this line was no less than 71 miles. On withdrawal in July 1962, No 5541 had amassed a recorded mileage of just under one million miles.

Preliminary cleaning up of the locomotive was undertaken at Barry before No 5541 was moved by rail to the Dean Forest Railway in 1972. Returned to traffic in just over three years, it now has a bright future on the 4-mile branch from Lydney to Parkend.

No 5541 prepares for a weekend programme on the Dean Forest Railway at Norchard in 1986. Fellow ex-Barry resident No 9681 stands alongside. (*Peter J. C. Skelton*)

94

26th: GWR 4-6-0 No 6960 *Raveningham Hall*

BUILT: March 1944
WITHDRAWN: June 1964

ARRIVED BARRY: July 1964
DEPARTED BARRY: October 1972

When F. W. Hawksworth was appointed Chief Mechanical Engineer of the GWR in 1941, Britain was in the grip of war and all normal locomotive development work at Swindon had been suspended. However, the Modified Hall or 6959 Class was introduced in 1944 to meet the demand for additional mixed-traffic motive power, Hawksworth taking the already successful Collett design and adding his own improvements, such as a higher degree of superheat, plate frames and a redesigned front bogie.

Completed at Swindon in March 1944, No 6960 did not carry the name *Raveningham Hall* until June 1947 when the wartime restrictions on the use of brass were lifted. Sent new to Old Oak Common it worked a variety of trains to most parts of the GW system, and in June 1951 was reported as being a regular performer on the Paddington to Weymouth Channel Islands boat trains. By 1953 No 6960 had moved on to Reading where, in addition to taking the semi-fast and stopping commuter trains up to London, it frequently worked as far north as Chester with the Margate to Birkenhead through services and even appeared on the Torbay Express

in the summer of 1954. The Halls at Reading were also used on general freight work with some of the rosters taking them away from their home depot for many days at a time. During August 1963, No 6960 was transferred to Oxford where its duties included the services to Paddington, Wolverhampton and Gloucester, as well as taking over the York to Bournemouth through train at Oxford and working it right down to the South Coast resort.

In late 1972, No 6960 was purchased by the directors of Steamtown, Carnforth and following a complete overhaul was one of the few GWR representatives in the 1975 Rail 150 cavalcade held at Shildon. Purchased privately by an enthusiast in 1977, *Raveningham Hall* is currently based on the Severn Valley Railway but has also made regular forays onto the BR main line including the GWR 150 specials between Swansea and Carmarthen in the late summer of 1985.

With a mixed collection of coaching stock in tow, No 6960 approaches Foley Park Tunnel with the 1.05pm Bridgnorth to Kidderminster in April 1987. (*John B. Gosling*)

27th: LMS 0-6-0T No 47493

BUILT:	February 1928	ARRIVED BARRY:	June 1967
WITHDRAWN:	December 1966	DEPARTED BARRY:	November 1972

Although the LMS Class 3F 0-6-0 tanks had many nicknames during their lives, it is as 'Jinties' that the class has commonly, if perhaps erroneously, become known by enthusiasts. Whatever you may wish to call them, they formed an integral part of the LMS scene, being used on a wide variety of duties from shunting in some remote yard to hauling six- or seven-coach local passenger trains on the main line.

No 47493 was constructed for the LMS by the Vulcan Foundry at its Newton-le-Willows workshops in Lancashire. After one week on test at nearby Warrington shed, it entered traffic as No 16576 in February 1928 and journeyed south to take up work from Devons Road, in East London. Here it joined several other members of the class engaged on the passenger services out of Broad Street to Poplar and up the GN main line as far as Potters Bar, but it also spent a good deal of time on shunting duties and transfer freights across London. After more than 26 years on this work, No 47493 was transferred to Speke Junction in November 1954, and helped out with local freight and shunting in the South Liverpool area until

December 1958, when it went on to the large shed at Newton Heath in Manchester. Just three months later it returned to Speke Junction for another spell before moving on again, in July 1962, to Wigan (Springs Branch) where its duties now included working in Bamfurlong sorting sidings and some of the other smaller yards in that district. Transferred finally to Liverpool (Edge Hill) in August 1965, No 47493 saw out its last months in service on trip freights down to the docks or occasionally on pilot duty at Lime Street Station.

In November 1972, No 47493 was transported by road to Radstock for temporary storage before moving on, by rail, to the East Somerset Railway one year later. Restoration was completed during 1976 and it had the honour of working the inaugural public passenger train out of Cranmore station on 4 April 1980.

The early morning sun glistens on the bunker side of No 47493 as it raises steam for the day's work ahead at Cranmore on the ESR. (*Steve Marcks*)

28th: GWR 2-6-2T No 4141

BUILT: August 1946
WITHDRAWN: February 1963

ARRIVED BARRY: November 1963
DEPARTED BARRY: January 1973

The history of this class of 2-6-2Ts dates back to 1903 when G. J. Churchward introduced the first of his designs for a large passenger tank engine. After the prototype had been thoroughly tried and tested, regular production of the class was commenced in 1905 and continued, with various modifications, until the early years of Nationalisation in 1949. Over 300 were built in their different forms, and they were mainly used on semi-fast and suburban passenger trains as well as on medium-distance freight traffic.

No 4141 represents one of the 5101 Class, an updated version of the original basic design, turned out from Swindon Works in August 1946. The whole of its career was spent allocated to Gloucester (Horton Road) although for much of this time it actually operated from Brimscombe (for banking duties up to Sapperton) or from the sub-shed at Cheltenham. At the latter depot it regularly worked the local passenger service across to Kingham and Chipping Norton, a route which took in the beautiful Cotswold village of Bourton-on-the-Water, while another interesting duty was the working of the London to Cheltenham expresses over the final part of their journeys from Gloucester. This gave the large prairie tanks an opportunity for some fast running over a fairly easy stretch of track with nine or ten coaches – on the return journey the train was reversed at Gloucester and generally worked onwards to Paddington by a Castle. During the periods when No 4141 was operating from the parent Gloucester shed it was often used on the stopping trains to Hereford, in addition to the occasional pick-up freight in the area. However, the closure of the line to Kingham at the end of 1962 together with the gradual introduction of diesels saw it finally declared surplus to requirements in February 1963.

Following purchase from Barry, No 4141 was taken in a convoy with several other locomotives to the Severn Valley Railway in early 1973 and since then it has undergone restoration on an isolated section of track at the quiet country station of Hampton Loade.

While funds are raised for its purchase No 4141 has had its chimney sheeted over in this early 1970s view at Barry.
(*D. K. Jones collection*)

29th: GWR 4-6-0 No 4930 *Hagley Hall*

BUILT: May 1929   ARRIVED BARRY: May 1964
WITHDRAWN: November 1963   DEPARTED BARRY: January 1973

After almost three years of evaluation tests with the converted Saint Class 4-6-0 No 4900 *Saint Martin*, general construction of the Halls was begun in December 1928, the first 80 being ordered in one lot. They were ideal mixed-traffic locomotives, deservedly earning a fine reputation for themselves.

No 4930 *Hagley Hall* was a product of Swindon Works in May 1929, and in the years leading up to World War II worked mainly from Wolverhampton (Oxley) and Chester sheds. During November 1939 it was transferred to Tyseley for use on the semi-fast passenger services out of Birmingham Snow Hill and Moor Street, as well as on the usual parcels and freight traffic. After brief spells at Weymouth and Bristol (St Philip's Marsh) it moved on to Westbury in 1953 where, in addition to working over the West of England main line, it also saw service on the routes to Bath, Swindon and Salisbury. At various times between May 1958 and July 1962, No 4930 fluctuated between Taunton and Exeter sheds and dealt with the slow, semi-fast and goods services between those two places and beyond, including many of the summer holiday expresses to resorts in Devon and Cornwall. July

1962 saw *Hagley Hall* transferred to Old Oak Common for two months before it moved on again, this time to the running shed at Swindon. Here it performed on the now familiar pattern of duties for the class and on one occasion in November 1962 it worked through to Yeovil town with a football excursion from Swindon. Withdrawn one year later, it had run just over 1¼ million miles during its 34 years of service.

Restoration of *Hagley Hall* to full working order was completed on the Severn Valley Railway in 1979 and it made its BR main line debut in September of that same year. Throughout the 1980s it has been a popular choice for these special trains, taking a prominent part in the GW 150 celebrations held during the summer of 1985 while more unusually perhaps it also saw service on BR's freight-only line between Andover and Ludgershall during March 1986.

Hagley Hall passes through Haresfield on the first day of the special Swindon to Gloucester trains in the summer of 1985. (*Peter J. C. Skelton*)

30th: GWR 2-6-2T No 5164

BUILT: November 1930
WITHDRAWN: April 1963

ARRIVED BARRY: November 1963
DEPARTED BARRY: January 1973

This class of large prairie tanks was built over a period of 46 years, thus effectively extending the construction of a 1903 design into the era of a Nationalised railway system! The 5101 series was introduced in 1929 as a more modern version of this original design and the locomotives were principally involved with passenger duties, although widespread dieselisation of suburban services from 1957 onwards displaced many from this work onto freight and banking turns.

Put into service from Swindon Works during November 1930, No 5164 was to spend the following 26 years based in the Wolverhampton area, operating mainly from Tyseley, although for short periods it did also work from Stafford Road and Wellington sheds. Tyseley always kept a large allocation of this class for dealing with the commuter trains from Birmingham to Leamington, Stratford-upon-Avon, Stourbridge and Kidderminster as well as in the opposite direction to Wolverhampton and Wellington. The class was also popular for working some of the long-distance trip freights between the marshalling yards at Oxley and Bordesley. In August 1956 No 5164 was trans-ferred to Newton Abbot, where its main purpose was to provide banking assistance for freight trains over the severe gradients between there and Brent; it was either kept at Aller Junction for banking trains to Dainton Tunnel or at Totnes station for use in both directions to Dainton or Rattery. When not employed on these duties, it could be seen working the local trains to Plymouth and Exeter, branch services on the line to Moretonhampstead, or during the summer peak, holiday expresses onward from Newton Abbot down to Torquay and Kingswear. In October 1961 No 5164 moved to Pontypool Road and worked out its last few months in South Wales before withdrawal in April 1963.

Taken to the Severn Valley Railway in early 1973 along with GWR locomotives Nos 4141, 4930 and 7819, No 5164 underwent extensive restoration at Bewdley which enabled it to re-enter traffic in time for the Christmas services in December 1979.

These handsome tank engines had a reputation for fast running and No 5164 is captured at speed while working a Bewdley to Bridgnorth train. (*Graham Wignall*)

31st: GWR 4-6-0 No 7819 *Hinton Manor*

BUILT: February 1939
WITHDRAWN: November 1965

ARRIVED BARRY: May 1966
DEPARTED BARRY: January 1973

The first 20 of Collett's Manor Class were constructed using the wheels and motion of withdrawn Churchward 43XX Moguls so as to produce a lightweight mixed-traffic locomotive which could replace earlier 4-4-0 and 2-6-0 designs.

No 7819 *Hinton Manor* was the last of the Manors to be built by the GWR at Swindon in February 1939, although it is quite possible that but for the intervention of World War II further examples of the class would have been turned out using parts from redundant locomotives. After an initial period of four years based at Carmarthen for work over the routes to Swansea and Aberystwyth, No 7819 was transferred to Oswestry in July 1943 and became a familiar sight on the Cambrian line services, in particular the stretch between Welshpool and Whitchurch. Despite being unusually recorded on the Lickey Incline with a 20-hopper wagon train of ballast in December 1956, it remained on these duties until February 1963, when a move to Shrewsbury was quickly followed by more permanent allocation to Machynlleth, although for most of the time at this latter shed it actually operated from Aberystwyth dealing with the passenger and

freight traffic from there across to Oswestry and Shrewsbury. For a while, *Hinton Manor* became the regular locomotive on the Cambrian Coast Express and was kept in spotless condition by the shed staff, this being one reason why it was chosen to haul the Royal Train between Barmouth and Chester in August 1963. No 7819 returned to Shrewsbury at the beginning of 1965 and worked out its last months on the remaining steam-hauled Cambrian line duties.

Arriving on the Severn Valley Railway in January 1973, *Hinton Manor* made its debut on SVR services in the late summer of 1977. In 1985, repainted in BR lined black livery, it worked several of the GWR 150 trains from Bristol and Swindon but in the summer of 1987 temporarily returned to its old Cambrian haunts with the special excursions between Machynlleth and Barmouth.

On its welcome return to the Cambrian, *Hinton Manor* shunts some stock back into the sidings at Machynlleth in May 1987. (*Steve Worrall*)

32nd: BR 4-6-0 No 73129

BUILT:	August 1956	ARRIVED BARRY:	February 1968
WITHDRAWN:	November 1967	DEPARTED BARRY:	January 1973

Although the BR Standard Class 5 was originally envisaged as a lightweight Pacific design, it was eventually developed as a conventional 4-6-0 largely based on the Stanier 'Black Five', in particular incorporating the excellent boiler. A total of 172 locomotives was built between 1951 and 1957 and they were perhaps the most widely distributed of all the Standard classes, being allocated to every Region of the BR network.

No 73129 emerged from Derby Works in August 1956 and was one of the last 30 steam locomotives ever to be built there; this particular batch was also chosen to be fitted with Caprotti valve gear, the locomotives so modified proving to be strong and reliable in the hands of experienced crews. No 73129 was sent new to Shrewsbury, where the duties were most varied and included working many of the North-to-West expresses right through to Plymouth, stopping services to Crewe, and parcels trains to South Wales which it normally took as far as Pontypool Road. No doubt due to the popularity of the class they were frequently borrowed by other sheds, and on one occasion in August 1957 No 73129 arrived at Buxton with a

local from Manchester Central. This was possibly a portent of things to come for in September 1958 it was transferred to Patricroft to deal with freight and coal traffic in the Manchester area, but was also frequently seen on passenger turns across to Leeds and during the summer months on excursions to the North Wales coastal resorts. Towards the end of steam, Patricroft became a refuge for the surviving members of the class and although by then they were mainly used on freight duties, they did occasionally deputise for Britannia Pacifics on the Manchester to Barrow parcels. When withdrawn in November 1967, No 73129 had lasted just eleven years in BR ownership.

Purchased by Derby Corporation, No 73129 was towed to Derby in January 1973 for storage, subsequently moving to the Midland Railway Centre in early 1975. Restoration commenced during 1982 and this 4-6-0 promises to be a welcome addition to the locomotive collection at Butterley.

The Caprotti valve gear is shown to advantage in this April 1979 view of No 73129 at Butterley. (*Midland Railway Trust Ltd*)

33rd: SR 4-6-2 No 34039 *Boscastle*

BUILT:	September 1946	ARRIVED BARRY:	September 1965
WITHDRAWN:	May 1965	DEPARTED BARRY:	January 1973

When O. V. S. Bulleid joined the Southern Railway as Chief Mechnical Engineer in 1937 he found that the company was depending on elderly locomotives for hauling many of its services. Thus he set about modernising the Southern steam fleet and the West Country lightweight Pacific was just one of the notable designs produced during his term of office, to try and remedy the situation.

Built at Brighton in September 1946, No 21C139 *Boscastle* was first allocated to Stewarts Lane depot. From there it worked many of the Kent coast expresses out of Victoria, becoming almost a daily sight on the Golden Arrow during the summer of 1948 before moving on to Brighton in November of that year. In May 1951 it was loaned to the former Great Eastern depot at Stratford for trials on the Liverpool Street to Cambridge services as well as on the Parkeston Quay boat trains, while on one occasion it even travelled through to Bury St Edmunds with a local passenger working from Ipswich! Returning to Brighton in January 1952, it appeared regularly on the few steam-hauled Central Division express turns such as the cross-country runs to Bournemouth and Plymouth in addition to

the night time mail and newspaper trains up to London. Following rebuilding at the start of 1959, *Boscastle* was transferred to Bournemouth, where in June it became the first rebuilt Bulleid Pacific to work over the Somerset & Dorset route to Bath with the Pines Express. Other duties at Bournemouth included the Waterloo and Weymouth services together with the through South Coast–Midlands expresses which it worked to and from Oxford. Its final move was to Eastleigh in September 1962, where *Boscastle* continued on the main line passenger turns to London, although in April 1963 it turned up at Birmingham Snow Hill with a football special from Southampton which it had worked right through via Oxford, Worcester and Kidderminster.

Purchased from Barry scrapyard in 1972 and moved to the Great Central Railway at Loughborough in January 1973, *Boscastle* has since undergone a complete mechanical overhaul in readiness for its return to revenue-earning service.

The fireman shovels coal forward as *Boscastle*, complete with Royal Wessex headboard, is prepared for duty at Nine Elms in the early 1960s. (*Andrew C. Ingram collection*)

34th: BR 2-6-4T No 80064

BUILT:	June 1953	ARRIVED BARRY:	October 1965
WITHDRAWN:	August 1965	DEPARTED BARRY:	February 1973

This handsome class of 2-6-4 tank engines is considered to be one of the most successful of all the Standard designs, generally receiving praise from their crews wherever they worked.

No 80064 was completed at Brighton Works in June 1953 and entered traffic on the London Midland region based at Watford where, with several other members of the class, it was used principally on the stopping and semi-fast commuter trains into Euston, although on one occasion in the summer of 1954 it was also noted piloting Patriot No 45534 on the down Shamrock express! At weekends it frequently dealt with the Saturday afternoon pick-up goods from Tring, calling at all stations between there and Willesden. Despite being officially transferred to the Southern region in December 1959, No 80064 did not actually leave Watford shed until the end of March 1960 when it took up duty from Ashford to help out with the stopping services to Maidstone, Ramsgate and Folkestone. As a welcome change from this relatively mundane work it was loaned to Bournemouth for a brief period in October 1960 to work the main line expresses between there and Weymouth while the turntable at the latter shed was undergoing repair. By May 1961, No 80064 was operating from Tonbridge depot dealing with the through trains to Eastbourne and Brighton as well as occasionally working some of the Oxted line traffic. During June 1962 it moved again, this time to Exmouth Junction from where it worked over the ex-Southern lines in Devon and Cornwall. It is known to have been used on passenger and freight services over both the Exmouth and Launceston branches together with the occasional banking duty up the incline between Exeter St David's and Central. Final reallocation came in June 1965 to Bristol Barrow Road.

After seven years at Barry, No 80064 was moved to Buckfastleigh on the Dart Valley Railway for restoration, a task which was successfully completed during 1981. Entering revenue-earning service on the Paignton to Kingswear line, it now operates on the Bluebell Railway, having moved to Sheffield Park in March 1984.

No 80064 and No 7827 *Lydham Manor* cross Broadsands viaduct with the stock of the Orient Express in April 1983. (*Peter J. C. Skelton*)

35th: BR 2-6-0 No 78019

BUILT: March 1954   ARRIVED BARRY: June 1967
WITHDRAWN: November 1966   DEPARTED BARRY: March 1973

When first introduced in 1952, the BR Standard Moguls were almost an exact copy of the Ivatt LMS design of 1946, but with various detail modifications and incorporating standard fittings. Their low axle-loading gave them a wide route availability and operating on all regions of BR except the Southern they proved to be just as economical and reliable as their predecessors.

No 78019 was built at Darlington Works during March 1954 and started its career based at Kirkby Stephen shed in Westmorland. From there it worked much of the freight and mineral traffic over the former North Eastern Railway lines to Tebay, Penrith and Barnard Castle, the latter route being particularly prone to blockage by snow, especially in the bleak moorland surrounding Stainmore Summit. As part of the general rundown of lines in the area, No 78019 was transferred to Wigan (Springs Branch) in April 1960, and although the rosters at this shed were mainly concerned with freight duties they also dealt with the local passenger services to Bolton and Rochdale. Just over one year later, in June 1961, it moved to Northwich and was used on trains to Chester Northgate and the Central stations at Manchester and Liverpool. A move south to London followed in May 1963 when it was sent to work from Willesden depot, principally dealing with the numerous empty stock trains in and out of Euston or as a standby for diesel failures. On closure of Willesden to steam in September 1965, No 78019 was re-allocated to Nuneaton for a few weeks before going on to its final shed, Crewe South, at the beginning of 1966. Here the Mogul found very little work to do, although it did appear on some of the summer excursion trains and occasionally act as station pilot before withdrawal in November 1966.

Having survived at Barry for many years in company with several others of the class, No 78019 was transported by road to Bridgnorth on the Severn Valley Railway in March 1973. Priorities elsewhere have dictated that renovation would be a long-term project, although a start was made during 1980.

Coupled to another member of the same class, No 78019 is pictured just after arrival at Barry in June 1967. (*Andrew C. Ingram collection*)

36th: GWR 4-6-0 No 6024 *King Edward I*

BUILT: June 1930   ARRIVED BARRY: December 1962
WITHDRAWN: June 1962   DEPARTED BARRY: March 1973

The Kings were perhaps the most famous of all Great Western locomotives and were designed to cope with the steadily-increasing train loads of the mid-1920s. They were the largest, heaviest and most powerful class of 4-6-0 ever built in this country, although the high axle-loading did mean that their initial sphere of operation was severely restricted. However, they are generally considered to have been among the more successful of British steam designs.

No 6024 *King Edward I* was built at Swindon in June 1930 and spent the first 24 years of its life operating from Plymouth (Laira) and Newton Abbot sheds. During this golden era of GWR steam power it was used on the crack expresses over the main line to Paddington including, of course, the famous Cornish Riviera Express. In October 1954 No 6024 moved on to Old Oak Common where it was frequently rostered for the main London to Bristol, Birmingham and Wolverhampton services such as the Bristolian and Inter-City, as well as continuing to work down to Plymouth with West of England trains. At the end of September 1961 it was transferred to Cardiff Canton principally to

deal with that depot's regular London turns, although other duties included the South Wales to Manchester trains, which it worked between Cardiff and Shrewsbury, and some of the fast milk trains up to Kensington. On withdrawal in June 1962 it was apparently sold for scrap (along with No 6023) to a firm at Briton Ferry but because of the restriction on King class locomotives over the South Wales main line west of Cardiff, they were re-sold to Woodhams and given special permission to move the short distance to Barry in November of that year. It is therefore ironic that a ban which had reduced their range of employment was eventually to save two of them from the cutter's torch.

No 6024 was an obvious choice for preservation and was accordingly delivered to the Buckinghamshire Railway Centre in early 1973. Rebuilding has been to the highest standards and *King Edward I* will make an impressive addition to those locomotives passed for running over the BR main line.

King Edward I passes through Hatton station with the 9.10 a m Paddington to Birkenhead in September 1957. (*M. Mensing*)

105

37th: BR 4-6-0 No 75069

BUILT:	September 1955	ARRIVED BARRY:	May 1967
WITHDRAWN:	September 1966	DEPARTED BARRY:	March 1973

Although overall responsibility for this class of 4-6-0s was attributable to R. A. Riddles, actual design work was entrusted to the drawing office at Brighton and general production took place almost continuously at Swindon between 1951 and 1957, a total of 80 locomotives being built.

No 75069 was completed at Swindon during September 1955 and allocated to the Eastern Section of the Southern Region at Dover. From here it worked alongside the Standard Class 5 4-6-0s on the services between the Kent Coast ports and London, while once or twice it was also recorded unusually on the Tonbridge to Brighton line. Due to a shortage of motive power at Redhill in August 1957, No 75069 was loaned to that shed for a two-week period and became almost a daily sight on the Margate to Birkenhead through train which it took as far as Reading. After four years at Dover it was transferred to the Central Section at Bournemouth for a brief spell between June and November 1959, but then moved on to Stewarts Lane where regular work for the class included the semi-fast trains from Victoria to Tunbridge Wells via Oxted. In August 1963 it moved across London

to the large shed at Nine Elms and dealt with an assortment of duties over the main line to Bournemouth until June 1965, when it was sent to Eastleigh for use on the locals between Portsmouth and Reading, but it also sometimes appeared on the heavy boat trains from Southampton to Waterloo. Although condemned in September 1966, No 75069 was re-steamed at Eastleigh in December of that year to give a final few days of service to its owners before being consigned to the scrapyard.

Taken to the Severn Valley Railway in early 1973 No 75069 returned to service during September 1984 and made its main line debut the following March with an excursion between Newport, Gloucester and Swindon. Since then it has made several more appearances on BR tracks, including the successful Cambrian line trains between Machynlleth and Barmouth in the summer of 1987.

No 75069 pulls away from Barmouth station and runs by the harbour with the return train to Machynlleth in May 1987. (*David Wilcock*)

38th: SR 4-6-2 No 35005 *Canadian Pacific*

BUILT: December 1941
WITHDRAWN: October 1965

ARRIVED BARRY: January 1966
DEPARTED BARRY: March 1973

The Merchant Navy Pacifics were Oliver Bulleid's first design for the Southern Railway, and incorporated many features novel to British steam locomotive development of that period. The prototype of the class was put into service during 1941, a most inopportune time for the introduction of such an unorthodox design; because of the many teething troubles that were encountered the early members of the class spent most of the war years on freight duties.

Southern Railway No 21C5 was turned out from Eastleigh during December 1941 and given the name *Canadian Pacific* at a ceremony held at Victoria Station in March 1942. The years up to Nationalisation were spent at Exmouth Junction but in March 1948 it was fitted with an American-type mechanical stoker and sent to work from Nine Elms where it was mainly rostered to the West of England services which included the Atlantic Coast Express. During March 1950, renumbered 35005, it went to Rugby for evaluation on the Testing Plant there, following which it was used on tests with the dynamometer car between Rugby and Euston. When trials with the stoker were concluded in April

1951 and the apparatus removed, *Canadian Pacific* returned to Exmouth Junction for working the expresses over the main line between Exeter and London, but by March 1954 had moved back to Nine Elms where it became a regular performer on the Devon Belle and the 'ACE' again. Shortly after rebuilding in June 1959 No 35005 was transferred to Bournemouth where the Merchant Navies were employed almost exclusively on Weymouth or Waterloo diagrams, particularly the faster-timed trains. The final move came in September 1964 to Weymouth where it continued on much the same duties, although in May 1965 it did head a special excursion throughout from Waterloo to Eastleigh and Swindon.

In March 1973, No 35005, was taken by road to Steamtown, Carnforth, for restoration, although it was to be several years before work actually started on returning this locomotive to full running order.

A down Ocean Liner Special bowls through Eastleigh station in August 1961 in charge of No 35005 *Canadian Pacific*. (*R. Greenwood*)

107

39th: BR 2-6-4T No 80135

BUILT:	April 1956	ARRIVED BARRY:	January 1966
WITHDRAWN:	July 1965	DEPARTED BARRY:	April 1973

This class of suburban passenger tanks eventually totalled 155, the majority being built at Brighton Works, although fifteen were constructed at Derby and ten at Doncaster. First introduced in 1951, they are generally considered to be one of the most successful of all the Standard designs.

No 80135 was completed at Brighton in April 1956 and although allocated initially to Plaistow depot for work over the former London, Tilbury & Southend lines, it was observed in May of that year performing on the Liverpool Street to Bishop's Stortford outer suburban services. It returned to Plaistow a few weeks later and took up duty on the busy commuter trains from Fenchurch Street to Southend and Shoeburyness. An opportunity to show its versatility came in June 1957 when it was chosen to haul the Railway Enthusiasts' Club 'London Suburban' railtour which took in the lines to North Woolwich, Chingford, Cheshunt and Hertford, returning via Stevenage to terminate at King's Cross; in May 1959 it was also specially groomed to work a P&O shareholders' special to Tilbury in connection with the SS *Iberia*. On the closure of Plaistow in November 1959, No 80135

moved on to Tilbury depot where it continued on the LT&S services until electrification of these routes in June 1962. After a short period in storage at Old Oak Common it was transferred to Shrewsbury to deal with the local passenger work in that area, which included trips down to Bridgnorth on the Severn Valley line. At the beginning of 1963 No 80135 was re-allocated to Oswestry where it spent most of its time operating services over the ex-Cambrian lines to Aberystwyth. Transferred back to Shrewsbury in September 1964 it was withdrawn in July of the following year.

No 80135 was moved to the North Yorkshire Moors Railway at Pickering in April 1973 and although returned to traffic in 1980 initial boiler problems were encountered. Following repairs on the Severn Valley Railway and now in private ownership, this locomotive has subsequently given several years of reliable service.

Framed by the footbridge at Goathland station, No 80135 heads off light engine for Pickering in May 1986. (*Brian Cooke*)

40th: GWR 0-6-2T No 5619

BUILT: March 1925
WITHDRAWN: June 1964

ARRIVED BARRY: September 1964
DEPARTED BARRY: May 1973

The 5600 Class mixed-traffic 0-6-2 tanks were a familiar sight throughout the Welsh valleys, 200 having been built by Swindon and Armstrong Whitworth of Newcastle between 1924 and 1928. With 4ft 7½in driving wheels and a boiler pressure of 200lb/sq in, their tractive effort of 25,800lb was quite remarkable for such small locomotives and was put to full use on both freight and passenger work.

No 5619 was turned out from Swindon during March 1925 and entered service from the shed at Chester, which nearly always had one or two members of this class for work in the area. After a few weeks there, followed by an even briefer period at Leamington, it moved on in June 1925 to the London Division, based variously at Old Oak Common and Reading for the next six months. During this time, as well as handling some of the freight traffic, it was also used on shunting and empty coaching stock duties in and out of Paddington. No 5619 returned to Leamington at the end of 1925, but after this rather unsettled first year in service, was transferred to the more familiar surroundings of South Wales in April 1926, initially

allocated to Cardiff (Cathays) but going on to Abercynon in December of that year. Except for short spells on loan to Barry, Cardiff, Dowlais and Merthyr, it remained at this former Taff Vale shed until 1950, working the heavy coal trains from Aberdare and Merthyr down to the docks and then returning up the valley with the empties. Its work was not limited to this coal traffic, for No 5619 frequently appeared on the scheduled local passenger services and workmen's trains. In October 1950, it was finally re-allocated to Barry shed, spending a good part of the time there on the locals to Pontypridd, Treherbert and Merthyr together with some freight work to Penallta and Treforest, before withdrawal in June 1964.

Purchased by Telford Development Corporation No 5619 was moved to the Telford Horsehay Steam Trust's site in 1973. Steamed for the first time just over seven years later, this 0-6-2T spent the summer of 1987 on loan to the Severn Valley Railway.

During its period on loan to the Severn Valley Railway No 5619 stands by the water column at Bewdley in company with Black Five No 5000 in June 1987. (*P. D. Jameson*)

41st: LMR 2-6-0 No 46512

BUILT: December 1952
WITHDRAWN: November 1966

ARRIVED BARRY: June 1967
DEPARTED BARRY: May 1973

First introduced in 1946, the Ivatt Moguls were one of the last new designs prepared for the LMS before Nationalisation. From the total of 128 locomotives eventually built over half were completed by Crewe, the remainder coming from Darlington and Swindon Works. After the last member of the class was built in 1953, the design was modified to incorporate BR fittings and became the Standard Class 2 2-6-0s, numbered in the 78000 series.

No 46512 was assembled at Swindon in December 1952 and went new to the shed at Oswestry in January of the following year. Here members of the class replaced Dean and ex-Cambrian 0-6-0s on the mid-Wales services to Moat Lane, Llanidloes and Brecon, as well as handling the local passenger workings to Welshpool. By the early 1960s it had become a common sight on the former Midland Railway line between Three Cocks Junction and Hereford with the stopping trains from Brecon. Oswestry shed closed at the beginning of 1965, and one of No 46512's final duties from there was to work the last passenger train over the Llanfyllin branch on 17 January 1965, the shed closing the next day. After a temporary move to

Shrewsbury it was subsequently transferred to the busy shed at Willesden in February 1965, and for most of the time there either acted as station pilot at Euston or dealt with the procession of empty coaching stock trains between there and the carriage sidings. By then the effects of dieselisation were catching up with No 46512, and following a move back to Shrewsbury in June 1965 and to Nuneaton in October, it eventually came to rest at Crewe South from June 1966 onwards. In those latter days of steam there were several other examples of the class at Crewe together with some of the Standard version, but there was little to keep them all occupied and by November 1966 they had been sold for scrap.

Purchased for use on the Strathspey Railway between Aviemore and Boat of Garten, No 46512 was initially moved to the Severn Valley Railway for restoration, but after a spell at a private site in Hereford it finally arrived in Scotland during 1982.

On familiar Cambrian territory No 46512 prepares to leave Oswestry with a Llanfyllin train in April 1963. (*Peter Cookson*)

42nd: GWR 2-8-0T No 5239

BUILT: August 1924
WITHDRAWN: April 1963

ARRIVED BARRY: November 1963
DEPARTED BARRY: June 1973

The fast development of mineral traffic in South Wales during the early part of this century saw the need for a tank engine suitable for heavy short-haul traffic. The prototype of the resulting design, a 2-8-0 tank, was built in 1910 and construction of the other locomotives continued up to 1940. However, as a result of the serious decline in the coal trade in the early 1930s, several members of this class were converted to 2-8-2 tanks with enlarged fuel capacity, this increasing their working range. These became the 72XX series.

No 5239 was built at Swindon Works in August 1924 and went to its first shed at Neath towards the end of that month, taking up work on the varied coal and mixed freight duties that were a familiar part of the Welsh railway scene. Following over-haul at Swindon during December 1928, it was transferred to the former Port Talbot Railway shed at Duffryn Yard and spent just under three years there before returning to Neath in November 1931. Apart from short intervals on loan to Danygraig in 1932, and Carmarthen in 1944, 5239 was destined to remain at this shed for over 30 years, although for a considerable part of this time it alternated

between the parent depot and the small, single-road sub-shed at Glyn Neath, eight miles away on the line to Aberdare and Merthyr. Normally four or five other members of the class were based at Glyn Neath to provide banking assistance for the succession of heavy westbound coal trains that used this route, and No 5239 continued on this sometimes punishing work right up to withdrawal in April 1963.

Having spent almost 50 years in South Wales (10 of them at Barry) No 5239 was taken to the old steam shed at Newton Abbot in June 1973 for restoration to working order. When this was complete it entered service on the Paignton and Dartmouth Steam Railway during the summer of 1978 and in June of the following year was named *Goliath* by the then Chairman of British Rail, Sir Peter Parker, at a special ceremony at Paignton (Queens Park) Station.

No 5239 *Goliath* enters Churston station with a Kingswear to Paignton train in August 1987. (*Roger Penny*)

43rd: GWR 4-6-0 No 5043 *Earl of Mount Edgcumbe*

BUILT: March 1936
WITHDRAWN: December 1963

ARRIVED BARRY: June 1964
DEPARTED BARRY: August 1973

The Great Western Castles were arguably amongst the finest ever steam locomotives built in Britain, greatly influencing locomotive design on the three other major railway lines. A total of 131 had been constructed before wartime conditions cut short the building programme, and it was not until 1946 that the remaining 40 were built under the direction of F. W. Hawksworth.

When turned out from Swindon Works in March 1936, No 5043 carried the name *Barbury Castle* but as a result of the decision to transfer the Earl series of nameplates from the rather elderly-looking 3200 class 4-4-0s to these more modern locomotives, it was renamed *Earl of Mount Edgcumbe* in September 1937. Beginning its career at Old Oak Common, No 5043 was a popular choice for that depot's top-link duties and it made several appearances on the world-renowned Cheltenham Flyer, as well as sharing the Paddington–Birmingham–Wolverhampton services with the more powerful Kings. After sixteen years working out of London it was transferred to South Wales in June 1952, staying for varying lengths of time at both Carmarthen and Swansea (Landore) where it found itself rostered to

most of the named Welsh expresses including the Capitals United and Red Dragon. Returning to Old Oak Common in February 1956, *Earl of Mount Edgcumbe* continued working the more important main line trains although the steady introduction of the Warship and Western diesel-hydraulics saw it spending more time on the semi-fasts from Paddington, particularly those to Reading and Didcot. In April 1962 it went back to South Wales, initially based at Cardiff Canton, but when that shed closed to steam a few months later it moved on to Cardiff East Dock, remaining there on secondary duties until withdrawn.

As one of only five Castles to reach Barry, No 5043 was purchased by the Birmingham Railway Museum in August 1973. It is unlikely that it will ever steam again, as it is primarily intended as a source of spares for the other members of the class at Tyseley.

In April 1962 *Earl Of Mount Edgcumbe* calls at Pontypool Road with the Liverpool portion of the through train to Cardiff. (*M. Mensing*)

44th: BR 2-6-4T No 80105

BUILT:	April 1955	ARRIVED BARRY:	January 1966
WITHDRAWN:	July 1965	DEPARTED BARRY:	October 1973

The first Standard Class 4 2-6-4 tank entered service in 1951 and construction of the remainder continued until 1957. They experienced relatively few teething troubles and were initially allocated to the London Midland, Southern, Eastern, and Scottish Regions of BR, the Western not receiving any until the early 1960s. Gradually displaced from their outer suburban workings by dieselisation or electrification, the first of the class was withdrawn as early as 1962.

Completed at Brighton Works in April 1955, No 80105 took up duty from Plaistow depot, being put to work on the busy commuter traffic between Fenchurch Street, Southend and Shoeburyness. These workings were considered almost unique, particularly with regard to the intensive morning and evening service, consisting of nine or 10 trains per hour over distances of up to 40 miles, many of them loading to 11 full coaches. It continued on this exacting work until made redundant by electrification of the route in June 1962, although by that time Plaistow had been shut and the entire allocation transferred to Tilbury. Following a brief period in store, No 80105 was re-allocated during

August 1962 to Machynlleth depot in Central Wales and shortly after arrival there was tried out with two other members of the class on the three-day Wrexham – Barmouth – Machynlleth – Shrewsbury – Wrexham cyclic roster; they proved unsuitable for the task and the duty was given back to tender locomotives. For most of its time in Wales, No 80105 was sub-shedded at Aberystwyth, frequently taking that resort's portion of the Cambrian Coast Express up to Dovey Junction, while on several occasions it also worked as far south as Carmarthen on passenger turns. Although spending a short time at Croes Newydd and Shrewsbury depots, it remained at Machynlleth until withdrawal in July 1965.

After more than eight years on the scrap lines at Barry, No 80105 was taken on the long journey north to its new home in Scotland, arriving at the Falkirk depot of the Scottish Railway Preservation Society in October 1973.

No 80105 waits to depart from Tilbury Riverside with a Southend train in July 1959. (*Frank Church*)

45th: LMS 2-6-0 No 42968

BUILT:	January 1934	ARRIVED BARRY:	June 1967
WITHDRAWN:	December 1966	DEPARTED BARRY:	December 1973

Soon after taking-over as Chief Mechanical Engineer of the LMS in 1932, W. A. Stanier produced his 'improved' version of the earlier 'Crab' 2-6-0s. This new class incorporated a GWR-style taper boiler together with other Swindon features, and 40 of them were constructed at Crewe between 1933 and 1934. At first their steam-raising ability was somewhat erratic, but eventually they settled down to a fairly undistinguished career, seen more often on freight than passenger duties.

This sole surviving representative of the class was built at Crewe in January 1934 as LMS No 13268. It arrived at Willesden depot towards the end of that month, and regularly worked up the West Coast main line to Crewe with some of the long-distance goods trains. After just 15 months based in London, this Mogul moved on to Liverpool Edge Hill in April 1935; between then and November 1938 it also had brief periods at Crewe, Aston, Bescot and Birkenhead sheds before returning to Edge Hill. During the early years of World War II it spent further periods at Willesden and Nuneaton, but in February 1942 found a more permanent home at Crewe, staying there for the next 19 years.

While there it handled some of the freight traffic to Wolverhampton and London, but throughout the busy summer periods it was a regular performer on the many holiday extras along the North Wales Coast to Llandudno and Bangor. The first move away from Crewe came in June 1961, to Birkenhead, and this was soon followed by additional spells at Nuneaton, Mold Junction, Wigan, Gorton and Heaton Mersey, its final allocation being to Wigan (Springs Branch) in January 1966. The last few members of the class ended their days there, dealing mainly with the local mineral and goods traffic but in August 1966, just four months before withdrawal, No 42968 was used to haul a brake-van tour of freight-only lines in the Wigan area.

Following acquisition by the Stanier Mogul Fund, No 42968 was delivered by rail to the Severn Valley Railway in December 1973. Entering Bridgnorth workshops for overhaul in 1980, it will increase the impressive complement of ex-LMS locomotives now working on this line.

Photographed here when just four years old, No 2968 stands at Llandudno Junction in May 1938. (*W. Potter/Stanier Mogul Fund Collection*)

46th: BR 2-6-0 No 76017

BUILT:	June 1953	ARRIVED BARRY:	January 1966
WITHDRAWN:	July 1965	DEPARTED BARRY:	January 1974

One hundred and fifteen of these Standard Class 4 2-6-0s were turned out from Horwich and Doncaster Works between 1952 and 1957. Based on the Ivatt LMS design of 1947 they embodied the usual BR Standard boiler fittings, together with some necessary changes to their external appearance to take away the rather severe lines of the earlier locomotives. The class as a whole was used mainly on light mixed-traffic duties throughout the BR system, although not reaching the Western Region until the latter days of steam.

Built at Horwich Works in June 1953, No 76017 was sent new to Eastleigh where it quickly took charge of the Southampton to Bournemouth semi-fast and local stopping trains. Other passenger duties included the services between Portsmouth and Salisbury, and less frequently the through train from Bournemouth to Brighton. It also saw use on various freight duties in the area. On one occasion in September 1954, while working the 7.00am Banbury to Eastleigh goods, the driver lost control of the train at Whitchurch and as a consequence No 76017 ran through the catch-points, ending up at the bottom of an embankment where it was to stay

for the next seventeen days awaiting the arrival of a breakdown crane. From March 1955, the Eastleigh Standard Class 4 2-6-0s also began working over the Somerset & Dorset line with local trains from Bournemouth to Templecombe and Bath, but during February 1960 No 76017 was transferred to Salisbury where it dealt with passenger turns to Portsmouth, Bournemouth and Weymouth, as well as appearing on the stopping trains to Yeovil and local freight work. Remaining at Salisbury until withdrawn in July 1965, it was among the first 10 or so of this popular class to be condemned.

No 76017 was acquired by the Standard 4 Preservation Group and taken to the Buckinghamshire Railway Centre at Quainton in January 1974. Just over four years later it moved to the Mid-Hants Railway and made its inaugural run in public service on that line in May 1984, receiving the name *Hermes* in June of the following year.

Before receiving the name *Hermes*, No 76017 poses for its portrait in sparkling condition in Ropley shed yard in June 1985. (*David Warwick*)

47th: SR 4-6-2 No 35029 *Ellerman Lines*

BUILT:	February 1949	ARRIVED BARRY:	March 1967
WITHDRAWN:	September 1966	DEPARTED BARRY:	January 1974

As the Southern Railway's first Pacific locomotive, Bulleid's design for the Merchant Navy class was certainly eye-catching with its air-smoothed casing and malachite green livery bearing three broad yellow lines running the full length of locomotive and tender. Twenty were built during the War years, the remaining ten coming out after Nationalisation, but the whole class was subsequently rebuilt by BR between 1956 and 1959.

No 35029 emerged from Eastleigh Works in February 1949 and went initially to Bournemouth, working the expresses between there and London. The stay here was fairly short, for just seven months later it was transferred to Dover, along with two other members of the class, as replacements for the Battle of Britain light Pacifics on the Night Ferry and other Continental boat trains. It was officially named *Ellerman Lines* at a special ceremony at Southampton Docks in March 1951 and shortly afterwards was chosen to haul the Royal Train conveying the King and Queen of Denmark from Dover Marine to Victoria. During 1956, No 35029 was re-allocated to Nine Elms and took up duty on the main line services to Southampton,

Bournemouth and Exeter including the well-known Bournemouth Belle and Atlantic Coast Express. Soon after rebuilding it also worked the inaugural Surbiton to Okehampton Car-Carrier in June 1960. By the end of August 1964 it had moved to Weymouth and continued on the services between there and Waterloo, although it also frequently appeared in Great Western territory at Oxford with the Bournemouth to York through trains. When finally withdrawn in September 1966 it had worked just under ¾-million miles, the lowest recorded mileage of any Merchant Navy Pacific.

After several years exposed to the sea air at Barry Docks *Ellerman Lines* were delivered by road to the Market Overton site of Flying Scotsman Enterprises in January 1974. Here it was carefully sectioned for display at the National Railway Museum in York, where it has now become one of the most popular exhibits.

Ellerman Lines storms through Brookwood station in September 1961 with the 13-coach Atlantic Coast Express. (*R. Greenwood*)

48th: SR 2-6-0 No 31874

BUILT: September 1925
WITHDRAWN: March 1964

ARRIVED BARRY: June 1964
DEPARTED BARRY: March 1974

Design work for the N Class Moguls had been started by the South Eastern & Chatham Railway in 1914, but the outbreak of World War I delayed completion of the prototype until 1917, general production beginning three years later. These Maunsell locomotives proved to be a useful asset to all three sections of the Southern Railway and the 80 that had been built by 1934 saw service on a wide variety of mixed-traffic duties.

No A874 was completed at Ashford Works in September 1925 from parts manufactured at the Woolwich Arsenal munitions factory some two years earlier, a fact which resulted in the class earning the nickname 'Woolworths'! Initial allocation was to Bricklayers Arms where it handled a good deal of the freight traffic between London and the Kent coast towns together with the occasional passenger turn, but for a short period in July 1935 it went temporarily on loan to the newly-opened shed at Norwood Junction to carry out freight trials designed to assess the suitability of the class for work in that area. Returning to Bricklayers Arms, it remained there until 1944, when the arrival of 50 War Department 2-8-0s saw it move first to

Guildford and then to Eastleigh. In the early years of British Railways No 31874 had brief spells at Exmouth Junction, Salisbury and Hither Green before coming back to Bricklayers Arms in 1951 to perform on much the same duties as before. Just under ten years later, in February 1961, it made its final move to Exmouth Junction where the Moguls were responsible for most of the freight workings on the Southern lines west of Exeter; thus No 31874 was seen on trains to Plymouth, Wadebridge and Barnstaple as well as to Newcourt Sidings on the Exmouth branch up to the time of its withdrawal in March 1964.

In March 1974 No 31874 was taken to the Mid-Hants Railway where, just over three years later, it headed the re-opening train between Alresford and Ropley. Originally named *Aznar Line* it was renamed *Brian Fisk* in 1979 and in May 1985 became the first steam locomotive to work back into Alton for 18 years on a special train.

The only remaining N class Mogul, No 31874, climbs Medstead Bank with the 13.02 Alton to Alresford in April 1987. (*David Warwick*)

49th: GWR 0-6-0PT No 3738

BUILT: September 1937
WITHDRAWN: July 1965

ARRIVED BARRY: October 1965
DEPARTED BARRY: April 1974

C. B. Collett's standard design for an 0-6-0 pannier tank was first introduced in 1929. Between then and 1950 no less than 863 locomotives of this type were constructed by Swindon Works and outside contractors. Collectively known as the 5700 class, they were used for shunting and light mixed-traffic duties over virtually the entire GWR system, earning for themselves a reputation of being exceptionally strong and free-steaming.

Built at Swindon in September 1937, No 3738 passed the majority of its life based in the London Division, going at first to Old Oak Common where it quickly settled into the routine of taking empty coaching stock to Paddington together with local shunting and pick-up freight duties. After many years working in the capital it went to Slough in October 1949, but less than 12 months later had moved on again to Reading where it principally acted as goods pilot or dealt with trip freights between the numerous yards in the Reading area. There were also several occasions when it was rostered for passenger work, including the stopping services to Basingstoke. During September 1960, No 3738 was transferred to the very different

surroundings of South Wales initially working from Tondu shed near Bridgend, where the pannier tanks often ventured up the Porthcawl branch to the limestone quarries at Cornelly as well as being used on shunting duties at the many local collieries. On the closure of Tondu in February 1964, it was stored for a short while before being sent to Llantrisant, taking up its share of the busy coal traffic dealt with there. In October 1964 when this shed was also closed No 3738 was re-allocated to Cardiff (Radyr) but actually finished its career with BR at Cardiff East Dock, being withdrawn in the summer of 1965.

Having left Barry in a convoy of three other locomotives during April 1974, No 3738 was steamed in the relatively short time of two years and now shares the task of hauling trains over the two demonstration lines at the Didcot Steam Centre in Oxfordshire.

Having completed its turn on the demonstration passenger line, No 3738 poses on the turntable at Didcot in August 1982. *(Alan Warren)*

50th: GWR 2-6-2T No 4144

BUILT: September 1946
WITHDRAWN: June 1965

ARRIVED BARRY: August 1965
DEPARTED BARRY: April 1974

The 5101 Class of 2-6-2 tanks was an updated version of an earlier Churchward design dating back to the start of this century. One hundred and forty locomotives of this particular series were built between 1929 and 1949, the majority of them initially going to the Wolverhampton division where they were the mainstay of suburban passenger services. Eventually they became more widespread but the gradual introduction of diesel multiple-units from the late 1950s onwards saw them relegated to more mundane duties, the last of the class being withdrawn in 1965.

No 4144 came out of Swindon Works in September 1946 and went new to the shed at Severn Tunnel Junction. A large proportion of the freight and coal traffic from South Wales came out via the Severn Tunnel, and the locomotives here were mainly employed on piloting or banking duties for the heavy trains that had to work through this steeply-graded tunnel. It was affectionately known as 'The Big Hole' to generations of GWR locomotive men and every foot of its 4 mile 628yd length could prove to be a living nightmare for the crew of a banking engine. After almost eleven years on this gruelling work No 4144 was transferred in August 1957 to Tondu depot, where it was principally used on the passenger duties from Bridgend including those to Maesteg and Cymmer Afan over the Llynfi Valley line and to Abergwynfi and Blaengwynfi, the latter turn involving a run over part of the former Rhondda & Swansea Bay route. In December 1962 it returned to Severn Tunnel Junction, and in addition to the familiar banking work also appeared on the tunnel car ferry service which consisted of some 'Carflats' and two coaches. By April 1965 this had reputedly become the last regular steam-hauled passenger train in South Wales, but following the opening of the Severn Bridge shortly thereafter the service ceased and No 4144 was sold for scrap.

In April 1974, with three other locomotives, it was towed to the Great Western Society depot at Didcot where it has now been dismantled for a complete overhaul to be undertaken.

No 4144 leaves Treherbert with an excursion for Porthcawl on a dull summer's day in 1962. (*Peter Cookson*)

119

51st: GWR 4-6-0 No 4942 *Maindy Hall*

BUILT:	July 1929	ARRIVED BARRY:	June 1964
WITHDRAWN:	December 1963	DEPARTED BARRY:	April 1974

The Hall Class 4-6-0s were one of the most versatile and successful mixed-traffic locomotives to be produced in the years between the two World Wars. They could quite happily run at 90mph with expresses, accelerate stopping trains rapidly away from stations, or trundle along with heavy goods trains; in fact there can be very little work that was not within their capabilities.

No 4942 *Maindy Hall* was built at Swindon Works in July 1929 and began its career in the West Country based at Newton Abbot. Just over a year later, in October 1930, it was transferred to Goodwick (Fishguard) and this marked the start of a period of operation in Wales, it subsequently being allocated to Swansea (Landore), Llanelly and Carmarthen. The years from 1936 to 1955 were spent in the Bristol Division, initially stationed at Weymouth, Swindon and Westbury but settling down at Bristol (St Philip's Marsh and Bath Road) from December 1940 onwards. During this latter period *Maindy Hall* was frequently used on the local services to Newport, Taunton and Exeter, together with the Southampton to Cardiff cross-country trains. After a few weeks at Exeter during

the summer of 1955, No 4942 moved on to Banbury in September of that year and became a common sight on the main line between London and Birmingham with freight and passenger workings. In November 1960 it returned to Bristol (St Philip's Marsh) for a brief spell before going on to Cardiff East Dock in August 1962, followed by a final transfer to Didcot three months later. Thus it worked out the last 12 months leading up to withdrawal at the shed that was destined to become its future home during preservation.

Maindy Hall was purchased by the Great Western Society in early 1974 with the intention of rebuilding it as a Saint Class 4-6-0, the forerunner of the Hall design. Although the initial appeal for funds to finance this challenging project was not as successful as hoped, plans still exist for the conversion to take place.

Maindy Hall nears Frome on a down empty coaching stock working in the summer of 1937 (*L and GRP*)

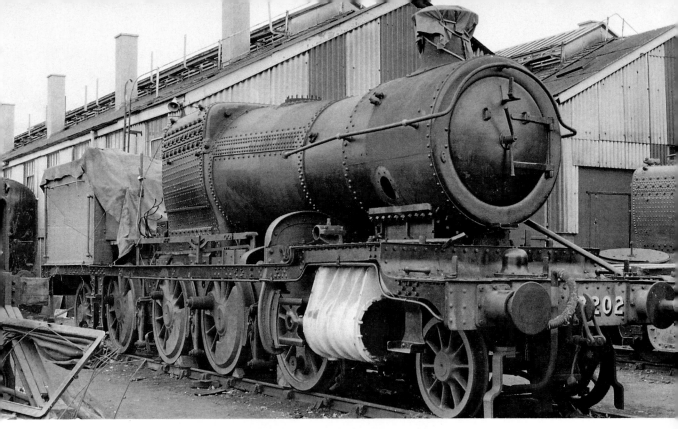

52nd: GWR 2-8-2T No 7202

BUILT: September 1934
WITHDRAWN: June 1964

ARRIVED BARRY: July 1964
DEPARTED BARRY: April 1974

As a result of the decline in the normally lucrative coal trade during the 1930s, several brand-new GWR 2-8-0 tanks built for this work were left with nothing to do and went straight into store. In 1934 it was decided to resurrect them for conversion to 2-8-2Ts with a fuel capacity nearer to that of a tender engine, thereby increasing their range. This proved to be so successful that further batches were converted right up to 1939.

Originally built as 2-8-0T No 5277 in 1930, No 7202 was altered to a 2-8-2T at Swindon in September 1934 and entered service in this form working out of Newport (Ebbw Junction) shed. In these early yars it was regularly employed on main line coal trains to London and Exeter, but the introduction of further 2-8-0 tender engines during the course of the war rendered its use on these trains unnecessary, resulting in a move on to Gloucester in April 1943 and then to Severn Tunnel Junction in January 1947. Just over a year later, in March 1948, No 7202 was transferred to Cardiff (Radyr) and between then and the early 1960s had a virtual monopoly along with No 7205 on the daily 2.35am through freight from Radyr to Salisbury,

returning with a load of empties destined for Penarth North Curve, Cardiff. When not on this duty it could be found working the coal trains from Nantgarw Colliery across to the newly-opened steel works at Margam, although once or twice it did stray far from home territory, arriving at Weymouth on an early-morning freight in October 1957 and at Paddington with a parcels train in the summer of 1959! No 7202 was finally re-allocated to Barry in September 1962, where it stayed for nearly two years before making the short journey across to Woodham's yard at Barry Docks following withdrawal in June 1964.

Fortunately, the Great Western Society realised the importance of including a representative of this class in its fine collection of locomotives and consequently in April 1974 No 7202 was brought to Didcot where restoration is now underway.

In July 1981 No 7202 stands outside the workshops at Didcot in partially dismantled state waiting its turn for rebuilding. (*Alan Warren*)

121

53rd: BR 4-6-2 No 71000 *Duke of Gloucester*

BUILT: April 1954
WITHDRAWN: November 1962

ARRIVED BARRY: October 1967
DEPARTED BARRY: April 1974

Destined to be the sole representative of its type, this Standard Class 8P Pacific was the result of a design prepared by R. A. Riddles and his staff in the early 1950s. Basically an enlarged Britannia but with three cylinders instead of two, it was considered to be a powerful locomotive yet rather heavy on coal consumption and was therefore not fully appreciated by its crews.

No 71000 emerged from Crewe Works in April 1954 and was named *Duke of Gloucester* to commemorate the Duke's Honorary Presidency of the sixteenth International Railway Congress held in London that May. It entered service from Crewe North shed and after a short period running-in on local trains to Holyhead, Shrewsbury and Manchester, graduated to the West Coast main line expresses, becoming a regular performer on the Mid-Day Scot. During April 1955, as a result of the various problems being experienced with 'The Duke', it went to Swindon Works for controlled road tests between there and Newbury as well as undergoing high-speed tests on the stationary plant. On completion of these trials, No 71000 returned to Crewe and resumed service on the more

important trains including those across to Perth and Aberdeen, but by 1962 it had been relegated to second-link duties although at summer weekends it did return to the main line with extras between Crewe and Glasgow. In November of that year the locomotive was finally withdrawn for preservation by BR and placed in store. Five years later, the strange decision was taken to preserve the left-hand cylinder only and scrap the remainder of the locomotive. So with the right-hand cylinder also removed to balance it for transportation, 'The Duke' was unceremoniously towed to Barry for cutting-up.

Undaunted by the considerable task ahead, No 71000 was purchased by a group of enthusiasts and taken to the Great Central Railway in 1974. Officially recommissioned by HRH Prince Richard the Duke of Gloucester in November 1986, this locomotive appropriately took part in the Crewe 150 celebrations during the summer of 1987.

The impossible dream comes true. *Duke of Gloucester* runs round at Rothley in preparation for The Carillon Special in November 1986. (*Graham Wignall*)

54th: SR 0-6-0 No 30541

BUILT:	January 1939	ARRIVED BARRY:	February 1965
WITHDRAWN:	November 1964	DEPARTED BARRY:	May 1974

The Class Q 0-6-0 goods locomotives were the last of Maunsell's designs for the Southern Railway, although they did not enter service until after his retirement. Their concept was one of providing an inexpensive modern replacement for the many old pre-Grouping 0-6-0s that the Southern had inherited, but only 20 of them were built between 1938 and 1939.

SR No 541 was constructed at Eastleigh Works during January 1939 and entered service from Guildford shed, helping to work much of the freight traffic on the Reading to Redhill line. After a short period at Horsham it then went on to Three Bridges, frequently being rostered to the commuter trains between Lewes and London Bridge as well as on goods duties over the Oxted line. By September 1953 it had been transferred to Bournemouth where there were usually two or three of the class for light mixed traffic duties, but they were not overpopular and numerous draughting experiments were carried out at this shed in an effort to improve their steaming abilities. During its time at Bournemouth No 30541 became a familiar sight in both Hampshire and Dorset, appearing on local passenger and freight work to the Southampton and Weymouth areas. At the beginning of 1963 it moved to Basingstoke for a few months before returning to Guildford in March of that year; at this stage of its career No 30541 was more normally seen on parcels and goods work, particularly on the Chessington branch but its final days in BR service were mainly spent acting as a stand-by on snow-plough duties. Following withdrawal in November 1964 it was towed to Barry in company with two similarly redundant Bulleid West Country Pacifics.

In May 1974 No 30541 was taken to the former Dowty Railway Preservation Society's site at Ashchurch in Gloucestershire but was subsequently moved to the Bluebell Railway in October 1978. Rebuilding took just over five years and it re-entered service in November 1983, fully restored in SR 1939 plain black livery.

Just a few days after making a welcome return to service, No 541 heads a 3-coach train on the Bluebell Railway in November 1983. (Mike Frackiewicz)

55th: LMS 4-6-0 No 45379

BUILT:	July 1937	ARRIVED BARRY:	October 1965
WITHDRAWN:	July 1965	DEPARTED BARRY:	May 1974

The true success of Stanier's 'Black Fives' can be judged from the fact that no fewer than 842 were built by Crewe, Derby and Horwich, as well as outside contractors, between 1934 and 1951. As powerful mixed-traffic locomotives they were ideal, putting in outstanding performances right up to the final days of steam in August 1968 and thereby earning the particular affection of many railway enthusiasts.

Built by Armstrong Whitworth of Newcastle in July 1937, No 5379 spent the years under LMS ownership primarily based at Crewe, although at the beginning of the War it was also loaned to Aston and Holyhead for a short period. There was a large allocation of the class at Crewe, which was used on a wide range of duties to London, Carlisle and along the North Wales coast line to Llandudno and Holyhead. On the formation of British Railways in January 1948 No 45379, as it was to become, was transferred to Rugby and began work on the passenger, parcels and semi-fitted freight trains to destinations including Wolverhampton, Liverpool, Peterborough and Derby, as well as arriving at Euston on one occasion in 1952 with the Northern

Irishman boat train. During June 1956 it returned to the Crewe area for another five years before moving on in April 1961 to Bletchley, where in addition to the London services it also worked across to Cambridge on some of the freight and passenger traffic, although the BR Standard locomotives in the 75000 series were generally preferred for this latter work. No 45379 moved to its last depot, Willesden, in March 1964 and throughout its short time there was a popular choice for special traffic, which resulted in appearances on the Great Central main line and at Hastings on the South coast before finally being declared redundant in the summer of 1965.

From six representatives of the class then at Barry No 45379 was considered in the best overall mechanical condition and was transported by road to Bitton on the Avon Valley Railway in May 1974 since when restoration has been progressing steadily.

With Nationalisation of the railways having taken place just eight months earlier, No 5379 stands in Northampton Castle station in August 1948. (*L. Hanson*)

56th: GWR 4-6-0 No 7812 *Erlestoke Manor*

BUILT: January 1939
WITHDRAWN: November 1965

ARRIVED BARRY: May 1966
DEPARTED BARRY: May 1974

Only 30 of these lightweight Manors were built between 1938 and 1950, making them the smallest class of 4-6-0 on the Great Western, yet no less than nine survive in the hands of preservation societies. Their axle loading was so low that they were able to run over secondary main lines previously restricted to 4-4-0 and 2-6-0 locomotives.

No 7812 *Erlestoke Manor* was completed at Swindon Works in January 1939 and after an initial spell working from Bristol (Bath Road) moved on to Tyseley in May 1943 to help out with the heavy wartime traffic in that area of the West Midlands. Shortly after the formation of British Railways in 1948 it was transferred to Newton Abbot and throughout the 1950s became closely associated with West Country services, spending periods at St Blazey, Laira and Truro sheds. Although basically a mixed-traffic locomotive, *Erlestoke Manor*'s chief task at Newton Abbot was to pilot the main line expresses over the steep banks at Dainton, Rattery and Hemerdon between there and Plymouth, replacing the ageing Bulldog 4-4-0s which had previously performed the duty. In October 1960 No 7812 joined several other members of the class working on the Cambrian section, initially allocated to Oswestry but subsequently based at Machynlleth, Croes Newydd, and finally Shrewsbury. During this period of its career No 7812 was immaculately maintained in lined-green livery and frequently worked the prestige Cambrian Coast Express between Shrewsbury and Aberystwyth as well as local services to Barmouth and Pwllheli, but in November 1965 Shrewsbury's entire fleet of six Manors were withdrawn.

Following purchase during 1973, *Erlestoke Manor* was moved by rail to the Dowty Railway Preservation Society's site at Ashchurch, arriving there in May 1974 after a one day stop-over at Parkend on the Dean Forest Railway. Subsequently transferred to the Severn Valley Railway, it re-entered service in September 1979 and made its long awaited return to main line duties in April 1982, double-heading with No 4930 *Hagley Hall* on the Welsh Marches Pullman.

Shortly after entering service on the Severn Valley Railway, *Erlestoke Manor* is prepared for the busy day ahead at Bewdley in 1980. (*Adrian Norman*)

57th: GWR 2-6-2T No 4150

BUILT: June 1947
WITHDRAWN: June 1965

ARRIVED BARRY: August 1965
DEPARTED BARRY: May 1974

The 5101 series of large passenger tanks was first introduced in November 1929 and subsequently constructed in batches right up to 1949. Collett made only minor detail changes to the original Churchward design of 1903, one of the pleasing additions being the revival of the copper-cap chimney and safety-valve brass bonnet. Withdrawals commenced in 1956 and the last of the class went for scrap nine years later, although one solitary member did survive as a stationary boiler until May 1967.

Turned out from Swindon Works in June 1947, No 4150 began its career working from Stourbridge Junction on the Birmingham and Wolverhampton area suburban services. By August 1953 it had moved on to the GWR shed at Weymouth and was used on banking duties up to Dorchester before being transferred to Taunton in September 1955 where, in addition to finding employment on local services over the main line, it also worked on the Minehead branch or occasionally acted as Taunton station pilot. Twelve months later No 4150 could be found working at Newton Abbot, where its main function was to provide banking assistance for the

many freight trains passing over the severe gradients between there and Brent. Although much of its time was spent on this work, this large prairie tank was also seen on stopping services to Exeter and Plymouth, and during the summer it frequently took holiday expresses onward from Newton Abbot to Paignton and Kingswear, as well as piloting several of the main line trains over the banks as far as Plymouth. After brief intervals at Exeter, Newton Abbot again and Westbury, between May 1960 and August 1962, No 4150 went to its final shed at Severn Tunnel Junction, performing on the arduous tunnel banking work.

After inspection at Barry, No 4150 was initially purchased for use on the Dean Forest Railway and taken to Parkend in May 1974. However, by early 1978 it had moved on to the Severn Valley Railway where it now waits its turn in the queue for rebuilding.

No 4150 stands in Exeter shed yard, adjacent to St Davids station during the summer of 1960. (*P. H. Groom*)

126

58th: LMS 0-6-0T No 47298

BUILT: December 1924
WITHDRAWN: December 1966

ARRIVED BARRY: June 1967
DEPARTED BARRY: July 1974

The LMS Standard 0-6-0T shunters led generally undistinguished careers, enthusiasts paying greater attention to the more celebrated main line locomotives, yet their participation in the everyday running of the railway was vital. The steady influx of diesel shunters during the 1950s saw them displaced from their traditional work but it took until 1967 before the last example went to the scrapyard.

As No 7138, this 0-6-0 tank was built by Hunslet of Leeds in December 1924 and spent the first few years based at the former LNWR depot at Camden, rubbing shoulders with many famous West Coast express locomotives while performing on its own unglamorous task of shunting in the carriage sidings or goods depot. By February 1928 it had been transferred to Northampton, principally for use on trip workings between the considerable number of yards in that area, but it also worked some of the light short-distance freight traffic to Bedford and Rugby. Fourteen years later, in May 1942, the renumbered 7298 moved on to Bletchley and frequently appeared in Swanbourne Yard or shunting elsewhere on the Bedford to Oxford line

until August 1954, when it travelled northwards to the shed at Sutton Oak near Liverpool. Here it regularly worked around the St Helens district or else helped marshal some of the main line fast freights in the goods yard at Pocket Nook, but the gradual decline in this freight traffic together with the further introduction of diesel shunting locomotives saw No 47298 declared redundant in December 1966. After a period in store at St Helens Shaw Street Station it was sold to Woodhams.

During July 1974, No 47298 arrived at the Steamport Museum in Southport, where it was successfully restored after five years' hard work. An undoubted highlight came in 1980 when it took part in the Rocket 150 Cavalcade at Rainhill, acting as 'shed pilot' at Bold Colliery, shunting the exhibits into their correct positions for the runs-past. In June 1983 it moved to the Llangollen Railway and now works services up the line to Berwyn.

A popular engine on the Llangollen Railway, Jinty No 7298 runs round its train at Llangollen station in September 1987 (*Steve Worrall*)

59th: BR 2-6-0 No 76079

BUILT: February 1957
WITHDRAWN: December 1967

ARRIVED BARRY: September 1968
DEPARTED BARRY: July 1974

The 76000 series Moguls were first introduced in 1952 and soon showed themselves to be good modern locomotives with a high route availability. Although the Southern-based members of the class were more often seen on passenger work, the design was biased towards goods traffic, as evidenced by the relatively small diameter driving wheels. However, like most BR Standard classes, they were destined to lead very short lives with the mass destruction of steam power in the late 1960s.

No 76079 was built at the Horwich works of the former Lancashire & Yorkshire Railway in February 1957 and entered service with the London Midland region at Sutton Oak shed. The five representatives of the class based there were mainly used on freight duties, although one of their regular diagrams took them from St Helens to Warrington and on to Chester with a local passenger service, working back home with the morning Hooton to Heaton Mersey freight empties. In December 1960, No 76079 was noted as far south as Bristol (St Philip's Marsh) but after having spent the night on Barrow Road shed it returned north with a parcels train. This was a fairly unusual incident, and the

2-6-0 could more normally be found in the Liverpool area, in particular on the sand trains for Pilkington's glass works at St Helens, although by mid-1965 it regularly travelled further afield with North Wales coal trains along the Chester to Holyhead line. After more than 10 years at Sutton Oak, No 76079 was transferred to Wigan (Springs Branch) in June 1967 where the duties were mainly concerned with mineral and general goods traffic, but it only lasted on this work for six months, being withdrawn at the end of the year. In company with three other Standard Moguls from Wigan, it was towed to Barry behind the inevitable diesel locomotive, arriving there in September 1968.

No 76079 was taken to Steamport, Southport in July 1974 and initially went on display as a static exhibit. Now privately owned it has been moved to a site under cover in Liverpool where rebuilding is being carried out.

Following overhaul at Eastleigh in May 1964, No 76079 spent a period running-in on trains from Waterloo and is seen here at Nine Elms shed. (*Andrew C. Ingram collection*)

60th: WR 2-6-2T No 4160

BUILT: September 1948
WITHDRAWN: June 1965

ARRIVED BARRY: August 1965
DEPARTED BARRY: August 1974

The history of the GWR large Prairie tanks is very involved, with more than 300 locomotives being built to the same basic design over a period of 46 years. G. J. Churchward was responsible for their initial production between 1903 and 1906, but his successor C. B. Collett perpetuated the class from 1929 onwards with detail modifications. The useful life of these later locomotives was much shortened by the advent of diesel multiple-units on to their traditional suburban workings.

No 4160 was part of the final batch of 20 locomotives built at Swindon Works during 1948/9, and although never carrying GWR livery, it was turned-out in unlined green and lettered *British Railways* in GWR-style Egyptian-serif shaded capitals. Initially allocated to Barry, No 4160 was frequently seen on the passenger services to Merthyr and Treherbert, as well as helping out with some of the excursion trains which were a regular feature of summer weekends in South Wales. By September 1953 it had been transferred away to Merthyr but for most of the time there was actually based at the sub-shed of Rhymney, working the locals down the valley to Caerphilly and Cardiff. In May 1958, No

4160 moved on again, this time to Cardiff (Radyr) where it continued on the same kind of work, although by now it was beginning to appear more frequently on goods duties such as those to Newport and Pontypool Road. Nevertheless, by the early 1960s passenger service closures and dieselisation gradually saw members of the class withdrawn for scrap and the few surviving 41XX tanks at this time congregated at Severn Tunnel Junction. No 4160 was transferred there in October 1964 to work out its last days on both the gruelling tunnel banking duties and the car ferry service across to Pilning.

No 4160 was moved from Barry to the Birmingham Railway Museum, Tyseley, in August 1974 but after only basic cleaning-up had been carried out, was put up for re-sale. Successfully tendered for by the Plym Valley Railway, it was moved initially in May 1981 to the Plymouth Exhibition Centre at Millbay prior to its transfer to the former Marsh Mills station site.

In sparkling ex-works condition No 4160 shunts the yard at Chalford with a Swindon to Gloucester pick-up goods in August 1963. (*Peter Cookson*)

61st: GWR 0-6-2T No 5637

BUILT: September 1925
WITHDRAWN: June 1964

ARRIVED BARRY: September 1964
DEPARTED BARRY: August 1974

By 1924 it was self-evident that many of the former Welsh railways' locomotives which had been absorbed by the GWR at the Grouping were obsolete and needed replacing with a new Standard class. The traditional 0-6-2 tank arrangement was an obvious choice for Collett and the first of his new design entered service during December 1924. Eventually totalling 200 locomotives, the class soon became popular because of their power, acceleration and speed capabilities on both passenger and freight work.

No 5637 was built at Swindon in September 1925 and arrived at its first depot, Cardiff Cathays, towards the end of that month. The stay here was very short, for only six weeks later it had moved on to Barry, mainly for use on the local services in the Cardiff and Newport districts. In October 1928, No 5637 was transferred to Abercynon, and apart from brief periods on loan to Merthyr and Cathays in the mid-1930s remained at this one shed for the next 28 years, principally taking the coal trains from Aberdare and Merthyr down to the docks at Cardiff, but also handling some of the passenger and workmen's trains. This long association with

Abercynon finally ended during 1956 when it was sent to Treherbert, chiefly to replace ageing Taff Vale 0-6-2 tanks on the stopping trains to Neath and Swansea over the former Rhondda & Swansea Bay route. Final move came in February 1960 when No 5637 returned to Barry shed for use on the passenger services from there to Merthyr (via Pontypridd) and Treherbert as well as the freight workings to Treforest and Penallta Colliery, but in the last few months before withdrawal in June 1964, it was more often confined to short-distance freight and shunting work.

In August 1974 No 5637 was purchased by the Birmingham Railway Museum at Tyseley, but without any subsequent restoration work being carried out it was put up for sale in March 1981 and bought by Thamesdown Borough Council for leasing to the Swindon & Cricklade Railway at Blunsdon.

Despite a missing safety valve bonnet, No 5637 seems to have survived its first four years at Barry remarkably well. (*Graham Wignall*)

62nd: GWR 4-6-0 No 5080 *Defiant*

BUILT: May 1939
WITHDRAWN: April 1963

ARRIVED BARRY: October 1963
DEPARTED BARRY: August 1974

The much-acclaimed Castle Class was Collett's first design for the GWR, and was basically an enlargement of Churchward's celebrated Star 4-6-0s. Construction of these new locomotives took place between 1923 and 1950, fifteen of them being rebuilt from withdrawn Stars, and one nominally rebuilt from the Great Western's only Pacific locomotive No 111 *The Great Bear*. They soon earned a fine reputation for themselves, and could stand in for the more powerful Kings on the Paddington to Wolverhampton or West of England turns.

Originally named *Ogmore Castle*, No 5080 was completed at Swindon Works in May 1939 and sent to its first shed at Old Oak Common shortly afterwards. From there it worked over most of the GW system with main line expresses out of Paddington to Plymouth, Penzance, Birmingham and Bristol. However, during August 1940 it was transferred to Cardiff (Canton) and in January of the following year was renamed *Defiant* to commemorate one of the many types of aircraft which had taken part in the Battle of Britain. At Cardiff it soon became established on the leading South Wales to London services, which from the early 1950s onwards

included several of the well-known titled trains such as The Red Dragon, Pembroke Coast Express, and South Wales Pullman, while it also travelled over the routes to Shrewsbury and the South West. Moved to Carmarthen in September 1956 and then to Landore a few months later, No 5080 continued to appear on top-link duties despite the arrival of further Britannia Pacifics in the area, which took over most of the principal London workings. By 1959 it had returned to Carmarthen, staying there until transferred for the last time to Llanelly in May 1961; even at this late stage of its career *Defiant* still found regular main line work up to the time of withdrawal in April 1963.

Although acquired for spares by the Birmingham Railway Museum, *Defiant* was considered to be worthy of restoration in its own right and following resteaming at Tyseley in July 1987 it has run trials over the main line and the Severn Valley Railway in preparation for a busy season on special trains during 1988.

Defiant makes its first main line trip on BR with a trial run from Tyseley to Stratford-upon-Avon on 18 August 1987.
(*John B. Gosling*)

131

63rd: LMR 2-6-2T No 41312

BUILT: May 1952
WITHDRAWN: July 1967

ARRIVED BARRY: January 1968
DEPARTED BARRY: August 1974

The first ten of these Ivatt 2-6-2 tanks were actually built under LMS auspices between 1946 and 1947, the remaining 120 members of the class coming out after Nationalisation. They were practically identical to the earlier Class 2 2-6-0s (Nos 46400–46527) but with the addition of side tanks and a bunker, resulting in a very modern locomotive ideal for light duties, with the emphasis on ease of maintenance and servicing.

Assembled at Crewe Works in May 1952, No 41312 spent the whole of its 15-year life based on the Southern Region of BR. First allocation was to Faversham in Kent, where it was mainly employed on secondary workings around the Margate and Dover areas, the shed actually sitting in the junction of the lines to those two places. Although transferred to Ashford in June 1959, it underwent a complete change of scenery six months later with a move to Barnstaple Junction on the North Devon coast, working a variety of duties from there over the route between Bideford, Torrington and Halwill Junction, as well as occasionally putting in an appearance on the Ilfracombe and Exeter line. During March 1963 No 41312 was re-allocated to

Brighton and became an established performer on the local passenger service up to Horsham, but by May of the following year had gone on to Bournemouth to take up work on the Wareham–Swanage and Brockenhurst–Lymington branches. However, as other forms of motive power gradually began to oust No 41312 from these lines, it was called on to work the very last booked steam service over the Lymington branch in April 1967. With only three months to go before withdrawal it was transferred away to Nine Elms, managing to survive on shunting duties in and around Waterloo until the final elimination of steam on the Southern Region in July 1967.

Although four members of the class were bought for scrap by Woodham Bros, only two of them lasted long enough to be purchased by preservation groups, No 41312 being acquired by the Caerphilly Railway Society during August 1974.

No 41312 runs light through Clapham Junction in June 1967 just a few weeks away from withdrawal. (*P. H. Groom*)

64th: GWR 0-6-2T No 6619

BUILT: January 1928   ARRIVED BARRY: November 1963
WITHDRAWN: February 1963   DEPARTED BARRY: October 1974

Although examples of the class were allocated at various times to most divisions of the GWR, this group of well liked 0-6-2 tanks is generally associated with the unique atmosphere of the South Wales coalfield. An interesting aspect of their operation in the Welsh valleys was that they generally worked chimney-first up the valleys and bunker-first when coming down, apparently because the guiding pair of wheels gave them greater stability at the obviously higher speeds.

Built at Swindon in January 1928, No 6619 spent a period running-in from Cardiff Cathays before going to Barry shed where it was destined to stay for the greater proportion of its working life. The 0-6-2 tanks here were used on passenger services to Treherbert and Merthyr (via Pontypridd), occasionally on the stopping trains between Cardiff and Swansea, plus the usual excursion and miners' traffic. They also dealt with some of the short-distance freight work, but after more than 28 years at Barry, No 6619 was transferred to Treherbert in August 1956, a shed which owed its existence to a Taff Vale Railway decision in the mid-19th century to diagram some of the coal train workings from the

head of the valleys instead of such trains commencing and terminating at Cardiff. Apart from the Treherbert to Neath and Barry passenger services, No 6619 was also used on mixed-traffic duties to Llanelly and Cardiff as well as frequently being recorded on the former TVR Ynysybwl branch with coal trains from Lady Windsor colliery. In February 1963, whilst shunting condemned locomotives in Woodham's yard, it became derailed and suffered minor front end damage, which it is thought led to No 6619 being withdrawn almost immediately.

Taken to the unfamiliar surroundings of the North Yorkshire Moors in October 1974 No 6619 underwent an extremely thorough rebuilding and made its public debut in steam at Grosmont in October 1984. In May of the following year it appeared at Didcot's GW 150 celebrations but returned north soon after to continue its work on this steeply graded line.

No 6619 blackens the North Yorkshire Moors sky as it heads away from Levisham in May 1986. (*John Hunt*)

133

65th: WR 4-6-0 No 7822 *Foxcote Manor*

BUILT: December 1950
WITHDRAWN: November 1965

ARRIVED BARRY: May 1966
DEPARTED BARRY: January 1975

The Manors comprised the smallest class of Great Western 4-6-0, both in size and number built, their axle loading of just over 17 tons enabling them to operate over secondary routes which were prohibited to heavier classes. First introduced in 1938, only 20 locomotives were built before the declaration of war put a stop to their construction, and the remaining 10 were therefore turned out after Nationalisation in 1950.

No 7822 *Foxcote Manor* emerged from Swindon Works in December 1950 and joined other members of the class at Oswestry for service on Cambrian line duties. During this time it came to be a regular performer on the Aberystwyth–Shrewsbury locals in addition to the Whitchurch–Welshpool–Aberystwyth trains. In April 1954, No 7822 was transferred to Chester where it appeared on the Wrexham–Barmouth and Chester–Pwllheli workings which took it over the former GWR route via Bala Junction and Llangollen. On returning to Oswestry in August 1958, *Foxcote Manor* worked out the rest of its days with BR operating services over the Cambrian lines, being subsequently based at Machynlleth from December 1963 and Shrews-

bury from January 1965. Throughout this period it continued on the usual pattern of local workings which at times included the Aberystwyth to Carmarthen trains but it was also regularly seen on the more important duties which covered the well-known Cambrian Coast Express. On two occasions in 1963, No 7822 was chosen for special duties, the first being in August when it worked the Royal Train on one stage of its journey from Barmouth to Chester, and the second in September when it double-headed with No 7827 on a Talyllyn Railway excursion between Ruabon and Barmouth. However, towards the end of 1965 all Shrewsbury's fleet of six Manors were withdrawn.

Bought by the Foxcote Manor Society in 1974, No 7822 was moved to a private site in Oswestry where preliminary restoration was carried out. Transferred to the Llangollen Railway in late 1985 it made a welcome return to service at the end of the 1987 season.

Over the weekend of 12/13 September 1987 *Foxcote Manor*, moved under its own power for the first time in almost 22 years, venturing outside its special shed at Llangollen. (*Steve Worrall*)

66th: BR 2-6-4T No 80151

BUILT: January 1957
WITHDRAWN: May 1967

ARRIVED BARRY: October 1967
DEPARTED BARRY: March 1975

As a direct development of the LMS Stanier and Fairburn designs, the Standard Class 4 2-6-4Ts were extremely good-looking locomotives, the smooth curved side tanks adding to their overall smart appearance. Several examples of the 155-strong class were based on the Southern Region, and those that worked the branch line services provided first-class accommodation for their crews compared with the ageing M7 0-4-4 tanks.

No 80151 was built at Brighton Works in January 1957 and went straight into service from the running shed there. Amongst its duties were the stopping trains from Brighton and Eastbourne to Victoria (via Eridge) together with the services to Tonbridge and Horsham, while occasionally it was recorded on the Bluebell line between Lewes and East Grinstead before that route's closure in 1958. Another regular working for the standard tanks there was the busy parcels traffic radiating out from the Brighton district to Bricklayers Arms, Portsmouth, Newhaven and Hastings. By December 1963, No 80151 had moved on to Redhill, where in addition to continuing on the Central Section parcels duties it worked the local trains across to

Tonbridge and Ashford, but during May 1965 it was transferred away to Salisbury and spent sixteen months there before making a final move to Eastleigh in September 1966. Apart from acting as station pilot, it was used on a mixture of duties in the Southampton area, including the Brockenhurst to Lymington branch, and in April 1967 was specially cleaned to work a Locomotive Club of Great Britain railtour of Hampshire branch lines. In the following month No 80151 sustained light damage while working a freight on the Ludgershall line and on its return to Basingstoke was withdrawn almost immediately.

Despite having been in service for only 10 years, No 80151 was unceremoniously dispatched to Woodhams and left to its fate. However, in 1975 it was purchased by a group of enthusiasts and taken by road to the Chappel and Wakes Colne base of the East Anglian Railway Museum.

Considered to be in excellent mechanical condition, work has yet to start on No 80151 seen here at Chappel in August 1987. (*Alan Warren*)

67th: BR 2-6-0 No 78022

BUILT: May 1954
WITHDRAWN: September 1966

ARRIVED BARRY: March 1967
DEPARTED BARRY: June 1975

The BR Standard Class 2 Moguls were designed by the drawing office at Derby under the supervision of R. A. Riddles, and 65 were turned out by Darlington Works between 1952 and 1956. Although they were allocated to all Regions except the Southern, the effects of Dr Beeching's branch line cuts together with the introduction of diesel multiple-units gradually displaced them from passenger work, their later years mainly being spent on freight duties.

No 78022 was completed at Darlington in May 1954 and entered service along with Nos 78023/4/5, from the former Midland shed at Sheffield (Millhouses). There it was used extensively on the South Yorkshire local passenger services, including those from Sheffield (Midland) to Chesterfield, Nottingham, Derby and Chinley, but on closure of Millhouses in January 1962 it was transferred to Doncaster, spending most of the time there as station pilot or else on light, short-distance freight duties. At the end of July 1962, No 78022 moved to Stratford in London, ostensibly to replace ex-GER J15s on local goods work, but after only a few weeks it had moved on to March in Cambridgeshire and

was placed in store there. Quite clearly there was little work for the Standard Moguls in East Anglia, so in December 1962 No 78022 was transferred to the London Midland Region, staying for short periods at Barrow and Aintree before settling down at Lostock Hall from December 1963 onwards. Its main job there was to act as Preston station pilot although from time to time it ventured down to Liverpool, Wigan or Blackburn with shunting and freight turns. It survived on this work until September 1966 and was then declared surplus to requirements, being dispatched to Barry early the next year.

Following a very rapid fund-raising effort, No 78022 was purchased by the Standard 4 Locomotive Preservation Society, (owners of another ex-Barry locomotive, No 75078), and moved to Oakworth on the Keighley & Worth Valley Railway in June 1975 for initial storage. Since then, restoration has been taking place in the yard at Haworth.

During its brief period at Doncaster in early 1962, No 78022 waits for the road in the station with a short trip freight. (G. Ibbetson)

68th: LMR 2-6-2T No 41313

BUILT: May 1952
WITHDRAWN: November 1965

ARRIVED BARRY: February 1966
DEPARTED BARRY: July 1975

The LMS introduced this class of light passenger tank in 1946 to the design of H. G. Ivatt and a total of 130 locomotives was built between then and 1952. Many of them were fitted with vacuum control gear for operating push-and-pull trains.

No 41313 emerged from Crewe in May 1952 and initially went to Brighton for work on the stopping trains to Lewes, Eastbourne, Tunbridge Wells and Horsham, together with a certain amount of pilot and trip working. By July 1952 it was based at Exmouth Junction, spending a couple of years operating over the former LSWR routes to Okehampton, Yeovil Junction and down the branches to Exmouth and Sidmouth, but during February 1955 No 41313 returned to Central Section duties, this time allocated to Three Bridges. However, just three months later it moved on again to Faversham where among its duties this time were the branch trains over the Sittingbourne to Sheerness line. In June 1959 it was sent to Ashford to assist with the services from there to Hastings, Gillingham, Ramsgate and Dover. At the beginning of 1960 it was transferred to Barnstaple Junction to join other members of the class which

had earlier replaced the ex-LBSCR E1 0-6-2Ts on local workings in that part of North Devon. While there, it became a regular sight on the Barnstaple–Torrington–Halwill Junction trains, over a line which had been opened to passenger traffic as late as 1925 and which was the last standard gauge rural branch line to be built in this country. Yet another move took place in March 1963 when No 41313 came back to Brighton for a year before finally being transferred to Eastleigh in May 1964, where it was used on the Brockenhurst to Lymington Pier branch together with pilot and trip working in the Southampton area right up to withdrawal in November 1965.

Purchased by the Ivatt Locomotive Trust, No 41313 was moved to the Quainton Road depot of the Buckinghamshire Railway Centre in July 1975 and joined sister locomotive No 41298 which had been bought direct from British Railways in 1967.

With just one Bulleid coach considered sufficient to cope with the branch traffic, No 41313 stands at Torrington during 1962. (*C. L. Caddy collection*)

69th: GWR 2-8-0 No 2857

BUILT: May 1918
WITHDRAWN: April 1963

ARRIVED BARRY: September 1963
DEPARTED BARRY: August 1975

The prototype of Churchward's successful heavy freight 2-8-0s was introduced in 1903 and became the first locomotive of that wheel arrangement to be built in this country. Subsequent production of the class took place between 1905 and 1942 with a total of 167 eventually being constructed, although the later locomotives incorporated all the improvements which C. B. Collett had introduced following his appointment as Chief Mechanical Engineer in 1923.

Built at Swindon Works during the latter stages of World War I in May 1918, No 2857 began work for the GWR at Salisbury where it performed on the heavy freight duties into South Wales, but after only a few months it was sent to the Newport Division, being based at both Pontypool Road and Aberdare between then and August 1922. The remainder of the 1920s were spent mainly at Old Oak Common and Newton Abbot, the duties at the latter shed including some of the china clay traffic from Cornwall as well as other heavy mineral workings. In May 1928 No 2857 returned to Aberdare for quite a long spell which was later followed by additional periods at Pontypool Road,

Cardiff and Plymouth, while the years from 1949 to 1958 were spent in the West Midlands, initially working from Stourbridge, but principally at Banbury where it was used on the important iron ore trains to Cardiff. After a short time operating out of Tyseley, it went back to Pontypool Road for the third time in June 1958 and then, apart from a few months allocated to Swindon, stayed for the remainder of its career in South Wales handling much of that area's considerable coal traffic until withdrawal from Neath shed in April 1963 after 45 years' service.

During the summer of 1975 No 2857 was moved by rail to the Severn Valley Railway and worked its first passenger train over this line some five years later. Following the replacement of a cracked cylinder block and other essential repair work, it re-entered service for the second time in 1985, heading a special demonstration freight train through Newport in September of that year as part of the GWR 150 celebrations.

No 2857 crosses Chepstow Bridge in September 1985 with its special freight train run in connection with the GW 150 celebrations that year. (*Brian Denton*)

138

70th: GWR 2-6-0 No 7325 (9303)

BUILT: February 1932
WITHDRAWN: April 1964

ARRIVED BARRY: November 1964
DEPARTED BARRY: August 1975

342 of these popular Churchward Moguls were built between 1911 and 1932, several of which were requisitioned for service in France during the 1914–18 War. They proved to be ideal mixed-traffic locomotives and although frequently overworked and overloaded, still managed to perform admirably when called upon to handle express passenger or heavy freights. In the late 1930s, 100 were withdrawn and certain parts, including the wheels and motion, were incorporated in new Grange and Manor 4-6-0s, but scrapping on a large scale did not really commence until 1958.

No 9303 represents one of the last batch of 20 locomotives built at Swindon in 1932 which were specially weighted at the front end to help reduce excessive tyre wear on the leading driving wheels. It began its career operating from the farthest outpost of the GWR system at Penzance, but by 1933 had moved 300 miles up the main line to Old Oak Common. From this date the 2-6-0 became a common sight throughout the London Division on both mixed freight and stopping passenger trains, being based at Oxford and Reading for a time – while at this latter depot it was regularly out-stationed at the sub-shed of Basingstoke, often working into Southampton as a result. In November 1953, No 9303 was transferred to Tyseley, where in addition to the familiar pattern of mixed traffic duties it helped pilot the summer Saturday expresses between Stratford and Birmingham as well as occasionally working through to Redhill with South Coast holiday services from the Midlands. After a short period at Banbury the extra front end weights were removed in June 1958 and the locomotive returned to service at Chester renumbered 7325. The remainder of the 1950s and early 1960s were spent in South Wales allocated to Pontypool Road, Newport (Ebbw Junction) and Severn Tunnel Junction, withdrawal coming while in store at Pontypool Road in April 1964.

Purchased for use on the Severn Valley Railway, No 9303 travelled to Bewdley together with No 2857 in August 1975 and a start was made on the long task of restoration during 1981.

Just as happy on passenger or freight workings, No 9303 heads a mixed goods train at an unknown location in the late 1930s. (Alan Warren collection)

71st: GWR 2-6-2T No 4561

BUILT: October 1924
WITHDRAWN: May 1962

ARRIVED BARRY: September 1962
DEPARTED BARRY: September 1975

The 4500 series of Churchward 2-6-2 tanks was designed for branch line work where route restrictions prohibited the use of heavier locomotives. The first 20 were built at Wolverhampton in the period 1906–8, the last new locomotives to be constructed there, and a further 55 were added by Swindon between 1909 and 1924.

A product of Swindon Works in October 1924, No 4561 went new to Tyseley depot on the outskirts of Birmingham where it was employed for a few years on the outer suburban services to Stratford-upon-Avon and Leamington. During September 1927 it moved on to Newport (Ebbw Junction), again for use on local passenger work in that part of Wales, but from then onwards it became a very unsettled locomotive, spending time at Plymouth (Laira and Millbay), Launceston, Moorswater, Bodmin, St Blazey, Exeter and Penzance between 1930 and 1938. However, No 4561 found a more permanent home in September 1938 when it was transferred to Truro and became firmly established on the Falmouth branch trains together with those to Newquay (via Chacewater) and other stopping trains over the Cornish main line. Twenty years

later, in November 1958, this 2-6-2 tank moved to Newton Abbot and was to be one of the regular locomotives on the Brent to Kingsbridge branch until the introduction of diesel railcars in the spring of 1961 saw it displaced from this line to spend a few weeks of working on the local goods up the Dart Valley between Totnes and Ashburton. Final allocation was to Plymouth (Laira) in July 1961 with withdrawal coming in May of the following year.

After having spent 13 years evading the cutter's torch on the scrap lines at Barry, No 4561 was rescued by the West Somerset Railway and unloaded at Bishops Lydeard, near Taunton, in September 1975. Although restoration began very slowly, the volunteers working on this engine received added incentive to achieve their objective with the appearance of sister locomotive No 5572 on loan from Didcot during the summer of 1986 and 1987.

Nos 4561 and 5573 double-head a return Buckfastleigh to Teignmouth excursion at Aller Junction in 1959. (*Real Photographs Co*)

72nd: GWR 2-6-2T No 5521

BUILT: December 1927
WITHDRAWN: April 1962

ARRIVED BARRY: September 1962
DEPARTED BARRY: September 1975

Following the success of the earlier locomotives, a further 100 2-6-2Ts were built between 1927 and 1929 – these had larger tanks with a sloping top which increased their water capacity to 1300 gallons. However, this added to their weight somewhat and they were therefore collectively known as the 4575 Class to distinguish them from the previous locomotives. Both types managed to survive complete until Nationalisation and 23 were eventually sold to Woodhams at Barry although 10 have since been cut-up.

No 5521 was turned out from Swindon Works in the last month of 1927, and after short periods at Newton Abbot and Truro found more permanent accommodation at Taunton from January 1930 onwards. For the first few years there it was based out at Bridgwater, but in July 1933 automatic staff-changing apparatus was fitted for working the Minehead branch as well as the Exe Valley route across to Barnstaple. For just over 21 years No 5521 operated in this part of North Devon and West Somerset before being put into store between February and May 1951. There then followed a brief spell on Cambrian Line services based at

Oswestry, but in October 1951 it was transferred to St Blazey where, apart from working the Par to Newquay branch passenger and freight trains, it would also pilot or bank the heavy holiday expresses up some of the steep gradients on this line. Other duties included the Padstow–Wadebridge–Bodmin Road services together with the pick-up goods on the freight-only Carbean branch. In August 1958 No 5521 returned to Taunton and resumed its business on the Minehead branch as well as becoming a regular sight on the local services to Chard, but in common with other members of the class it finished its days at Plymouth (Laira), going there in November 1961, only to be condemned five months later.

Although originally purchased for use on the West Somerset Railway, No 5521 subsequently moved to the Dean Forest Railway and has undergone rebuilding as part of an MSC employment scheme based at Lydney Trading Estate.

With one of the earlier 45XX tanks behind, No 5521 stands in a row of small prairies at Barry in 1966. (*B. J. Miller collection*)

73rd: GWR 2-6-2T No 5542

BUILT:	July 1928	ARRIVED BARRY:	March 1962
WITHDRAWN:	December 1961	DEPARTED BARRY:	September 1975

The tremendous acceleration which these small prairie tanks possessed made them great favourites for local passenger or branch line work, and the class as a whole monopolised many branches right up to the end of steam working in the early 1960s. In these later years several engines received fully lined-out BR green livery, a pleasing choice which certainly enhanced their attractive lines. Scrapping commenced in 1950, but the bulk of the class were withdrawn between 1957 and 1962 as dieselisation or the closing-down of local services curtailed their activities.

Built at Swindon in July 1928 No 5542 spent the first 15 months based at Gloucester and Cheltenham (Malvern Road) where it worked the local passenger services between those two places, as well as the stopping trains to Kingham and Honeybourne. In October 1929 the 2-6-2T was transferred to Bristol (Bath Road) for use on the routes to Wells, Radstock and Bath, although for a few months it was known to have operated from the sub-sheds at Yatton and Weston-super-Mare. Like sister locomotive No 5521 previously described, No 5542 was fitted with automatic staff-changing

equipment in the summer of 1933 and allocated to Taunton for working over the Minehead and Barnstaple branches. Apart from short stays at St Blazey, Kingsbridge and Truro in the late 1930s and a slightly longer period at Newton Abbot between 1953 and 1955, it remained at Taunton for 24 years, working a variety of passenger and goods trains in the area, including an occasional sprint down the main line to Exeter. Final allocation was to Westbury in September 1957 and No 5542 spent its remaining days in regular service on the trains to Bristol Temple Meads via Frome and Radstock before withdrawal at the end of 1961.

Thirteen years in Barry scrapyard were to prove lucky for No 5542 because in September 1975 it was moved to the West Somerset Railway for use on the Taunton–Minehead line, familiar territory indeed! It has since been bought by the '5542 Group' which is now responsible for its restoration and eventual operation on the WSR.

Standing at Bishops Lydeard shortly after arrival from Barry, No 5542's condition bears testimony to its long sojourn in the scrapyard. (*Christopher Redwood*)

74th: WR 0-6-0PT No 9466

BUILT: February 1952
WITHDRAWN: July 1964

ARRIVED BARRY: November 1964
DEPARTED BARRY: September 1975

The Hawksworth 94XX pannier tanks were introduced in 1947 as an updated version of the ubiquitous 57XX locomotives. The first 10 were built at Swindon and the remaining 200 by outside contractors, but as British Railways was studying the possibility of a complete changeover to diesels for shunting work, the life expectancy of the class was destined to be short right from the beginning, and all were withdrawn whilst still having several years of profitable life left in them.

No 9466 was built at the Newcastle works of Robert Stephenson & Hawthorn Ltd and went to its first depot at Gloucester in February 1952. The stay here was short, for only two months later it had been transferred to Worcester to find employment on heavy shunting work, short transfer freights between the many goods yards in that district and banking duties at Honeybourne for the main line freights up to Campden. Although the 57XX panniers were regularly seen on passenger duties, the Hawksworth locomotives were considered to be unsuitable, and No 9466 was only rarely used in this capacity, mainly on the local services to Stratford and Leamington Spa. In January 1961 it

moved to Bristol (St Philip's Marsh) and performed the customary pilot and transfer duties although it was mainly occupied on shunting in the large yards at Stoke Gifford and elsewhere. A complete change of scenery followed in July 1962 when it was transferred to South Wales, going initially to Tondu near Bridgend but subsequently moving on to Cardiff (Radyr) in July of the following year. However, the effects of the BR modernisation scheme saw its everyday work taken over by 350hp diesel-electric shunters and so by the summer of 1964 it was declared surplus to requirements and sold for scrap.

As the only one of 19 representatives of the class to have survived the scrapman at Barry, No 9466 was resteamed at the Buckinghamshire Railway Centre in February 1985 and 3 months later appeared at Didcot's GW 150 festivities in the guise of No 9404. In the summer of 1986 it went on loan to the Swanage Railway but can now be seen operating the passenger shuttle service back at Quainton.

Light duties for No 9466 as it works the shuttle service at the Buckinghamshire Railway Centre in May 1987. (*Alan Warren*)

75th: WR 0-6-0PT No 9681

BUILT: May 1949
WITHDRAWN: July 1965

ARRIVED BARRY: August 1965
DEPARTED BARRY: October 1975

As a replacement for the many hundreds of Victorian saddle and pannier 0-6-0Ts, Collett's design for a new shunting and light freight tank engine was an undoubted success, with no less than 863 examples being built between 1929 and 1950. Not surprisingly, this made them the most numerous type to run on the GWR, and although the last one was not withdrawn until 1966 several of them managed to survive into the 1970s under the ownership of the National Coal Board and London Transport.

Completed at Swindon Works in May 1949, No 9681 began work for British Railways at Tondu in South Wales where it was engaged on a wide variety of mixed-traffic duties, including general freight and coal trains to the Cardiff, Bridgend and Swansea areas, together with the limestone traffic from Cornelly on the Porthcawl branch destined for the steelworks at Margam. It was also quite frequently rostered for passenger work and regularly handled the stopping services between Bridgend, Maesteg and Cymmer and those between Tondu and Blaengarw. During December 1955 it spent a brief period at Abergavenny sharing pilot

duties with Ivatt 2-6-2T No 41203, but shortly after this was re-allocated to Oswestry where it became a familiar sight on transfer freights, and of course pilot work, in the Welsh border country. From December 1960 onwards No 9681 passed its declining days based back in South Wales allocated to Cardiff Canton, Barry and finally Cardiff East Dock. During this time it performed on the normal trip and colliery shunting duties, only occasionally seeing use on passenger workings. In the week before closure of East Dock in August 1965, No 9681 was put into steam and worked under its own power to Woodhams at Barry where the fire was dropped and the locomotive left to its fate.

Fortunately this was not the end of the story because in October 1975 No 9681 was delivered by low-loader to the Dean Forest Railway, where it made a gratifying return to steam during September 1984, resplendent in British Railways black livery.

No 9681 climbs up from the branch line with a train for Norchard on the Dean Forest Railway in 1986.
(*Peter J. C. Skelton*)

76th: WR 4-6-0 No 6990 *Witherslack Hall*

BUILT: April 1948
WITHDRAWN: December 1965

ARRIVED BARRY: February 1966
DEPARTED BARRY: November 1975

Seventy-one Hawksworth Modified Halls were turned out between 1944 and 1950, this bringing the grand total of Hall Class locomotives to 330. Like their predecessors, they were very successful machines. They incorporated many improved features, such as a higher degree of superheat to combat the effects of poor fuel on performance. The modified locomotives were officially known as the 6959 Class to distinguish them from the earlier Collett design.

No 6990 *Witherslack Hall* was built at Swindon just after Nationalisation in 1948 and went straight to its first shed at Old Oak Common. After a period of running-in, it was selected to take part in the famous Locomotive Exchanges of 1948 which were held to compare the relative merits of existing types before commencing design work on the new BR Standard locomotives. During these trials it regularly took charge of the Marylebone to Manchester expresses over the Great Central main line and also worked some trains on to Sheffield via Penistone, a journey which took it through the notorious Woodhead Tunnel. On conclusion of the tests No 6990 returned to Old Oak Common where

it stayed, apart from 14 months at Oxford in 1950/1, until the early 1960s. For most of its time there, the Hall operated on the semi-fast expresses out of Paddington to several destinations, but throughout the summer of 1956 it was regular locomotive on the 'Oxford Flier', alias the 5.35pm Oxford to Paddington, which quite often attained speeds up into the high eighties. In October 1963, *Witherslack Hall* was transferred to Bristol (St Philip's Marsh) yet when that shed closed in June 1964 it moved across the city to Barrow Road. Even though the days of steam were now numbered it still managed to turn up at Eastleigh with a freight in July 1965, but just six months later No 6990 performed its final task of hauling a rake of condemned locomotives to Barry scrapyard.

Rescue was at hand, however, for in November 1975 No 6990 was moved to Loughborough on the Great Central Railway and following successful resteaming in August 1986 it once again hauls trains over part of the route of the 1948 Exchanges.

Reviving memories of the 1948 Exchanges, *Witherslack Hall* pilots 0–6–0ST No 68009 just south of Loughborough in August 1986. (*Graham Wignall*)

77th: LMS 2-8-0 No 48151

BUILT: September 1942
WITHDRAWN: January 1968

ARRIVED BARRY: September 1968
DEPARTED BARRY: November 1975

The Stanier Class 8Fs dominated heavy freight work over most of the LMS system, although they could still show a good turn of speed when required and were occasionally used on passenger turns or on summer excursions. In addition to those built to LMS orders, the class was also built in quantity for the Ministry of Supply, the Railway Executive Committee and the LNER, a total of 852 eventually being constructed.

LMS No 8151 was turned out from Crewe in September 1942 and immediately went to Carlisle (Kingmoor) to help with the heavy wartime freight traffic over the West Coast main line but by February of the following year it had been transferred to Grangemouth to perform on the equally significant oil trains to Perth, Dundee and the large yards surrounding Glasgow. In February 1949 the locomotive, by now renumbered 48151, journeyed south to Wellingborough and established itself on the heavy Toton–Brent coal trains, a duty which it shared with the Garratt 2-6-6-2 locomotives. Together these two classes virtually monopolised the more important freight workings over the Midland main line. A further move came in June

1955, this time to Canklow, near Rotherham, where it was principally employed on goods duties throughout South Yorkshire as well as to Healey Mills and Dringhouses Yard (York) and it continued operating in this area when transferred to Staveley (Barrow Hill) at the beginning of 1963. Just over 16 months later, in April 1964, No 48151 went on to Liverpool Edge Hill before making its final move to Northwich in Cheshire during March 1966 – here it was mainly used on the ICI limestone trains across to the Peak Forest quarries, but also appeared on the North Wales coastal route with more general goods taffic. When withdrawn in January 1968 it was amongst the last 350 steam locomotives remaining in service during this final year of standard gauge steam on British Railways.

Although originally moved to Embsay on the Yorkshire Dales Railway, No 48151 was restored at Wakefield and Butterley before returning to steam in June 1987 and taking part in the following month's Crewe 150 celebrations.

Fresh from its appearance at the Crewe 150 celebrations, No 48151 makes an impressive sight at Butterley in the late summer of 1987. (*Midland Railway Trust Ltd*)

78th: S&DJR 2-8-0 No 53809

BUILT:	July 1925	ARRIVED BARRY:	August 1964
WITHDRAWN:	June 1964	DEPARTED BARRY:	December 1975

The Midland Railway was responsible for the locomotive stock of the Somerset & Dorset Joint Railway, so when larger and more powerful locomotives were required to handle the ever increasing mineral traffic, Derby produced six of these elegantly-proportioned 2-8-0s in 1914. A further five were added in 1925, and although several of them did work on the Midland Division of the LMS in 1931, the class as a whole remained firmly associated with the Somerset & Dorset line.

Built at the Darlington Works of R. Stephenson & Co in July 1925, S&D No 89 spent most of its life working the freight traffic between Bath, Evercreech Junction and Templecombe. In fact, it was while on an Evercreech Junction to Bath goods in November 1929 that this locomotive was involved in a serious accident – the crew was overcome by smoke and fumes while passing through the mile-long unventilated Combe Down Tunnel and when the runaway train became derailed in Bath goods yard, three railway employees were killed. Because the locomotive was virtually brand-new it was not declared a write-off but, even so, Derby Works almost had to rebuild it. The freight workings over

the S&D were quite considerable, for in addition to the general goods traffic large quantities of coal were carried from the collieries centred on Radstock and Midsomer Norton, while stone traffic from the many quarries was also substantial. However, during the 1950s the Class 7F 2-8-0s began to appear on many of the Midlands to South Coast holiday expresses which they worked between Bath and Bournemouth, frequently taking 10 coaches unassisted over the Mendips, but generally No 53809 remained on the goods trains for which it was designed.

In late 1975, No 53809 was moved by road to Kirk Smeaton near Doncaster, initial restoration being carried out in the old station yard there. This work was completed at the Midland Railway Centre, Butterley in time for it to take part in the cavalcade of locomotives at Rainhill during 1980. It has since worked several excursions over the BR main line as well as making appearances on the Keighley & Worth Valley and Severn Valley Railways.

No 53809 on the main line at Kirkby-in-Ashfield when returning from an open day at Shirebrook in June 1987. In tow are No D4, *Electra* and No 55015 *Tulyar*. (*Midland Railway Trust Ltd*)

79th: LSWR 4-6-0 No 30506

BUILT: October 1920
WITHDRAWN: January 1964

ARRIVED BARRY: October 1964
DEPARTED BARRY: April 1976

The S15 Class was the third of R. W. Urie's ouside-cylinder 4-6-0 designs for the London & South Western Railway, and he built 20 in 1920–1 for fast heavy goods working. Even though Maunsell perpetuated the class in the late 1920s and 1930s these handsome and useful locomotives never exceeded 45 in number, and the two examples rescued from Barry are the only two representatives of Urie's work to survive into preservation.

As LSWR No 506, this 4-6-0 was turned out from Eastleigh Works in October 1920, and after entering traffic from Nine Elms in London moved just down the line to Strawberry Hill the following year. In 1923 when the new shed at Feltham was opened to serve the adjoining marshalling yards, it was transferred there and, apart from a short stay at Exmouth Junction in 1926/7, remained at this one depot for the rest of its working life. The S15s as a whole became the mainstay of Western Section heavy goods services and No 30506, as it was renumbered after Nationalisation, helped work Feltham's freight turns to Salisbury, Portsmouth, Southampton and Bournemouth, together with several of the cross-London transfer workings.

Nevertheless, during the peak holiday periods it was frequently pressed into main line passenger duty, appearing on Waterloo to Basingstoke and Salisbury stopping services as well as on the occasional express, such as the Southampton boat trains, when Nine Elms motive power resources were stretched to the limit. Withdrawn in January 1964, No 30506 was to have towed three other S15s to Barry in June, but failed en route and did not make this final journey until four months later.

No 30506 arrived at Alresford on the Mid-Hants Railway in April 1976 and preliminary restoration work was commenced almost straight away. However, in early 1980 the boiler was found to be beyond economical repair and so a replacement was obtained from Maunsell S15 No 30825 which still then languished at Barry. This boiler was taken to Ropley in February 1981 and fitted into the frames of No 30506 allowing restoration to continue with an eventual return to traffic taking place in July 1987.

No 506 climbs Medstead bank in July 1987 with its first passenger train following an 11-year overhaul at Ropley. (*David Warwick*)

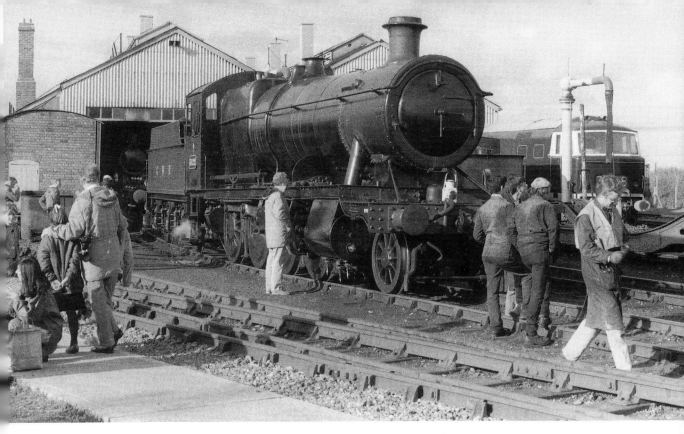

80th: GWR 2-8-0 No 3822

BUILT:	April 1940	ARRIVED BARRY:	July 1964
WITHDRAWN:	January 1964	DEPARTED BARRY:	May 1976

Heavy coal traffic was the *raison d'être* of this class of 2-8-0 locomotives, but their range of duties gradually expanded so that in post-war days they could even be seen on local goods workings or, more rarely, on the occasional passenger turn during a busy summer period. All 167 were taken into British Railways stock on 1 January 1948 and the first to go, No 2800 itself, was not withdrawn until 1958 after a life of 55 years.

No 3822 was built at Swindon in April 1940 and began operating for the GWR in the Neath Division, initially at Llanelly but later from Neath itself. As the war progressed it moved on to Cardiff (Canton) in October 1942 and was put to work on the important iron-ore trains between Banbury and South Wales together with the usual coal traffic, even more vital in wartime. Between February 1947 and June 1960, this 2-8-0 was based at Pontypool Road from where it regularly journeyed up to London with heavy trains of general freight or locomotive coal destined for Old Oak Common depot, but like so many other members of the class, No 3822 would spend several days at a time away from its home shed, frequently appearing in

Birmingham, Shrewsbury or the West Country on goods workings. In June 1960 it was transferred to Severn Tunnel Junction and continued on the same sort of duties as before, which also included setting foot in Southern territory at Salisbury with heavy freight (via Westbury). The stay there was comparatively short, for in September 1962 No 3822 went on to Aberdare, quickly followed by further periods at Neath and Cardiff East Dock. Thus after spending its whole career based in South Wales, this locomotive was sold to Woodhams for scrap having covered almost 650,000 miles in revenue-earning service.

The sum necessary to purchase No 3822 was raised in only five months and after several years' exposure to the corrosive effects of sea air, it was towed by rail to the Didcot Railway Centre in May 1976 to undergo rebuilding. Making its public debut in steam at Didcot in July 1985, No 3822 has been restored to wartime black livery.

No 3822 attracts passing interest while on display at Didcot in May 1987. (*Alan Warren*)

81st: GWR 4-6-0 No 5029 *Nunney Castle*

BUILT:	May 1934	ARRIVED BARRY:	May 1964
WITHDRAWN:	December 1963	DEPARTED BARRY:	May 1976

The batch of ten Castles built in 1934, Nos 5023–5032, were the first locomotives on the GWR constructed to a high standard of accuracy using special optical instruments to set up the frames, axlebox guides and cylinders. Increased mileages between repairs were achieved and this only added further to the already fine reputation of the Castle class 4-6-0s, which were to dominate main line passenger duties to the West of England for almost forty years.

No 5029 *Nunney Castle* emerged from Swindon Works in May 1934 and went new to Old Oak Common, where it was destined to remain for the greater part of its working life. Initially the locomotive was a common sight on the Paddington to Bristol and South Wales expresses, and records also show that in September 1939 it took part in the wartime evacuation of children from London to the West Country, working one of the many specials from Ealing Broadway during that month. In the post-war years No 5029 was put to work on the Western Region crack expresses and seems to have hauled most of the named trains of that era including the Bristolian, Red Dragon, Merchant Venturer, Pembroke Coast Express and Cambrian

Coast Express, while in September 1957 it was chosen to haul the Royal Train conveying the present Queen between Newbury and Shrewsbury. In April 1958, *Nunney Castle* was transferred to Worcester, where it was kept in immaculate condition, but by the following year it had moved on to Shrewsbury and then Newton Abbot before ending up at Plymouth (Laira) from November 1959 onwards. For three years there it continued on the main line trains to London together with the important milk traffic from Penzance to Kensington, which it would have worked forward from Plymouth. In December 1962, No 5029 was re-allocated for the last time to Cardiff East Dock where it still worked the most important trains right up to withdrawal.

As the last Castle to remain in Barry, No 5029 joined the fast growing collection of GWR stock at the Didcot Railway Centre in May 1976. Restoration to main line standards is now well under way.

Nunney Castle gets ready to leave Birmingham Snow Hill with the 4.8 p m to Paddington in February 1958. (*M. Mensing*)

150

82nd: GWR 4-6-0 No 4920 *Dumbleton Hall*

BUILT: March 1929
WITHDRAWN: December 1965

ARRIVED BARRY: February 1966
DEPARTED BARRY: June 1976

The GWR Halls were a perfect illustration of the mixed-traffic concept, performing equally well on fast passenger or heavy goods workings as the occasion demanded. However, they rarely wandered off their home lines due to the loading gauge restrictions imposed by the width across cylinders, but there were some foreign routes on which they regularly appeared, including the Great Central main line to Nottingham or over Southern metals to Bournemouth.

No 4920 *Dumbleton Hall* is the oldest member of the Hall class preserved, having been built at Swindon in March 1929. After an initial period at Old Oak Common it was sent to work in South Wales in May 1929 based at Carmarthen, but just over 12 months later had moved on again, this time to Truro where it chiefly operated over the West of England main line between Plymouth and Penzance. The years between 1932 and 1939 were spent in the London Division located at both Oxford and Old Oak Common, and there then followed fairly lengthy intervals at Cardiff and Reading before settling down at Taunton in June 1953. While there, No 4920 would have worked

slow, semi-fast and freight services to Bristol, to Exeter or beyond and occasionally something more ambitious such as the nightly Acton goods. Transferred to Newton Abbot in December 1958 it continued on the usual pattern of duties for the class, which now included piloting the weighty holiday expresses over the three well known South Devon banks at Dainton, Hemerdon and Rattery but just under six years later, in June 1964, this Hall made its final move to Bristol (Barrow Road). These latter days were mainly occupied on freight workings or as a stand-by for diesel failures and so, shortly after condemnation in December 1965, No 4920 made its 'last' journey to the scrapyard.

After lying at Barry for more than ten years, *Dumbleton Hall* arrived at Buckfastleigh on the Buckfastleigh and Totnes Steam Railway during June 1976. Restoration is expected to be completed in 1988 and the engine will then enter service on the Paignton and Dartmouth Steam Railway.

Back to June 1976 and *Dumbleton Hall* is on display at a Dart Valley Railway Steam Gala at Buckfastleigh. (*Roger Penny*)

83rd: LNER 4-6-0 No 61264

BUILT: December 1947
WITHDRAWN: November 1965

ARRIVED BARRY: September 1968
DEPARTED BARRY: July 1976

Sir Nigel Gresley's successor as Chief Mechanical Engineer of the LNER in 1941 was Edward Thompson who is best known for his two-cylinder B1 4-6-0s, 410 of which were built by Darlington, Gorton and outside contractors between 1942 and 1952. As mixed-traffic locomotives they were highly successful, helping to replace many earlier designs which were beginning to show their age.

Built in December 1947 by the North British Locomotive Company at its Queen's Park Works in Glasgow, No 61264 entered service from Parkeston shed on the Essex coast. Here it was put to work on the heavy boat trains between Harwich and Liverpool Street as well as some of the London–Norwich services. The B1s at Parkeston were always smartly turned-out for working the top-link turns which included the Hook Continental, the Scandinavian and the North Country Continental, the latter train being worked by No 61264 as far as Sheffield. After 13 years on the GE Section it was transferred to Colwick depot near Nottingham in November 1960 and appeared on almost every duty imaginable: passenger, freight, parcels, station pilot or even shunting! Its working area took in the Great Central

main line to Marylebone and the routes across to Grimsby and Immingham, while on several occasions it was used on excursion traffic from the Midlands to Skegness. Following withdrawal in November 1965 No 61264 was transferred to Departmental stock and renumbered No 29 remained as a stationary boiler at Colwick until July 1967.

No 61264 was transported by road to the Great Central Railway in 1976 where it joined the only other surviving B1 No 61306. However, when the locomotive was dismantled it was discovered that the boiler and firebox were beyond economic repair and at one stage No 61264 could have been the first engine to return to Barry for scrap. Fortunately, advances in modern welding techniques mean that repairs are now possible and although the boiler was initially removed to Resco Railways at Woolwich it has subsequently been delivered to a specialist firm in Devon for repairs to be carried out.

No 61264 approaches Bestwood Junction from the Annesley direction with a freight for Colwick yards in April 1965. (*D. B. Swale*)

84th: BR 2-6-4T No 80078

BUILT:	February 1954	ARRIVED BARRY:	June 1966
WITHDRAWN:	July 1965	DEPARTED BARRY:	September 1976

The Standard Class 4 2-6-4 tank was developed from the very similar Fairburn and Stanier engines of the LMS, but to enable it to pass the universal L1 loading gauge, the cylinders had to be reduced in size, which necessitated a corresponding increase in boiler pressure. The addition of slightly curved side tanks produced one of the most attractive large tank engines seen in Britain, well equal to its intended use on heavy suburban passenger work.

No 80078 emerged from Brighton Works at the beginning of 1954 and went straight to Plaistow shed to take up work on the former London Tilbury & Southend Railway commuter services between Fenchurch Street, Barking and Shoeburyness. Eventually there were no less than 28 representatives of the Standard 80000 series based at Plaistow for these trains, but from the mid-1950s onwards they began drifting away to one of the other main sheds on the system at Tilbury, No 80078 making this move in December 1956. Apart from a major overhaul at Darlington Works in late 1959, it continued on the routine of LT&S stopping services until the summer of 1962 when electrification made No 80078 and its sister locomotives

redundant. Following a period in store at Old Oak Common during July 1962, it was transferred to Shrewsbury and spent a short time there before moving up to Croes Newydd, Wrexham, in January 1963. At this depot it replaced the ageing 43XX Moguls on Cambrian line duties and thus found employment on the routes from Oswestry to Welshpool, Machynlleth, Aberystwyth and Pwllheli, as well as from Wrexham Central to Chester Northgate and New Brighton. Its work included the local passenger and pick-up goods trains over these lines.

After spending almost the same amount of time in Barry scrapyard as it had working for BR, No 80078 was purchased by the Southern Steam Trust and moved to Swanage in September 1976 as part of the future motive power necessary to assist in the scheme to re-open the line to Wareham.

Taking a break from its hectic duties on the LT&S services No 80078 rests on Plaistow shed in the mid 1950s.
(*C. L. Caddy collection*)

85th: SR 2-6-0 No 31806

BUILT: June 1928
WITHDRAWN: January 1964

ARRIVED BARRY: June 1964
DEPARTED BARRY: October 1976

The design for the Southern Railway U Class Moguls was already on the drawing board at the time of the notorious Sevenoaks accident in August 1927, when K class 2-6-4T No A800 derailed at speed, killing 13 passengers. As a result of this accident the decision was taken to rebuild all the tanks as 2-6-0 tender locomotives and to complete the outstanding K class orders in a similar fashion. The resulting U class eventually totalled 50, of which 20 were rebuilds from the ill-fated tank design.

This particular locomotive was originally built at Brighton in October 1926 as one of the K class 2-6-4 tanks No A806 *River Torridge* and initially worked at Redhill and on Eastern Section duties until withdrawn from service in 1927 following the accident at Sevenoaks. After conversion at Brighton Works in June 1928, during which time the name was removed, it was sent to work from Nine Elms on semi-fast and stopping passenger trains down the main line plus a certain amount of freight traffic. By the end of World War II this Mogul was operating out of Guildford, but shortly after Nationalisation was transferred to Faversham for secondary duties in the Margate and Dover areas together with some of the passenger workings up to London Victoria. After an additional short spell at Nine Elms No 31806 moved on to Basingstoke in June 1955; this depot's main turns were on the semi-fasts to Waterloo and Salisbury, although on several occasions the locomotive appeared at Swanage with holiday expresses from the north which it had worked onwards from Basingstoke. The last re-allocation was to Guildford in March 1963 and No 31806 spent its last year in BR service on the Reading to Redhill trains, a line on which the Maunsell Moguls became very familiar during their final days.

Although moved to the Mid-Hants Railway in October 1976, No 31806 was put in store for nearly 3 years before restoration began in 1979. Re-entering service in April 1981 it now looks extremely smart in lined-out BR black livery.

No 31806 enters the tidy Medstead and Four Marks station with a morning Alresford to Alton train in May 1987. (*David Warwick*)

86th: SR 4-6-2 No 34081 *92 Squadron*

BUILT: September 1948
WITHDRAWN: August 1964

ARRIVED BARRY: April 1965
DEPARTED BARRY: November 1976

By the end of 1946, 48 West Country Pacifics had been built by the Southern Railway and as the next batch was destined for use away from the West of England, a different sequence of names was introduced. These commemorated the squadrons, personalities and aerodromes involved in the Battle of Britain fought in the skies over Southern England during 1940, and 44 locomotives proudly carried such names.

No 34081 *92 Squadron* was constructed at Brighton Works during September 1948 and entered service at Ramsgate, where it spent the first 10 years of its life on the Kent Coast expresses to Victoria, Cannon Street and Charing Cross, including some of the well-known continental boat trains such as the Golden Arrow and Night Ferry. By 1957 there was a reputed shortage of maintenance staff at Ramsgate to deal with the frequently troublesome unrebuilt Bulleid Pacifics, so in September of that year No 34081 was transferred westwards to the large depot at Exmouth Junction near Exeter. There it seems to have been regularly used on the local stopping services to Ilfracombe and Plymouth and is recorded at having taken one

of the last trains out of Plymouth (Friary) before the station's closure to passengers in September 1958. Some of its other jobs included working the various portions of the Atlantic Coast Express onwards from Exeter to their destinations in North Devon and Cornwall, together with Waterloo-bound expresses in the opposite direction which it would normally have taken right through. *92 Squadron* was not always seen on passenger workings, for it also frequently appeared on the main line with fast goods trains, more so in its last few years. In July 1964 it was transferred to Eastleigh but apparently did little work there, being condemned almost immediately.

After purchase by the Battle of Britain Locomotive Preservation Society in 1976, No 34081 was moved to Wansford on the Nene Valley Railway in Cambridgeshire, and when restoration has been completed it will work alongside steam locomotives from Sweden, Denmark, France and Germany.

Making one of its rare appearances outside its shed, *92 Squadron* sits in the sun at Wansford during the summer of 1987. (*Rob Bellamy*)

87th: LMS 0-6-0 No 44422

BUILT:	October 1927	ARRIVED BARRY:	August 1965
WITHDRAWN:	June 1965	DEPARTED BARRY:	April 1977

Over a period of 30 years between 1911 and 1941 no fewer than 772 of these Fowler Class 4F 0-6-0s were built. Obviously such a numerous class could be seen in almost all parts of the extensive LMS network but although somewhat unglamorous and not as efficient as they could have been, their robust and simple construction made them ideal for the rigours of intensive freight diagrams. Out of this large total only four have survived into the hands of preservation societies, but at least they should keep alive the tradition of these unassuming 0-6-0s.

Turned out from Derby Works as LMS No 4422 in October 1927, this locomotive spent most of its early life in the Leicester district working heavy coal and other general freight traffic down the Midland main line to London. It is worth noting that this was in the days before the advent of the Stanier Class 8F 2-8-0s, so many of these trains had to be double-headed, a feature which largely disappeared when the Stanier locomotives were introduced. By 1940 this Class 4F was operating in the Bristol and Bath area, and throughout the 1950s it became strongly associated with the Somerset & Dorset route between Bath and Bournemouth,

where its principal duty was to assist summer expresses, including the famous Pines Express, to and from the South Coast resort over the steep Mendip gradients. There is one recorded instance in August 1953 when it left Evercreech Junction unaided with a Midlands-bound eight-coach relief, despite this train being over the limit laid down for a Class 4F! In November 1960, No 44422 was transferred to the small shed at Templecombe where it essentially remained on S&D services for the next four years, finally going on to Bristol (Barrow Road) and then Gloucester prior to condemnation in June 1965.

After several years of neglect at Barry, No 44422 was bought by the North Staffordshire Railway Co and moved to their Cheddleton site in April 1977 since when progress on its rebuilding has been continuing steadily.

After its last overhaul at Horwich Works in June 1963 No 44422 spent a short while working in the north and is seen here on the Burnley to Todmorden line with a coal train. (*Mike Mitchell*)

88th: WR 4-6-0 No 6989 *Wightwick Hall*

BUILT: March 1948
WITHDRAWN: June 1964

ARRIVED BARRY: August 1964
DEPARTED BARRY: January 1978

Following successful testing of the prototype, production of the Hall Class commenced in 1928, and continued with only minor changes until 1943. F. W. Hawksworth then introduced his own modified version to take account of the difficult wartime operating conditions, and when construction finally stopped in 1950, three hundred and thirty representatives of the class were in service. Apart from one locomotive destroyed during the war, withdrawals commenced in 1959 and the last survivors were all condemned at the end of 1965.

No 6989 *Wightwick Hall* was built at Swindon in March 1948 and spent its whole life based in the Welsh border country, staying for 10 years at Hereford, four at Worcester and finally two at Gloucester (Horton Road). Throughout this time it was used on almost every sort of mixed-traffic duty imaginable, but the main work involved local passenger and freight services between those three places as well as to Swindon, Cardiff, Bristol, Weston-super-Mare, Banbury and London. However, there are several recorded sightings of No 6989 on slightly more interesting duties, such as in November and December 1959 when it made

numerous appearances on the Cambrian Coast Express between Shrewsbury and Wolverhampton, or in September 1962 when it was taken off a goods train to replace the failed pioneer Western diesel-hydraulic locomotive No D1000 on a Birmingham to Paddington express. The Hall was also employed on excursion and similar traffic as required and many times worked into Wembley with football or hockey specials, but as diesels and diesel multiple-units began to take over the various duties, the shed staff were hard pressed to find work for No 6989 and in June 1964 it was withdrawn from service, having travelled almost 650,000 miles for BR.

The Wightwick Hall Appeal Fund was set up in 1975 to rescue the locomotive and after two years of hard fund raising it was purchased from Woodhams in 1977. No 6989 was taken to its new home at the Buckinghamshire Railway Centre in two parts, the tender arriving in July 1977 followed by the engine itself in January 1978.

Wightwick Hall hurries an evening train from Birmingham Snow Hill near Malvern Wells in May 1958. (*M. Mensing*)

89th: LMS 0-6-0T No 47324

BUILT: June 1926
WITHDRAWN: December 1966

ARRIVED BARRY: June 1967
DEPARTED BARRY: February 1978

Henry Fowler based his design for a shunting tank directly upon the Johnson Midland Railway 0-6-0T of 1899. Construction of these new locomotives took place between 1924 and 1930, mainly by private contractors, and eventually 422 examples were put to work. They all led fairly undistinguished careers although eight were transferred to the War Department in 1940 for service in France, while another two were altered to 5ft 3in gauge and sent to the LMS-operated Northern Counties Committee line in Ireland during 1944.

LMS No 16407 emerged from the North British Locomotive Company's Hyde Park Works in June 1926 and entered service from the former Caledonian Railway shed at Dawsholm, to the west of Glasgow, where it was used extensively on shunting work in the many private industrial yards and sidings. In February 1931, this 0-6-0 tank was reallocated to Ayr, and apart from being employed as station pilot there it also worked the Ayr Harbour branch together with other trip freight and shunting duties in the area. However, in August 1933 it left Scotland and travelled south to take up work in the Liverpool district, going initially to Edge Hill

but later moving on to Speke Junction, and while there it was renumbered 7324 in accordance with the new scheme introduced by the LMS during 1934. At the beginning of 1939 it was transferred across the Mersey to Birkenhead, joining other members of the class on the busy dock pilot and shunting work, a task on which it remained for the next 27 years right up to withdrawal. No 47324's last year in service was 1966 and during these final months it often found employment away from Birkenhead, such as on station pilot duty at Chester General. After six months of waiting for the call to the scrapyard it made the ignominious 'final' journey to South Wales during June 1967 in company with four other locomotives from the same depot.

No 47324 was bought from Barry by the Fowler 3F Society and moved to the Mid-Hants Railway for overhaul to begin. However, in May 1986 it was transferred to the Avon Valley Railway at Bitton for this work to be completed.

No 47324 spends a quiet Sunday away from its routine shunting work on Birkenhead shed in 1961. *(Fowler Society)*

158

90th: SR 4-6-2 No 34105 *Swanage*

BUILT: March 1950
WITHDRAWN: October 1964

ARRIVED BARRY: February 1965
DEPARTED BARRY: March 1978

The overall concept of the Bulleid West Country and Battle of Britain Pacifics was of a scaled-down version of the Merchant Navy Class, reduced in both weight and width to give it the greatest possible route availability. No less than 70 were ordered at one go and these emerged from Brighton Works in 1945/6, while the remaining 40 were constructed by BR between 1948 and 1951.

Built at Brighton in March 1950, 34105 *Swanage* was based at Bournemouth depot for almost the whole of its comparatively short working life. Light Pacifics there consistently dealt with expresses on the Bournemouth–Southampton–Waterloo route as well as frequently deputising for the larger Merchant Navies on the more important trains. No 34105 itself had the honour of hauling the inaugural Royal Wessex between Weymouth and Waterloo on 3 May 1951, but generally it settled down to the everyday routine of main line work, which also included trips down the Swanage branch with the through trains from London. Later on in the 1950s it began to appear more regularly on the Somerset & Dorset route to Bath with northbound expresses, including the Pines Express, while other duties saw it working over Great Western metals into Oxford.

Around 1961/2, *Swanage* appears to have earned the reputation of being an indifferent performer and thus was little used on main line work, its time being filled-in on the Brockenhurst–Christchurch school trains, or even as substitute for a failed tank engine on the Bournemouth West–Brockenhurst push-pull train in September 1961! This situation had obviously changed by 1963 when it returned to top-link duties including the Pines Express, although by then this train was routed via Southampton, Basingstoke and Oxford. After more than fourteen years at this one shed it was transferred to Eastleigh in September 1964, but condemned only a few weeks later.

Purchased in 1976 and moved to the Mid-Hants Railway two years later, *Swanage* made a welcome return to service in August 1987 after an extensive rebuild at Ropley.

In its second week of service on the Mid Hants Railway, *Swanage* climbs towards Ropley with an Alresford to Alton train in September 1987. (*David Warwick*)

91st: LMS 2-6-0 No 42765

BUILT:	August 1927	ARRIVED BARRY:	June 1967
WITHDRAWN:	December 1966	DEPARTED BARRY:	April 1978

The design for these 2-6-0s was prepared at Horwich during the period when George Hughes was Chief Mechanical Engineer of the LMS, but he retired before construction of the first locomotive had started, leaving the way clear for his successor, Henry Fowler, to add a few of his own modifications. The result was an efficient and highly popular mixed-traffic class eventually numbering 245, all of which survived into the last decade of steam operation on BR.

Completed at Crewe Works in August 1927, LMS No 13065 was turned out wearing the attractive Crimson Lake passenger livery, and entered traffic at Kentish Town depot in North London, working a mixture of general goods and mineral trains on the West Coast and Midland main lines. It continued on much the same sort of jobs when transferred to Leicester in April 1932, but was not limited to freight work and could often be seen on excursion and relief trains. Next move was to Belle Vue (Manchester) in February 1935. It was while working an express fitted freight between Manchester and London two years later that this 2-6-0 was derailed outside West Hampstead Station,

destroying much of its train but suffering little damage itself. Belle Vue's rosters were mainly concerned with goods workings, although there was the odd passenger turn such as the Saturday Manchester to Blackpool service together with excursions to the same place from a variety of starting points. After a period at Rose Grove (Burnley) between September 1950 and August 1951, No 42765 went on to Fleetwood on the Lancashire coast, staying there for the next 13 years before making its final move to Birkenhead in May 1964. One of the Mogul's regular duties at this shed was to work the Birkenhead–Paddington trains to and from Chester, together with some of the local freight, and when withdrawn at the end of 1966 it was amongst the last five 'Crabs' to remain in service.

After 12 years in Barry, No 42765 was purchased privately and moved to the Keighley & Worth Valley Railway in April 1978 where restoration to its original LMS maroon livery is well under way.

A rather grubby No 42765 rests on Warrington (8B) shed on a Saturday in June 1966. (*Peter J. C. Skelton*)

92nd: SR 4-6-2 No 34101 *Hartland*

BUILT: February 1950
WITHDRAWN: July 1966

ARRIVED BARRY: October 1966
DEPARTED BARRY: July 1978

The decision to rebuild the Bulleid Pacifics was made in 1955 in an attempt to reduce their comparatively high running and maintenance costs. The Merchant Navies were tackled first, while work on the West Country and Battle of Britain classes commenced in June 1957 and continued for almost four years, by which time 60 locomotives had been dealt with.

No 34101 *Hartland* was one of only six Bulleid light Pacifics to be built at Eastleigh Works, all the others being products of the Brighton workshops. It went to its first shed at Stewarts Lane in London during February 1950, where it immediately took charge of the expresses from Charing Cross and Victoria to the Kent Coast towns of Ramsgate, Folkestone and Dover, which of course included several of the important boat trains. Although generally associated with these more prestigious workings, *Hartland* was also used on some of the semi-fast and local services, including those to Tunbridge Wells and Margate, while on one occasion in September 1956 it travelled the Horsham–Shoreham branch as far as Bramber with a ramblers' excursion. Following No 34101's

rebuilding in September 1960 it returned to Stewarts Lane, but on completion of the Kent Coast electrification in mid-1961, it was transferred to Bricklayers Arms. When that shed closed to steam in May 1962 it moved on again to Brighton, finding employment on the through trains to Plymouth, one of the longest continuous locomotive workings on the Southern Region. Yet another move came in June 1963 to Nine Elms, and this was quickly followed by a final allocation to Eastleigh from August 1964 onwards, during which time it often appeared on the Southampton Docks to Waterloo boat trains. After withdrawal in the summer of 1966, it journeyed to South Wales to join the fast growing collection of 'unwanted' Bulleid Pacifics at Barry.

Hartland was taken to the private premises of Shaw Metals Ltd, Derby, in summer 1978 for restoration, and when this is completed a decision will be made on its future home in preservation.

The rebuilding of *Hartland* is almost complete at Eastleigh Works in September 1960. The re-use of the original smokebox door during the rebuilding is quite apparent in this photograph. (*L. R. Peters*)

93rd: BR 2-10-0 No 92240

BUILT: October 1958
WITHDRAWN: August 1965

ARRIVED BARRY: October 1965
DEPARTED BARRY: October 1978

The Class 9F 2-10-0 was last of the dozen BR Standard designs to appear, yet it is generally considered to have been the most successful, with 251 examples being built between 1954 and 1960. Essentially freight locomotives, they were also capable of showing a good turn of speed when required on passenger duties. Regrettably the Modernisation Plan saw to it that many of them were destined to lead very short lives.

No 92240 was among the last batch of steam locomotives ever to be built at Crewe, emerging from the Works there in October 1958 and initially going to Newport (Ebbw Junction) to assist with the heavy South Wales iron ore and coal trains. After only a few weeks it was transferred to Old Oak Common to be rostered for the fast freight duties to Oxford, Banbury and further afield, but it was not long before the shed staff discovered the capabilities of 9Fs to help out at summer weekends when passenger traffic was at its height, and as a result No 92240 was recorded leaving Kensington Olympia with a Hastings to Wolverhampton holiday express in August 1959. Just over a year later, in September 1960, it moved down the main

line to Southall shed and continued on the same sort of heavy goods work for which it was so well suited. Class 9Fs had a tractive effort of almost 40,000lb and could haul prodigious loads single-handed. No 92240 still managed to appear on passenger trains from time to time, and in July 1962 it worked as far as Acton with a return excursion from Gloucester to East Anglia. Nevertheless, in August 1965 after less than seven years' service, this almost brand-new piece of machinery was dispatched to the scrapyard – hardly an economic use of railway equipment.

Nine of these 2-10-0s ultimately arrived in Woodham's yard, and it is perhaps surprising that it took until 1978 before one of these popular and efficient locomotives was saved, the first being No 92240, taken to Sheffield Park on the Bluebell Railway in October of that year.

No 92240 stands ready for work in Southall shed yard, its home depot, in September 1962. (*P. H. Groom*)

94th: BR 2-6-4T No 80100

BUILT: January 1955
WITHDRAWN: July 1965

ARRIVED BARRY: January 1966
DEPARTED BARRY: October 1978

First introduced in 1951, the Class 4 2-6-4Ts were the most numerous of all Standard tank engines, with 155 being built over a period of six years. Although the first was withdrawn as early as 1962, general scrapping did not commence until the summer of 1964, with several of the Southern Region examples lasting up to the final months of steam in July 1967.

Built at Brighton Works in January 1955, No 80100 was just one of many Standard tanks allocated to Plaistow in East London for duty on the ex-LT&SR lines out of Fenchurch Street, work which they shared with 37 Stanier LMS three-cylinder 2-6-4Ts based at Shoeburyness depot. Although spending most of its time on these busy suburban services, No 80100 was sent to Darlington Works for overhaul in April 1958, following which it was noted being run-in on a parcels train from Darlington Bank Top to Crook in County Durham, quite a change of scenery indeed! Moving on to Tilbury in November 1959 it remained on the LT&SR route right up to electrification in June 1962, following which it was put into store at Old Oak Common while the Western Region decided

what to do with it. This decision came a few weeks later when No 80100 was sent to Shrewsbury, where it found extensive use on the local passenger services in that area, initially on the Severn Valley line to Bridgnorth prior to closure in September 1963, as well as putting in occasional appearances on some of the workings over the Central Wales route to Swansea. Soon after, it began working regularly on the Hereford–Grange Court–Gloucester local trains, but when this line was also closed in November 1964 it became more and more difficult to find work for No 80100 to do, a fact which led to its withdrawal seven months later.

It is quite appropriate that No 80100 was rescued for further use on the Bluebell Railway in October 1978 because, as well as the class being designed at Brighton, many of them also worked over that line in its last few years before complete closure.

Following overhaul at Darlington in April 1958, No 80100 returns south through Doncaster on its way back to the LT&S. *(P. Tait)*

163

95th: SR 4-6-0 No 30847

BUILT: December 1936
WITHDRAWN: January 1964

ARRIVED BARRY: June 1964
DEPARTED BARRY: October 1978

The Maunsell S15s were a development of the earlier Urie design dating back to 1920 and were built at Eastleigh Works in two batches during 1927/8 and 1936. Like their forebears, these were extremely useful mixed-traffic locomotives and because of their simple and robust construction gave very little trouble in service, the whole class lasting until the general run-down of Southern steam in the early 1960s.

As the very last 4-6-0 to be built for the Southern Railway, Class S15 No 847 went to its first shed at Exmouth Junction in December 1936 and soon became established on that depot's long-distance freights, secondary passenger workings, holiday reliefs and parcels traffic, several of these duties taking it up as far as London. After a 15-year spell there, it moved on to Salisbury in June 1951 and was chiefly rostered to main line goods trains, but it also frequently appeared on the stopping passenger services from Salisbury to Basingstoke and Waterloo as well as those between Templecombe, Axminster and Exeter Central. Following this lengthy period on Western Section activities, No 30847 was transferred to Redhill on the Central

Section in early 1960 and spent the greater part of its time there on freight work across to Guildford and Reading; because these were much shorter distance turns than it had previously worked, as well as the Central Section's turntables being slightly smaller, the 4-6-0 lost its 5000-gallon eight-wheeled tender in exchange for a 4000-gallon six-wheel version from a withdrawn King Arthur Class locomotive. In June 1963, this S15 made its final move to Feltham, dealing with much of the traffic from there down to the goods yards at Eastleigh, although right up to withdrawal at the beginning of 1964 it could still be seen working various stopping passenger services in that locality.

No 30847 was the third locomotive to be transported from Barry to the Bluebell Railway within the space of five days, arriving at its new home on 8 October 1978, where it will fill an important gap in this predominantly Southern Railway collection of motive power.

No 30847 seems to be going well near Winchfield with a stopping train for Waterloo in May 1953. (*K. W. Wightman*)

96th: GWR 2-8-0T No 5224

BUILT: May 1924
WITHDRAWN: April 1963

ARRIVED BARRY: August 1963
DEPARTED BARRY: October 1978

The first of these Churchward eight-coupled tank engines was built at Swindon in 1910 and was to form the basis of a well-liked class ideal for heavy, short-distance freight work. They operated almost exclusively in South Wales although there were a few at St Blazey in Cornwall for the china clay traffic, while one was even tried out on banking duties up the Lickey Incline in 1960!

No 5224 began working for the GWR in May 1924 based at Newport, but this was quickly followed by short periods at Llantrisant and Tondu before ending up at Barry shed five months later. The stay here was to prove a long one and for the next 15 years the 2-8-0T normally busied itself on the coal trains up and down the valleys as well as on general freight along the coast between Cardiff, Bridgend and Swansea. In March 1940, it was transferred to Newport (Ebbw Junction) and would have banked or been at the front of heavy iron-ore trains from Newport Docks up to the Ebbw Vale Steel Works, while the development of the petroleum products industry also created more work for it to do on tanker trains to and from the oil refineries. During February 1954, No 5224 moved

to Severn Tunnel Junction where, in addition to the usual run of mixed freight trains, it assisted with the sometimes punishing tunnel banking duties but after eight years of this work was re-allocated to Cardiff Canton at the end of February 1962. Following closure of this shed in September 1962, it moved for the last time to Cardiff East Dock, remaining there until condemned in April 1963.

On arrival at the Great Central Railway's headquarters at Loughborough in 1978, No 5224 was soon dismantled to allow a thorough investigation of the work required to return it to operating condition. Despite 15 years' exposure to the elements, many parts were found to be in excellent condition and accordingly it became the first locomotive from Barry to be resteamed on the GCR in October 1984. In May of the following year it was taken down to Didcot to participate in their GWR 150 celebrations but returned to Loughborough shortly afterwards.

The fireman looks out for the 'right away' as No 5224 prepares to leave Rothley with a train for Loughborough during Easter 1985. (*Graham Wignall*)

97th: BR 2-6-0 No 78018

BUILT:	March 1954	ARRIVED BARRY:	June 1967
WITHDRAWN:	November 1966	DEPARTED BARRY:	October 1978

The Standard Class 2 Moguls were similar in almost all respects to the Ivatt LMS design of 1946, and like all the BR Standard locomotives were much appreciated by shed staff because of their many aids to easy maintenance, fire-cleaning and the like. Presumably these features will be equally welcomed by the future generations of footplatemen on our private railways!

Completed at Darlington Works in March 1954, No 78018 entered traffic at West Auckland shed in County Durham, although this was soon followed by a re-allocation down the line to Kirkby Stephen. For most of its time on the North Eastern Region, this 2-6-0 was employed on mineral and general goods workings over the route between Tebay and Barnard Castle, a difficult line to operate because of the long gradients and the wild exposed moorland traversed. On one occasion in February 1955, No 78018 stuck in a deep snowdrift near Bleath Gill while heading a Kirkby Stephen to West Auckland goods; the crew was forced to abandon the locomotive, which was not reached by a snowplough until two days later. As part of the run-down of lines in that area, it was transferred away to the

shed at Chester Midland in April 1960 and stayed there until the summer of 1962, when it was sent north to Workington to help out with the local passenger and freight workings from there across to Keswick and Penrith, as well as sometimes standing in for diesel failures on the services to Carlisle. At the end of the summer season No 78018 returned to Chester for a few months before moving down to Willesden in May 1963 where it was chiefly used on empty coaching stock and station pilot duties at Euston, but on closure of this shed to steam in September 1965 it was transferred to Nuneaton and then to Shrewsbury before withdrawal.

No 78018 arrived at Shackerstone on the Market Bosworth Light Railway in November 1978, but little restoration work was carried out there and it has since been re-sold and moved to a private site at Darlington, appropriately quite near to the works where it was originally built.

After almost three years based at Shackerstone, No 78018 gets ready to leave for its new home at Darlington in July 1981. (*B. Lamb*)

98th: GWR 0-6-0PT No 3612

BUILT: March 1939
WITHDRAWN: October 1964

ARRIVED BARRY: March 1965
DEPARTED BARRY: December 1978

The Great Western pannier tanks, so called because their water tanks were fitted both sides of the boiler and not directly attached to the frames, could be seen shunting in almost every yard on the GWR system, but they proved to be equally effective on branch line or short-distance main line passenger duties. Fortunately a large number of this fine class have been preserved although all of them were purchased from sources outside BR, such as scrapyards, London Transport or the National Coal Board.

No 3612 was built at Swindon Works in March 1939 and allocated initially to Aberbeeg, a medium-size shed situated around half-way on the line between Newport and Ebbw Vale. Its main source of employment there was on the vital wartime goods and coal traffic from the valley stations down to the docks at Newport, work on which the pannier tank continued until transferred to Tondu in May 1943. In addition to mineral trains on the Porthcawl branch, No 3612 now found itself regularly handling some of the local passenger duties, particularly those to Cymmer and Blaengarw while it often spent short periods working from the tiny

sub-shed at Bridgend a few miles south of Tondu. Shortly before Nationalisation, in August 1947, this locomotive returned to Aberbeeg for a few years before making its final move to Llantrisant in May 1950. There were several pannier tanks here for shunting in the nearby collieries and yards plus a certain amount of general mixed-traffic duties. No 3612 itself regularly worked the branch service from Llantrisant to Penygraig until that line's closure in 1958. Despite the introduction of diesel shunters and overall decline of railway operations in South Wales, No 3612 remained at this shed until it, too, was closed down in October 1964.

No 3612 was purchased by the Severn Valley Railway in December 1978 as a source of spares for its other 57XX pannier tanks and was broken-up on site at Eardington station in early 1979. Although, strictly speaking, this locomotive has not been 'rescued', its spirit lives on in two other working examples of the class.

Shortly after transferral from Aberbeeg No 3612 stands in the open at Llantrisant in the early 1950s. (*Real Photographs Co*)

99th: GWR 0-6-2T No 6695

BUILT: October 1928
WITHDRAWN: July 1964

ARRIVED BARRY: September 1964
DEPARTED BARRY: May 1979

The 56XX Class 0-6-2 tanks were built primarily for both freight and passenger service in the South Wales Valleys where they soon established a splendid reputation for their power, acceleration and speed capabilities. Two hundred examples were constructed by Swindon and outside contractors between 1924 and 1928, and although many did find their way to other areas, the bulk of the class remained in the Welsh Valleys until the final elimination of steam.

Built by Armstrong Whitworth of Newcastle in October 1928, No 6695 initially took up work on the outer-suburban services from Birmingham (Snow Hill) to Stratford-upon-Avon and Leamington, and for several years it was based at the latter shed to operate these trains. However, the steady drafting of the larger 5101 class 2-6-2 tanks to the region in the early 1930s saw No 6695 displaced from these workings to Oxley, near Wolverhampton, where it earned its keep on that depot's freight rosters for five years between September 1934 and September 1939. The outbreak of war led to its transfer for the first time to the more familiar surroundings of South Wales, where by far the greatest proportion of its time was spent at Swansea East Dock and Landore sheds on the local passenger and goods workings. When Landore closed to steam in June 1961, No 6695 travelled the short distance to Neath for a few years before making its final move to Cardiff (Radyr) in October 1963. At this time, however, the supremacy of the 56XX class was being challenged by the newly introduced Class 37 diesel-electric locomotives which quickly began to take over many of their traditional freight duties and so by the summer of 1964 this 0-6-2T was withdrawn for scrap and duly consigned to Woodham's yard.

The Barry phenomenon has led to several locomotives appearing in extremely unusual surroundings, perhaps none more so than the moving of No 6695 to former Southern Railway territory at Swanage in May 1979. When restored, it should make a fine, if somewhat strange, sight at the head of a train of green Bulleid coaches!

A close-up of No 6695 waiting time at Treherbert with a local train to Swansea in the early 1960s. (*Peter Cookson*)

100th: GWR 2-6-2T No 4110

BUILT: October 1936   ARRIVED BARRY: August 1965
WITHDRAWN: June 1965   DEPARTED BARRY: May 1979

In 1903 the first of these 'large prairies' was turned out of Swindon Works but it was not until 1949 that the last of the series, No 4179, was completed. During that 46-year period of construction the design was essentially unaltered, apart from some minor modifications in detail; it is therefore quite fitting that several of the class have survived into the preservation era, the locomotives already restored proving to be extremely capable machines.

Part of a batch of 10 2-6-2 tanks built during 1936, No 4110 was dispatched to its first shed at Severn Tunnel Junction in October for use on the exacting tunnel banking duties, but after only two months it was relieved from this rigorous work and transferred to the Wolverhampton Division. Here it was to stay for the next 26 years working the intensive local passenger services from Birmingham (Snow Hill and Moor Street) to Leamington and Stratford-upon-Avon as well as those to Stourbridge and Kidderminster, Dudley, Wolverhampton Low Level and Wellington – not forgetting the occasional appearance on some of the Worcester stopping trains! There was a brief period at Birkenhead between March 1942 and April 1943

for secondary duties in that area, but generally No 4110 moved around from shed to shed in the Birmingham district until June 1962 when the high-density diesel multiple-units began to take over the suburban services. This 'large prairie' then moved to Taunton where it was employed on the Minehead branch for a while before going on to Neath in May 1963 for passenger work across to Hengoed and Pontypool Road. After a few months at Cardiff Radyr, No 4110 ironically was transferred back in April 1965 to the shed where it began its career, Severn Tunnel Junction.

In May 1979, No 4110 became the one hundredth locomotive to leave Barry scrapyard, going to the GWR Preservation Group's site at Southall. Although originally intended to be restored for use on a private railway in Devon, it will remain here as part of the Steam Centre being developed around the former locomotive depot.

As a change from its normal suburban passenger duties, No 4110 passes The Hawthorns Halt, West Bromwich, with an up coal train in September 1961. (*M. Mensing*)

101st: LMS 0-6-0T No 47279

BUILT: April 1924
WITHDRAWN: December 1966

ARRIVED BARRY: June 1967
DEPARTED BARRY: August 1979

Between 1924 and 1930, more than 400 of these standard shunting locomotives were built for the LMS, their design dating back to the Midland Railway 0-6-0T of 1899. They were simple and straightforward machines which could often be seen on passenger duties during their early years, particularly on the North London line out of Broad Street, but generally they led somewhat humble lives, never quite receiving the same attention as their much larger workmates.

LMS No 7119 emerged from the Newton-le-Willows workshops of the Vulcan Foundry in April 1924 and spent a good part of its early days based at Toton, near Derby, for work in the marshalling yards, where it was principally employed on preparing for dispatch the seemingly endless procession of southbound coal trains. In May 1934 it was transferred the short distance to Nottingham followed by a further move to Wellingborough almost exactly four years later, by which time it had also been renumbered 7279. This 0-6-0T was to stay at this latter shed for quite some length of time, being kept busy on the customary routine of shunting duties, pilot work and more regularly on

the transfer workings between the former London & North Western and Midland Railway goods yards. Renumbered for the third time shortly after Nationalisation, No 47279 remained at Wellingborough right up to August 1957 when it was sent to Bedford for shunting work in and around the Bedfordshire brickfields as well as trip freights between the Midland and St John's stations. Towards the end of 1963, after almost 40 years based in the East Midlands, it was transferred up to Workington on the Cumberland coast for a short period before finally ending its days in the Liverpool district from November 1965 onwards, initially allocated to Aintree but ultimately at Sutton Oak, St Helens, prior to withdrawal in December 1966.

In spite of its derelict condition, the South Yorkshire 3F Fund was set up in 1979 to try and save No 47279 for posterity, an aim achieved in August of that year when it was moved to Haworth on the Worth Valley Railway for rebuilding.

No 47279 waits in Haworth yard in July 1980 while fund raising and other preparations were made prior to it entering the workshops there for a full overhaul. (*Alan Warren*)

170

102nd: BR 2-6-4T No 80136

BUILT: May 1956
WITHDRAWN: July 1965

ARRIVED BARRY: June 1966
DEPARTED BARRY: August 1979

Out of the 155 BR Class 4 2-6-4Ts to enter traffic between 1951 and 1957, 130 were built at Brighton Works, the remainder coming from Derby and Doncaster. Classified as mixed-traffic locomotives, they were intended for short-distance freight and suburban passenger work but soon showed themselves to be fast, powerful machines which performed their duties well and whose extra adhesive weight was much appreciated compared with some of the older designs they replaced.

Built at Brighton in May 1956, No 80136 was just one of a large fleet of tank locomotives operating the busy passenger services from Fenchurch Street to Southend and Shoeburyness. For most of the time on these workings it was based at Plaistow, but when that depot closed its doors in November 1959 it moved to Tilbury, staying there until finally displaced by electrification in June 1962. Transferred to the Western Region as a result, No 80136 spent a short interval out of use before being allocated to Shrewsbury to assist with the local passenger workings, including those to Buildwas and Bridgnorth on the Severn Valley line. However, after only a few months there it was sent to Oswestry. The Standard tanks took a major part in handling the stopping trains over the former Cambrian route, their surefootedness proving to be a blessing when it came to some of the difficult starts from stations on that line. There then followed a three-month spell at Machynlleth during the summer of 1964 when it was rostered to some of the all-stations trains to Barmouth, Pwllheli and Aberystwyth as well as on the local pick-up freight work. Nevertheless, No 80136 was finally transferred back to Shrewsbury in September 1964, but found little to keep it occupied in the period up to withdrawal in July 1965.

As the eighth Standard 2-6-4T to leave Barry scrapyard No 80136 was taken by road to Cheddleton, near Leek, in August 1979 to form part of the North Staffordshire Railway Museum based on the attractive station site there.

No 80136 takes water at Purfleet after having worked a train up from Fenchurch Street in February 1959. (*Frank Church*)

171

103rd: GWR 2-6-2T No 5193

BUILT: October 1934
WITHDRAWN: June 1962

ARRIVED BARRY: September 1962
DEPARTED BARRY: August 1979

Although these well-proportioned 2-6-2 tanks were generally employed on passenger work, it is probably fair to say that they were originally conceived as general-purpose machines for all secondary duties, the examples at Severn Tunnel Junction, Taunton and Newton Abbot even being used on banking work. However, dieselisation of their traditional activities from the late 1950s onwards saw many of them finishing their days on more humble freight work.

No 5193 was built at Swindon Works in October 1934 and sent new to Stourbridge Junction primarily for use on the suburban services to Birmingham Snow Hill and Wolverhampton Low Level, an area with which this class was long associated. Apart from a few months on freight duties at Oxley between July and September 1939, it continued on these workings until transferred to the West Country in October 1952, staying for varying lengths of time at Truro, St Blazey and Plymouth (Laira) sheds. An opportunity to show its adaptability came in May 1956 when the turntable at Penzance was being repaired; to avoid tender-first running by main line locomotives, No 5193

and eight other 2-6-2 tanks were drafted to Truro (where the tender locomotives were turned and serviced) for working the expresses on to Penzance although on many occasions these were so heavy that they had to be double-headed. During the period allocated to St Blazey, it was often seen on the Par to Newquay branch trains but in October 1960, at which time several other 51XX tanks were being withdrawn, it returned to Plymouth presumably to await a decision as to its future. Fortunately No 5193 survived, being sent to Neyland the following month where it appeared on a mixture of duties in the Tenby and Pembroke areas before condemnation in June 1962 and subsequent storage at Severn Tunnel Junction.

Following purchase by the '5193 Fund', the locomotive was removed from Barry in August 1979, being hauled onto its low loader by a veteran Sentinel steam tractor and unloaded at the Steamport Transport Museum, Southport, by fellow ex-Barry resident, LMS 0-6-0T No 47298.

Taking a break from its duties on the line to Newquay No 5193 stands in Par station yard in July 1956. (*D. K. Jones collection*)

104th: WR 4-6-0 No 7820 *Dinmore Manor*

BUILT: November 1950
WITHDRAWN: November 1965

ARRIVED BARRY: May 1966
DEPARTED BARRY: September 1979

Construction of the first 20 GWR Manor 4-6-0s was begun in 1938 utilising the wheels and motion of withdrawn 43XX 2-6-0s, while the remaining 10 locomotives were built new by BR during 1950.

No 7820 *Dinmore Manor* was first of the BR-built Manors to be turned out from Swindon in November 1950. Its initial allocation was to Oswestry for working local services over the Cambrian lines, in particular the routes from Whitchurch to Welshpool and Aberystwyth, and from Shrewsbury to Aberystwyth. This was then followed by a move to Chester at the end of 1953 before going on to Plymouth (Laira) one year later. The Manors there and at Newton Abbot were responsible for replacing the old GWR Bulldog 4-4-0s on banking and pilot duties over the notorious Devon gradients, but although this formed a major part of No 7820's work there are several recorded instances when it strayed far from Plymouth. For example, in July 1955 this locomotive was noted on a Paddington to Reading semifast, presumably working its way gradually back home after a trip up to London, but even more strange was when it arrived on the Southern Region

at Portsmouth with an excursion during the summer of 1958! Transferred to Truro in November 1959 and then to St Blazey the following year, *Dinmore Manor* eventually found its way to South Wales in September 1960, allocated to Cardiff Canton and Cardiff East Dock between then and May 1963. Even now No 7820's wanderings were not over, for it was to spend the next two years or so at Shrewsbury and Oxley (Wolverhampton) sheds before being withdrawn at Shrewsbury in November 1965.

Originally acquired by the Gwili Railway at Bronwydd Arms in September 1979, No 7820 was put up for sale during 1984 to raise much needed funds for other restoration projects. Several locomotive groups tendered but the Dinmore Manor Fund based on the West Somerset Railway were successful and it was accordingly moved to Bishops Lydeard in March 1985.

Showing its mixed traffic pedigree, *Dinmore Manor* works a down coal train at Aller Junction in August 1957. (*Peter Cookson*)

173

105th: BR 2-10-0 No 92212

BUILT:	September 1959	ARRIVED BARRY:	September 1968
WITHDRAWN:	January 1968	DEPARTED BARRY:	September 1979

Design work for this, the most numerous of all the Standard classes, was carried out at Brighton under the supervision of R. A. Riddles but none was ever built there. Of the total of 251, 198 were turned out from Crewe and the remainder at Swindon, including the last steam locomotive of all, No 92220 *Evening Star*. It is a sad fact that despite being considered by many to be among the finest locomotives ever built in this country they arrived too late, with some lasting only five years.

Constructed at Swindon Works in September 1959, No 92212 entered traffic from Banbury shed in Oxfordshire and immediately began work on the iron-ore trains across to the South Wales steelworks, a duty which it gradually took over from the Churchward 28XX Class; loadings on this working were limited by Hatton bank, north of Leamington and the Class 9Fs were capable of handling up to six more 27-ton hoppers than the 2-8-0s could manage. No 92212 stayed at Banbury until May 1961 when it was loaned for the summer season to Bath Green Park, along with three other Class 9Fs, for use on the large number of holiday expresses that used the Somerset & Dorset route between

Bath and Bournemouth. Their presence on this line substantially reduced the amount of double-heading normally required, and thus they were very popular with shed staff who always had problems trying to find enough locomotives during these peak periods. No 92212's next move was to Tyseley in July 1962 and there it could be seen at work on heavy freight duties throughout the West Midlands, frequently appearing on that part of the main line between Birmingham and Crewe. During May 1963 it even reached Weymouth with a pigeon special! Just over three years later, in November 1966, it was transferred north to Carnforth and when withdrawn in January 1968 had just survived into the very last year of steam operation on BR.

No 92212 was removed from Barry in September 1979 and taken to the Great Central Railway at Loughborough where restoration has been progressing to a very high standard.

Following its long road journey from Barry, No 92212 is pictured here just a few hours after unloading at Quorn in September 1979. (*Graham Wignall*)

106th: LMR 2-6-0 No 46428

BUILT: December 1948   ARRIVED BARRY: September 1967
WITHDRAWN: November 1966   DEPARTED BARRY: October 1979

As Ivatt's first design for the LMS, these Class 2MT tender locomotives heralded a new era in branch line motive power, proving to be ideal for this and other similar light work. Fast, economical and with excellent powers of acceleration, the 128 representatives of this class saw service on all regions of BR except the Southern.

A product of Crewe Works in December 1948, No 46428 spent its early years on secondary duties in the Wigan and Manchester areas, part of this time being spent on loan to Heaton Mersey where it worked local freight turns in place of the ageing ex-LNER J10 0-6-0s. Apart from the summer of 1954 when it worked from Rhyl on the North Wales coast, No 46428 was based at Wigan (Springs Branch) continuously from April 1952 to February 1962. For much of this time it seems to have worked the 8.30pm Manchester Central to Wigan Central stopping passenger train almost single-handed for several years although it is also known to have been employed on similar services to Liverpool, Bolton and Rochdale. At the beginning of 1962 it was transferred to the Wolverhampton district, initially for a few weeks at Bescot before moving on to the former LNWR shed at Bushbury. Once again this 2-6-0 became a popular choice for the local 'all station' trains in that part of the West Midlands, including those between Wellington and Stafford, while at various times it also appeared on lightweight freight duties. In October 1964 it went to Leamington Spa to take over from ex-GWR engines on the local goods and parcels workings but when this shed closed in June 1965, No 46428 was re-allocated to Tyseley and then to Crewe South, being withdrawn from that latter depot in November 1966.

No 46428 was originally purchased by the Strathspey Railway at Aviemore in October 1979 to provide a replacement boiler for its other Ivatt Mogul, No 46464. By 1986 it was no longer required for this purpose and accordingly put up for sale, being acquired by the East Lancashire Railway at Bury shortly afterwards.

Under cover of a road bridge just outside Bury (Bolton Street) station, the sad remains of No 46428 await attention in September 1987, just after delivery from the Strathspey Railway. (*Richard Fox*)

107th: BR 4-6-0 No 73082 *Camelot*

BUILT: June 1955
WITHDRAWN: June 1966

ARRIVED BARRY: November 1966
DEPARTED BARRY: October 1979

Construction of the 172 BR Standard Class 5 locomotives was shared between Derby and Doncaster Works, with the first one coming off the production line in the spring of 1951 and the last during 1957. In traffic they were sure-footed and reliable, often overloaded but still managing to put in some outstanding performances comparable with their equally successful counterparts, the LMS Stanier Class 5s.

No 73082 was built at Derby Works in the summer of 1955 and allocated to Stewarts Lane in London for work on the Victoria to Kent Coast expresses, including many of the Dover and Folkestone boat trains. The Standard Class 5s did some of their best work in Kent, eventually taking over many services from the worn-out LSWR N15 4-6-0s, but as the initial stages of the electrification programme were being completed No 73082 was transferred away to the Western Section at Nine Elms in June 1959. Shortly after this move the Southern Region decided to revive the names formerly carried by the Urie King Arthurs, so in August 1959 this particular locomotive was given the name *Camelot* which had formerly been carried

by No 30742. In this new guise No 73082 was responsible for many of the semi-fast workings from Waterloo to Salisbury, Bournemouth and Southampton, while it was also frequently seen on some of the parcels and newspaper trains over the same routes. After several years on this work it was re-allocated to Guildford in May 1965 and saw service on the stopping trains over the Reading to Redhill line before withdrawal in mid-June 1966; even so this was not the end of *Camelot*'s career with BR because just two weeks later it was put back into steam and hauled three condemned locomotives to their South Wales graveyards before being put into store at Eastleigh to await its own call to the cutter's torch.

Following several years of intensive fund raising No 73082 was delivered by road to the Bluebell Railway in October 1979 where a start was made on its restoration, a job which has included the fabrication of a new tender as one was not available at Barry.

Camelot strides away from Faversham with the 3.22 p m Ramsgate to Victoria in March 1959. (*D. R. Hagan*)

108th: SR 4-6-2 No 34059 *Sir Archibald Sinclair*

BUILT: April 1947
WITHDRAWN: May 1966

ARRIVED BARRY: October 1966
DEPARTED BARRY: October 1979

O. V. Bulleid's West Country Class was introduced in 1945, towards the end of World War II, the mechanical layout being identical to his earlier Merchant Navy design but with the overall weight further reduced to give the best possible route availability and to allow running over routes restricted by the limited Southern Railway loading gauge.

No 21C159 emerged from Brighton Works in April 1947 and was officially named *Sir Archibald Sinclair* at Waterloo Station early the next year. Sent new to Nine Elms it had a brief period on the Waterloo–Basingstoke–Salisbury semi-fasts but was soon rostered for top-link duties including the Bournemouth Belle and Atlantic Coast Express, while it also became the first light Pacific to work into Southampton Docks in July 1947 with the Channel Islands boat train. Just after Nationalisation it was considered that the Southern Region had a surplus of Pacific locomotives, and to explore the feasibility of moving several of these to the Eastern Region, No 34059 was allocated to Stratford in April 1949; it appeared on the services from Liverpool Street to Cambridge, Norwich,

Yarmouth and Parkeston Quay but returned to the Bournemouth main line just one month later with the idea apparently dropped. In mid-1951 *Sir Archibald Sinclair* was transferred to Exmouth Junction, and as well as working the more important trains from Exeter to Plymouth it was also recorded on the short-lived Devon Belle together with some of the local stopping services to Barnstaple and Ilfracombe. During 1955 it moved to Salisbury and resumed work on the passenger and fast fitted-freight duties over the London to Weymouth and London to Exeter routes. Shortly after rebuilding in March 1960, No 34059 operated for a while on the South Eastern Section between Charing Cross and Ramsgate before returning to Salisbury from where it was withdrawn.

Following thorough examination by representatives of the Bluebell Railway, No 34059 was purchased and moved to Sheffield Park on the same day as No 73082 previously described, restoration being essentially a long-term project.

As if ashamed of its condition, *Sir Archibald Sinclair* hides among the trees at Sheffield Park in August 1981. (*Alan Warren*)

109th: GWR 4-6-0 No 7802 *Bradley Manor*

BUILT: January 1938
WITHDRAWN: November 1965

ARRIVED BARRY: July 1966
DEPARTED BARRY: November 1979

The Grange and Manor 4-6-0s of the late 1930s were primarily built to replace life-expired 43XX Moguls, but in order to provide a locomotive that could go almost anywhere on the system the Manors were fitted with a smaller boiler that helped reduce the axle-loading to just over 17 tons.

No 7802 *Bradley Manor* came off the production line at Swindon Works in January 1938 and went to its first shed at Old Oak Common towards the end of the following month. The Manors were always a fairly rare sight in the London area and it was not long before No 7802 was transferred away to Bristol, spending time at both St Philip's Marsh and Bath Road depots from May 1938 onwards; there it worked alongside the Halls on both passenger and freight trains to Taunton, Exeter and South Wales while it also spent a brief period based at the sub-shed of Weston-super-Mare. Just eight years later, in May 1946, *Bradley Manor* went on to more accustomed territory for the class on the former Cambrian main line, allocated at first to Aberystwyth and then Machynlleth in the period up to November 1962. While here it seems to have been a popular choice for the Cambrian Coast

Express, the line's most prestigious train, while other work included the Welshpool to Whitchurch services and the locals across to Shrewsbury; these routes provided some hard tasks for the locomotives although the frequency of station stops gave an opportunity if required to regain boiler pressure. Unusually perhaps, No 7802 was transferred to Tyseley in November 1962 but returned to the Cambrian in the following September, finishing its days at Machynlleth and Shrewsbury sheds.

Following the successful return to steam of its first Barry acquisition, the Erlestoke Manor Fund purchased *Bradley Manor* in late 1979 and moved it to the Severn Valley Railway to provide an interchangeable boiler and other long-term 'reserve' spares for No 7812. However, in early 1983 the decision was made to return No 7802 to working order as well and following the successful raising of funds to this end great progress has now been made in this locomotive's rebuilding.

During a Stephenson Locomotive Society Cambrian farewell railtour in 1965, No 7802 is turned on the turntable at Whitchurch for the very last time. (*R. Greenwood*)

110th: SR 4-6-2 No 35018 *British India Line*

BUILT: May 1945
WITHDRAWN: August 1964

ARRIVED BARRY: December 1964
DEPARTED BARRY: March 1980

The 30 Merchant Navies built between 1941 and 1949 are considered by many to have been the most advanced design ever to run in regular service in this country. Certainly they contained several innovations new to British practice but some of these did give quite serious problems in traffic, and this was the major factor which led to the decision to rebuild the entire class from 1956 onwards.

British India Line was built as Southern Railway No 21C18 at Eastleigh Works in May 1945 and spent its entire life, apart from two months at Bournemouth in 1960, allocated to Nine Elms shed in London. Initial work included the Waterloo to Basingstoke and Bournemouth West services; when the all-Pullman Bournemouth Belle resumed running after the War it was No 21C18 that worked the first down train on 7 October 1946. In June 1948, locomotive interchange trials took place between the various regions of the newly-formed British Railways, and No 35018 remained on the Southern working trains between Waterloo and Exeter in competition with a Royal Scot, a Duchess and one of the legendary A4s. On conclusion of these trials it soon returned to normal service, yet in July 1955

there came the opportunity to work an impromptu Royal Train, for while heading the Bournemouth Belle it was stopped specially at Winchester to pick up the Queen following her visit to the city. Shortly after, No 35018 became the first Merchant Navy to enter Eastleigh Works for rebuilding, this task being completed in February 1956. After a few teething troubles had been sorted out it settled down on the Bournemouth line trains together with the Waterloo to Exeter services, and continued on these important workings until it was finally condemned in August 1964.

After fifteen years' inactivity on the scrap lines at Barry, No 35018 moved to the Mid-Hants Railway during 1980, an appropriate destination, for it was frequently seen on this diversionary route when engineering works were taking place on the main line.

Merchant Navy at rest. *British India Line* shows off its impressive lines in Nine Elms shed yard in May 1963. (*P. H. Groom*)

111th: SR 2-6-0 No 31625

BUILT:	March 1929	ARRIVED BARRY:	June 1964
WITHDRAWN:	January 1964	DEPARTED BARRY:	March 1980

Including those locomotives rebuilt from the ill-fated River tanks, there were 50 of Maunsell's 2-6-0 Class U passenger locomotives, and as a general rule these tended to gravitate to the lines of the former LSWR. They were seldom used on freight duties, but their ability to adapt to a variety of working conditions ensured that they all had long lives, the first being withdrawn in 1962.

Completed at Ashford Works in March 1929, Southern Railway No A625 was sent to Nine Elms to deal with a number of secondary duties out of Waterloo including those to Salisbury, Portsmouth and Southampton. By 1933 it had been transferred to Guildford where there were always several Moguls for passenger duties in the area, but for a while in the mid-1930s it did operate along with two sister locomotives out of Salisbury shed, their most important duty there being to work over 'foreign' metals to Bristol, returning from Temple Meads with a mail train – for this working they were kept in spotless condition in an effort to impress their GWR colleagues! After a period at Basingstoke during the War this particular locomotive was one of two U Class 2-6-0s converted at Ashford in 1947

to oil-burning in an attempt to overcome the then shortage of good steam coal, but after just one year in this condition based at Fratton the idea was abandoned and it reverted to coal firing. The early years of Nationalisation were spent at Nine Elms and Eastleigh but in September 1953 it was transferred back to Guildford to resume work on the local passenger services, although in November 1955 when a Merchant Navy failed at Basingstoke with the Bournemouth Belle No 31625 was commandeered to work this heavy train on to Southampton where another locomotive took over. As steam working declined, the last regular passenger duty for the Maunsell Moguls was that from Redhill to Reading and No 31625 often appeared on these services until withdrawn in January 1964.

Purchased privately for the Mid-Hants Railway, No 31625 arrived there in March 1980 and became the second U Class locomotive to be rescued for eventual use on this popular line.

Taking a break from its normal duties on the line up from Guildford, No 31625 basks in the sun on Reading shed during the summer of 1963. (*P. H. Groom*)

112th: SR 4-6-2 No 34027 *Taw Valley*

BUILT: April 1946   ARRIVED BARRY: December 1964
WITHDRAWN: August 1964   DEPARTED BARRY: April 1980

The 110 locomotives that formed the West Country and Battle of Britain Classes were turned out almost continuously between 1945 and 1951, and when taken with the 30 Merchant Navies gave the Southern Region the second largest fleet of Pacifics in this country, beaten only by the combined ER collection of A1, A2, A3 and A4s!

Built at Brighton in April 1946, No 21C127 *Taw Valley* began its career at Ramsgate shed, normally working the services to Victoria and Cannon Street as well as between Margate and Charing Cross (via Dover). Shortly after the formation of British Railways in 1948 it moved away to Exmouth Junction, finding employment on the Atlantic Coast Express and Devon Belle workings to and from Ilfracombe, together with the express and stopping services from Exeter to Plymouth over both the LSWR and GWR main lines, this latter working being to familiarise Southern crews with the road via Dawlish in the event of it having to be used as a diversionary route. After nine years in the West Country, No 34027 was despatched to East-leigh Works in 1957 for rebuilding and when this was completed in September it returned to Eastern

Section duties, going at first to Bricklayers Arms and then back to Ramsgate a few months later. However, when Stage 1 of the Kent Coast electri-fication was finished in the Ramsgate area during June 1959, the Pacific became redundant and returned to Bricklayers Arms to work the com-muter trains via Tonbridge. In May 1961, as Stage 2 neared completion, *Taw Valley* was made redun-dant again, this time being transferred to Brighton where it performed on the shed's few remaining steam duties, including replacing the Schools Class 4-4-0s on one of the London Bridge business trains. The final re-allocation for No 34027 came in September 1963 to Salisbury.

Although originally delivered to the North Yorkshire Moors Railway during 1980, *Taw Valley* was subsequently transferred to the Bury Transport Museum in November 1982. However, in August 1985 it was moved in partially restored condition to the Severn Valley Railway where the work was completed in the autumn of 1987.

Still in undercoat *Taw Valley* waits to leave Kidderminster in the gathering dusk with one of its first public appearances since restoration in September 1987. (*John B. Gosling*)

113th: LMS 4-6-0 No 45699 *Galatea*

BUILT: April 1936
WITHDRAWN: November 1964

ARRIVED BARRY: May 1965
DEPARTED BARRY: April 1980

191 of these Stanier three-cylinder 4-6-0 express locomotives were produced by Crewe, Derby and an outside contractor between 1934 and 1936. Performance of the initial locomotives was most disappointing and it took an extensive series of trials to show that alterations to the draughting arrangements and a change to high superheat could improve the situation. Further experiments were carried out on one or two others of the class but generally the Jubilees put in around 30 years of good service on main line duties.

Galatea, named after a warship of the Royal Navy, was built at Crewe Works in April 1936 and appears to have spent much of its early life in the Derby area, although by 1947 it was based at Leeds for working expresses over the Midland main line to St Pancras as well as over the difficult but highly scenic route to Carlisle via Settle. Around the time of Nationalisation No 45699 was transferred to Bristol (Barrow Road) where its main work was on the cross-country services from there to Birmingham, Sheffield and York. While heading a Bradford to Bristol train in August 1953 it was involved in a derailment near Tamworth, and although thrown

on its side the locomotive suffered mainly superficial damage, which was soon repaired at Derby. During the summer peak, *Galatea* was often seen on excursion traffic with the result that it arrived at the East Coast resort of Cleethorpes in July 1958. As time passed by it was used on almost any sort of duty, being recorded at such diverse places as Crewe, Cardiff, Llandudno and Aylesbury in 1960 alone! Following dieselisation of the Bristol to Birmingham line, No 45699 was transferred to Shrewsbury in September 1961 where it performed on a variety of local workings up to the time of withdrawal in November 1964, following which it was stored at Eastleigh.

Brought to Steamtown, Carnforth in April 1980 as a source of spares for sister locomotive *Leander*, the remains of *Galatea* were subsequently acquired by the Severn Valley Railway and moved south to Kidderminster in April 1987 where a decision has still to be made as to their eventual fate.

On one of its regular workings, *Galatea* leaves Pontefract (Baghill) with a Newcastle to Bristol train in 1958. (*Peter Cookson*)

114th: SR 2-6-0 No 31638

BUILT: May 1931
WITHDRAWN: January 1964

ARRIVED BARRY: June 1964
DEPARTED BARRY: July 1980

Maunsell's design for the U Class Moguls was basically similar to his N Class mixed-traffic locomotives, although with 6ft 0in coupled wheels as against 5ft 6in. They were excellent value for money, being just right for medium-weight passenger trains on sharply-graded routes where the heavier 4-6-0s were prohibited, and although officially limited to 70mph, they were free-steaming locomotives which could easily exceed this speed in service.

As Southern Railway No A638, this 2-6-0 emerged from Ashford Works in May 1931. Following an initial period at Redhill it was soon moved to Guildford shed, principally for use on the semi-fasts up to Waterloo together with the local passenger services and the very occasional freight duty. After a few years of operating from Exmouth Junction during the latter period of the War, No 31638 was transferred to Faversham in Kent and performed on the secondary duties in that district, which also included certain of the passenger trains to Victoria. For about three or four weeks in 1952 it was noted working along with some other U Class 2-6-0s on the service between Cheltenham and

Andover Junction over the former MSWJR route, presumably as a forerunner to their introduction on these trains a few years later. At the beginning of 1953 it briefly returned to Redhill, but in September of that same year went on to Fratton, being employed there on the passenger turns from Portsmouth to Brighton and to Salisbury (via Southampton). No 31638's last move was in November 1959 when it returned to Guildford for working the Reading to Redhill trains – the Maunsell Moguls were the mainstay of these services for many years, proving to be ideal locomotives on this hilly cross-country line. Following withdrawal in January 1964, No 31638 was stored at Fratton for almost five months before being towed dead to its intended place for cutting-up in South Wales.

As the last U Class to remain at Woodhams, this locomotive was purchased for use on the Bluebell Railway in 1980, and arrived at Sheffield Park in July of that year to await its turn for rebuilding.

No 31638 rests between duties at its home shed of Fratton in May 1958. (*P. H. Groom*)

183

115th: BR 2-6-4T No 80080

BUILT:	March 1954	ARRIVED BARRY:	January 1966
WITHDRAWN:	July 1965	DEPARTED BARRY:	November 1980

Built at Brighton, Derby and Doncaster Works over a period of six years, these 2-6-4Ts entered service with very few problems and soon found their way to most parts of the country. They steamed exceptionally well and were able to maintain the full boiler pressure of 225lb/sq in at whatever rates of working were required.

Constructed at Brighton Works in March 1954, No 80080 is one of the 11 Standard 2-6-4 tanks to reach Barry scrapyard which had begun their careers at Plaistow to deal with the busy commuter service from Fenchurch Street to Barking, Tilbury, Southend and Shoeburyness. Although the vast majority of its time was spent on this sometimes hectic work, there are two recorded instances of No 80080 being rostered to special traffic. The first of these was in April 1955 when it worked a West Ham United football special off the Tilbury line to Luton (Bute Street) via Hatfield, and the second in March 1956 when it headed the Railway Correspondence & Travel Society's 'East London Railtour No 2' out of Fenchurch Street. Following electrification of the LT&S lines in June 1962, No 80080 was put in store for a few weeks before being

allocated to Croes Newydd, Wrexham, where it found use on the local passenger service from Wrexham Central to Chester Northgate and New Brighton. However, its main area of employment was on the lines of the former Cambrian Railway from Oswestry to Welshpool, Machynlleth and along the coast to Pwllheli and Aberystwyth where these tanks became a familiar part of the local scene. In fact they were an extremely successful choice for service on the Cambrian, their powers of adhesion and overall strength being ideal when it came to tackling the climb up to Talerddig Summit, but by the summer of 1965 they were no longer required and No 80080 was declared redundant.

Released from the scrap lines in November 1980, No 80080 was taken to the Peak Railway at Matlock. However, during 1983 and 1984 the semi-restored boiler and chassis were moved to the Midland Railway Centre at Butterley where final reassembly took place in time for it to guest at a BR Open Day at Ripple Lane depot in October 1987.

Steam returns to the LT & S! No 80080 stands ready with its shuttle train at the Ripple Lane depot open day in October 1987. (*Steve Worrall*)

116th: BR 2-10-0 No 92134

BUILT: May 1957
WITHDRAWN: December 1966

ARRIVED BARRY: June 1967
DEPARTED BARRY: December 1980

The original concept of these Class 9 freight loco-motives had been as a 2-8-2, but the 2-10-0 wheel arrangement was finally agreed as the best for heavy freight duties, the extra adhesion being essential when it came to handling loose-coupled mineral trains of up to 1000 tons or more. Construction began in late 1953 and continued until 1960, with the later Swindon examples ironically being built alongside the now-defunct Warship diesel-hydraulics.

Turned out from Crewe in May 1957, No 92134 entered service from Saltley shed on the outskirts of Birmingham where it was initially kept busy on heavy goods work to the Gloucester, Nuneaton and Derby areas, but it soon progressed further north-wards, finding a regular duty on the Water Orton–Glasgow Class C freight which it worked as far as Carlisle via Sheffield and Skipton. In December 1957 it was transferred to Wellingborough where the Class 9Fs were used extensively on the Toton to Brent coal trains and return empties, but in addition to this it travelled to the Sheffield district with the weekday Wellingborough to Rotherwood service and handled other more general freight

traffic over the Midland main line, this latter work including some of the longer-distance duties from Carlisle to St Pancras. Transferred to Leicester in February 1964, No 92134 journeyed south the following September to undergo its last major overhaul at Eastleigh Works, and when this was completed it returned to Leicester for use on that depot's heavier goods workings which took it all over the Midlands and up to South Yorkshire. In April 1965, No 92134 changed sheds for the last time, taking up residence at Birkenhead on South Merseyside.

The delivery of No 92134 to the North Yorkshire Moors Railway in 1980 took five days at a maxi-mum speed of 12mph! However this engine's travels were not yet over for in early 1984 it moved down to the workshops of Shipyard Services Ltd at Brightlingsea. When restoration is complete, No 92134 will be the only single-chimney Class 9F preserved.

Subsequently moved to Essex for restoration, No 92134 is seen here while at Grosmont in June 1981, six months after arrival from Barry. (*Alan Warren*)

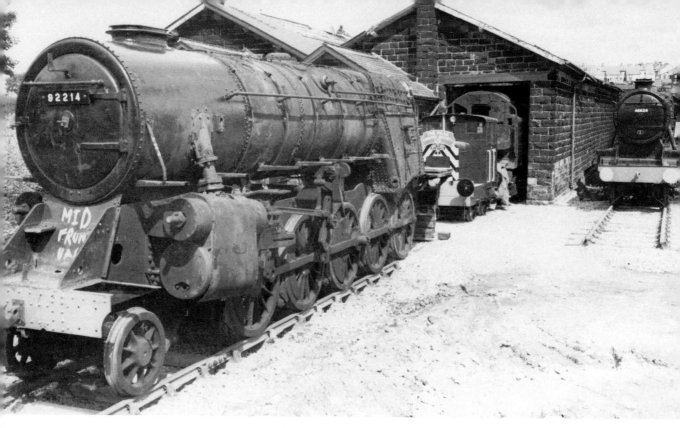

117th: BR 2-10-0 No 92214

BUILT:	October 1959	ARRIVED BARRY:	October 1965
WITHDRAWN:	August 1965	DEPARTED BARRY:	December 1980

In service the Class 9Fs proved remarkably trouble-free locomotives, and the excellent boiler was matched by an ability to run very fast, one example topping 90mph while working an express passenger service. However, this excess of speed was officially frowned upon as it caused heavy wear on the running gear, bringing down the period between overhauls to an unacceptably low mileage, with the result that the practice was actively discouraged.

No 92214 was among the final batch of steam locomotives ever to be built for British Railways, having been completed at Swindon in October 1959. The first allocation to Cardiff Canton only lasted a few weeks, for in November it was sent to Banbury to handle the heavy ironstone trains from the Oxfordshire quarries across to the furnaces of the South Wales steelworks, a duty which it shared with the GWR 2-8-0s. Additionally it appeared on the fast goods work up to Old Oak Common but the iron-ore trains remained No 92214's main source of employment until transferred to Newport (Ebbw Junction) in November 1961. The jobs there chiefly consisted of the usual coal and other mineral traffic, but a chance to break away from this relatively

uninteresting work came in the summer of 1964 when it was loaned to Bath Green Park to help out with the almost endless succession of holiday expresses which travelled to and from the South Coast via the Somerset & Dorset route. The 2-10-0s were ideally suited for this steeply-graded line but the lack of steam-heating equipment precluded their use other than during the summer, and it is believed that No 92214 was the last of the class to traverse this line between Bath and Bournemouth. On completion of this stint on passenger work it returned to more sedate duties, based at Severn Tunnel Junction until withdrawal.

Having spent twice as long in the scrapyard as it had in BR service, No 92214 was delivered to the Peak Railway Society at Buxton in December 1980, this making two Class 9F departures from Barry in the space of a few days (*see No 116*).

After a working life of less than six years, No 92214 stands outside its shed at Buxton in 1982 waiting for the chance to show its true potential on the Peak Railway. (*D. and S. E. Barratt*)

118th: SR 4-6-2 No 34067 *Tangmere*

BUILT:	September 1947	ARRIVED BARRY:	April 1965
WITHDRAWN:	November 1963	DEPARTED BARRY:	January 1981

The first Bulleid light Pacific to be rebuilt was No 34005 *Barnstaple* in 1957, and a further 59 underwent the same treatment in the period up to 1961, when the cost of the modifications could no longer be justified. This meant that 50 worked out their remaining days in original form but only a handful of these managed to survive into the last year of Southern steam in 1967.

Named *Tangmere* after the fighter station in West Sussex, No 21C167 came out of Brighton Works in September 1947 and immediately took up duty at Ramsgate on the express workings from the Thanet coast to London. It continued on these duties when transferred to Stewarts Lane in November 1949, but its sphere of operation now widened considerably to take in the Dover and Folkestone boat trains as well as the Kentish Belle Pullman express. Although spending most of its time on the Eastern Section, this did not stop No 34067 from appearing elsewhere on the Southern Region, and at various times during the 1950s it was unusually recorded on trains at Brighton, Plymouth and Eastleigh, while on three occasions it also worked through to Wembley with football and hockey specials before

travelling to Watford to turn on the triangle there. *Tangmere* remained at Battersea until the Kent Coast electrification was completed in May 1961, when it was transferred to Salisbury for both passenger and freight traffic over the main line between London and Exeter. It made its only known appearance on the Somerset & Dorset in April 1963 with a Southampton FA Cup special which it worked as far as Bath. In October of the same year No 34067 was transferred to Exmouth Junction, only to be condemned almost straight away; it was to be some time before this locomotive actually reached Barry for it spent almost 16 months in store there and at Eastleigh prior to the journey to its future Welsh home of the next 16 years.

Acquired for use on the Mid-Hants Railway, *Tangmere* arrived at Alresford in January 1981 and following substantial sponsorship from a local firm, it should not be long before this fine locomotive is in action again.

In filthy external condition, *Tangmere* races through Tonbridge with a down express in August 1959. (*Peter Cookson*)

187

119th: GWR 0-6-0PT No 4612

BUILT: February 1942
WITHDRAWN: July 1965

ARRIVED BARRY: October 1965
DEPARTED BARRY: January 1981

The 57XX Class of 0-6-0 pannier tanks constituted the largest single group of locomotives on the GWR and was also one of the biggest classes built in Britain, with a grand total of 863 machines. They remained the system's workhorses for many years until soon after Nationalisation, when the ever-increasing quantity of BR diesel shunters saw them find new areas of employment, several going to the Southern and London Midland regions.

Built at Swindon Works in February 1942, No 4612 began work at Bristol (St Philip's Marsh) on the busy wartime shunting and short-distance freight duties but it also managed to fit in some of the local Bristol passenger services which it shared with the 45XX 2-6-2Ts and GWR diesel railcars. Six months after Nationalisation, in June 1948, it moved on to Swindon and spent several years here based at the sub-shed of Chippenham for mixed-traffic duties on the short branch to Calne, while other jobs included working the shuttle service from Swindon main line station to Swindon Town on the MSWJR route, branch freights to Malmesbury and Faringdon, together with general shunting and yard pilot duties. Although transferred to

Taunton for a short period in 1961, No 4612 remained at Swindon until August 1962 when it went briefly back to Bristol for a few months before moving on to Neath in October. Here it soon settled on the normal pattern of duties for the class and by early 1965, although there had been a marked decline in the number of regular steam workings in South Wales, there still remained a nucleus of pannier tanks at Neath to power local trip freights as far east as Bridgend. Nevertheless, in April of that year, No 4612 was beautifully turned out to work an enthusiasts' railtour of the Welsh valleys along with sister locomotive No 9675 but just over a month later was transferred for the last time to Cardiff East Dock, where it stayed until withdrawn in July 1965.

At the beginning of 1981, No 4612 was moved to the Keighley & Worth Valley Railway to provide spare parts for that line's other pannier tank, and dismantling for this purpose began in mid-1982.

Just a few months after arrival from Woodhams, No 4612 stands in Haworth yard in March 1981. (*Alan Warren*)

120th: GWR 2-6-2T No 4121

BUILT: December 1937
WITHDRAWN: June 1965

ARRIVED BARRY: August 1965
DEPARTED BARRY: February 1981

Although initial construction of this large group of 2-6-2 tanks took place between 1903 and 1908, it was to be a further 20 years before the class was multiplied by the introduction of the 5101 and subsequent series. These updated versions of the original design were extremely effective locomotives and the 6100 series in particular were to dominate the London Division commuter services for many years.

No 4121 was assembled at Swindon Works in December 1937 and like so many others of the class began its career on the Birmingham and Wolverhampton outer suburban services, being based at Leamington to perform this task. However, after only three months it was sent to the joint LMS/GWR shed at Birkenhead, along with Nos 4120/2-9, for use on a miscellany of duties in that area and was frequently seen on trains to Chester and Wrexham until being put in store between May and September 1949. There then followed a major overhaul at Swindon after which No 4121 was sent to Pontypool Road to deal with the passenger services across to Aberdare and Neath, a job on which it remained until transferred to Severn Tunnel

Junction in February 1953. Here the difficult tunnel banking duties were its principal source of work for the next five years, and it must have been a welcome relief to return to passenger work when transferred to Tondu in July 1958, the local services worked including those from Bridgend to Blaengwynfi and Abergwynfi. It did occasionally travel further afield but line closures gradually reduced the scope of No 4121's employment with the result that in April 1964 it was sent away to Aberdare. From that depot it reputedly hauled the last westbound passenger train across the well-known Crumlin viaduct, but when Aberdare closed in March 1965 it spent a few months in store up to the time of withdrawal in June.

After almost 16 years exposed to the corrosive effects of the sea air at Barry, No 4121 was moved to Norchard on the Dean Forest Railway in January 1981, where several other ex-residents of this scrapyard are now gathered.

No 4121 stands at Pyle with the branch train for Porthcawl in July 1959. (*H. C. Casserley*)

189

121st: BR 4-6-0 No 75014

BUILT:	December 1951	ARRIVED BARRY:	October 1967
WITHDRAWN:	December 1966	DEPARTED BARRY:	February 1981

The 80 Standard Class 4 4-6-0s turned out from Swindon between 1951 and 1957 were designated mixed-traffic locomotives, but could more often be seen on passenger working during their time on the Western, Southern and Midland Regions of BR. With a maximum axle-load of 17¼tons and a greater working range than their 2-6-4 tank counterparts, they were extremely versatile locomotives capable of going practically anywhere.

Completed in December 1951, No 75014 began work for BR based at Patricroft to handle the many stopping and semi-fast passenger services out of Manchester, but by September 1953 it had been transferred with the rest of the Patricroft Standard Class 4s to Llandudno Junction. There they were mainly concerned with the local services on the North Wales coastal line between Holyhead, Chester and Crewe, while the additional traffic generated during the holiday period to resorts such as Rhyl and Colwyn Bay always made sure there was plenty for them to do. No 75014 remained in this area when transferred to Chester in September 1957 and it was even loaned back to Llandudno Junction for a few months during the summer

season of 1959. However, as more diesels began to appear on the scene, No 75014 moved the short distance to the mainly freight depot at Mold Junction in April 1960. Just over two years later it resumed passenger working based at Bletchley, where it dealt with the stopping services to Euston together with the local trains between Oxford and Cambridge. This was then followed by 12 months in the Midlands, based at both Stoke and Tyseley between September 1963 and September 1964 before finally moving to Shrewsbury where No 75014 began perhaps the most memorable phase of its career on the trains across to the Cambrian Coast; these Standard Class 4s excelled on this difficult cross-country route, but No 75014 itself did not survive until the end of steam working on the Cambrian, having been withdrawn three months earlier in December 1966.

No 75014 was taken to the North Yorkshire Moors Railway in 1981 where restoration was begun just over four years later.

Looking rather tired and certainly ill kept, No 75014 waits for its next turn of duty at Shrewsbury in July 1966, its final year on BR. (*D. K. Jones collection*)

122nd: SR 4-6-0 No 30828

BUILT: July 1927
WITHDRAWN: January 1964

ARRIVED BARRY: June 1964
DEPARTED BARRY: March 1981

When additional heavy goods locomotives were required for use on the Western Section of the Southern Railway in the mid-1920s, Maunsell took the already proven Urie S15 4-6-0s and made his own modifications to the design; fifteen of these new locomotives were then turned out from Eastleigh Works in 1927/8 and a further 10 followed in 1936. The operating department was thus provided with a thoroughly modern machine, which continued to give excellent service right up to the first withdrawals in 1962.

Costing around £10,500 to build at Eastleigh in July 1927, No 30828 was allocated to Salisbury shed from new where it was to remain for all 36 years of its working life. Along with the other S15s based there, this locomotive saw use on the heaviest freight turns over the main line between London and Exeter as well as those from Salisbury to Southampton and Eastleigh goods yards, while in later years it was also seen on local pick-up freight duties at the various stations on these routes. Although primarily a freight locomotive, No 30828 was frequently rostered to passenger duties and these included the stopping and semi-fast trains

from Salisbury up to Waterloo, while in the opposite direction it usually dealt with the local services to Templecombe, Yeovil, Axminster and Exeter Central. In the mid-1950s one of its regular jobs was to travel right down to Yeovil with the 6.54pm from Waterloo so that it was available to work back to Salisbury the following day with an early morning freight. At the busier times of year No 30828 was also seen on express holiday reliefs which were sometimes worked up to speeds of 75mph, but generally it remained on main line freight and stopping passenger duties until withdrawn at the beginning of 1964.

Purchased by the Eastleigh Railway Preservation Society with the aid of a loan and grant from the local borough council's lottery fund, No 30828 was unloaded at Eastleigh in March 1981 and towed through the station to the Works yard where it was the star attraction at a BR open day two months later.

In ex-works condition, No 30828 stands on Bournemouth shed during the early 1960s. (*C. L. Caddy collection*)

123rd: GWR 2-8-0 No 2885

BUILT: March 1938
WITHDRAWN: January 1964

ARRIVED BARRY: March 1964
DEPARTED BARRY: March 1981

Considered by many to be amongst the best heavy freight locomotives in Britain, the first of Churchward's 2-8-0s took to the tracks in 1903 and construction of the batches continued until 1919. It was then to be another 20 years before further 28XXs appeared and these later ones, known as the 2884 Class, were an up-to-date edition with outside steampipes, side-window cab and modified framing.

No 2885 was the second of this more modern version to be constructed at Swindon Works in March 1938 and it entered service from Pontypool Road. This shed was responsible for a considerable number of regular goods and mineral trains, with the result that No 2885 travelled to many parts of the GWR system with fast freights or other general traffic – just a few of the places to which it worked included the Birmingham area, Oxford, Birkenhead, Bristol and Exeter. In June 1942, the 2-8-0 was transferred to Banbury to play its part in hauling the extremely important wartime flow of iron-ore to the South Wales steelworks, and this class all but monopolised these workings for many years. However, the greatest proportion of No

2885's life was spent in the Midlands based at Stourbridge Junction where it was sent in April 1948; once again it worked to a great variety of destinations and an interesting fact is that because these locomotives tended to be absent from their home sheds for lengthy periods, a small box was welded to the footplate which contained a report card informing when the next boiler wash-out was due! Apart from 10 months at Tyseley in 1958/9, No 2885 stayed at Stourbridge until September 1962 when it moved back to South Wales, this time allocated to Newport (Ebbw Junction). This was not its last move, because in May 1963 it was transferred to Severn Tunnel Junction and carried on there until condemned just over six months later.

In March 1981, No 2885 was moved to the GWR Preservation Group's site in the former goods depot at Southall but has now moved the short distance to the Steam Centre being set up in the old locomotive shed there.

No 2885 approaches Chipping Campden with a lengthy freight train in May 1963. (*M. Mensing*)

124th: GWR 2-6-2T No 5532

BUILT: June 1928
WITHDRAWN: July 1962

ARRIVED BARRY: November 1962
DEPARTED BARRY: March 1981

When first introduced in 1906, the 4500 Class of 2-6-2 light tanks provided good modern machines capable of handling branch line work together with certain secondary duties over the main line. The later 4575 series, built between 1927 and 1929, had a larger water capacity and were generally more widespread in their activities than the earlier locomotives, although all 175 of these 'small prairies' were to be the mainstay of Great Western branches for many years.

No 5532 was turned out from Swindon during June 1928 and went to its first shed at Stourbridge Junction to take up duty on the stopping trains to Wolverhampton and Birmingham, work on which it continued until November 1934. It then moved to Worcester and soon settled down on the local services to Gloucester, Kingham and back to Birmingham, while this also included brief spells working from the small sub-shed at Evesham in the heart of the Cotswolds. In July 1937 No 5532 was transferred to the very different surroundings of Newport (Ebbw Junction) and this began a long association with South Wales that was to last for the next 16 years and which also involved allocations

of varying lengths to the sheds at Tondu, Aberbeeg and Pontypool Road. During this period, the tank was principally used on the valley passenger services within the Newport Division, but it also saw some use on freight and pilot work. At the end of 1953, No 5532 moved on to Bristol (Bath Road), remaining there until transferred to Swindon in November 1958 and then to Westbury in June the following year. One of its final duties at Westbury was to work the last local passenger train from Bristol to Frome on 31 October 1959, after which it was sent to work out its own last days at Plymouth (Laira). There No 5532 appeared on the branch services up to Launceston, but it was also known to have been employed on shed pilot duties at Laira before withdrawal.

No 5532 was purchased by the Dean Forest Railway as a future supply of spare components for its two other prairie tanks, and arrived at Norchard late in March 1981.

Obviously never having received the new BR totem introduced from 1957 onwards, No 5532 silently awaits its fate at Barry in 1966. (*B. J. Miller collection*)

125th: GWR 4-6-0 No 5972 *Olton Hall*

BUILT: April 1937
WITHDRAWN: December 1963

ARRIVED BARRY: May 1964
DEPARTED BARRY: May 1981

The Hall Class was just what the GWR required for a mixed-traffic locomotive, and the first production order placed in 1928 was for no fewer than 80, so confident must Collett have been about their suitability for the job! In this he was proved quite correct for they were excellent and useful machines, able to work all types of train except perhaps the heaviest freights, and ultimately 330 were built over a period of 26 years.

No 5972 *Olton Hall* was built at Swindon in April 1937 and after a running-in period of one month based at Neath, moved up the line to Carmarthen where it was often used on the stopping passenger services between Fishguard and Swansea as well as on fast freights to Gloucester and Bristol. No 5972 was stabled at Carmarthen throughout the war, and it was not until January 1951 that this locomotive was transferred away, at first to Plymouth (Laira) and then on to the Wolverhampton Division just eight months later. For most of the time in this part of the Midlands it was allocated to the predominantly freight depot at Oxley, but a chance to return to more regular passenger duties came in July 1954 when *Olton Hall* commenced a spell in

the West Country. Based at Truro, Penzance and Plymouth during this phase of its career, No 5972 could be seen on the local stopping trains between those three places as well as on the numerous summer Saturday specials that were a feature of this part of the country, and on several occasions it was recorded leaving Penzance with the Cornishman express. Other work included both fitted and mixed freight traffic over the main line, but in August 1959 No 5972 returned to South Wales and dealt with the usual miscellany of mixed-traffic duties from Severn Tunnel Junction, Neath, Fishguard and finally Cardiff East Dock sheds before withdrawal at the end of 1963.

Purchased privately from Barry, No 5972 was taken to the premises of Procor (UK) Ltd at Horbury Junction near Wakefield in May 1981, and is undergoing restoration in the workshops there.

Running 45 minutes late, *Olton Hall* nears Treverrin Tunnel with the down Cornishman in June 1956. (*M. Mensing*)

126th: GWR 4-6-0 No 4936 *Kinlet Hall*

BUILT: June 1929
WITHDRAWN: January 1964

ARRIVED BARRY: June 1964
DEPARTED BARRY: May 1981

With the exception of the Modified Halls introduced by Hawksworth from 1944 onwards, only minor alterations were ever made to the basic Hall design, although in the late 1940s eleven did run temporarily as oil-burners. The first withdrawal was actually in 1941 when No 4911 received a direct hit from a German bomb near Plymouth, but scrapping proper commenced in 1959 with the prototype No 4900 *Saint Martin*.

Coming off the assembly line at Swindon Works in June 1929, No 4936 *Kinlet Hall* entered service from Chester and quickly became established on an assortment of mixed-traffic duties from that shed. These included some of the passenger workings into South Wales, and in *The Railway Magazine* of March 1930 there is a log of a run with No 4936 on a Pontypool Road–Hereford–Shrewsbury train – judging from the timings quoted, No 4936 gave an excellent account of itself on the North-to-West route. *Kinlet Hall* remained in the Wolverhampton Division for most of this early period of its life and spent time at Shrewsbury, Oxley and Wolverhampton (Stafford Road) depots before being transferred to Oxford during 1933. For the next seven

years it alternated between there, Banbury and Old Oak Common before being sent to the West Country in April 1940, located initially at Truro from where it was used over the main lines in Devon and Cornwall. No 4936 stayed in this area when transferred to Plymouth Laira in October 1954 and then on to Newton Abbot at the end of 1958, one of its regular duties at this latter shed being to pilot expresses over the notorious Devon banks. However, by the early 1960s steam was in retreat in the West of England, and so in May 1962 *Kinlet Hall* moved to Cardiff, based at both Canton and East Dock sheds in the last few months before withdrawal in January 1964.

No 4936 arrived on the Peak Railway at Matlock in May 1981 and although subsequently moved to the Gloucestershire Warwickshire Railway at Toddington during 1985, negotiations are in hand for a possible move to the Llangollen Railway in Clwyd.

Kinlet Hall approaches Bentley Heath Crossing on the Birmingham to Leamington main line with an up empty stock working in June 1961. (*M. Mensing*)

127th: SR 4-6-2 No 34007 *Wadebridge*

BUILT: August 1945
WITHDRAWN: October 1965

ARRIVED BARRY: May 1966
DEPARTED BARRY: May 1981

The three West Country Pacifics that participated in the 1948 Locomotive Exchange Trials put in some truly fine performances, no doubt helped by the enthusiastic approach of their Southern crews. No 34004 in particular excelled over the difficult Highland main line between Perth and Inverness, putting its LNER B1 and LMS Class 5 competitors in the shade, albeit at the expense of heavy coal and oil consumption.

Completed at Brighton Works towards the end of the War, No 21C107 *Wadebridge* was sent to take up duty from the shed at Exmouth Junction in August 1945. Here it was mainly rostered to the depot's top-link duties which included the Devon Belle and Atlantic Coast Express, but the West Countries at this time rarely penetrated as far as London, normally coming off these trains at Wilton near Salisbury. The light Pacifics at Exmouth Junction were also used on the local passenger and goods work within North Cornwall and Devon, frequently appearing at Padstow or Ilfracombe with stopping trains to Exeter. During mid-1951, now renumbered 34007, it was transferred to Nine Elms and in July of the following year worked the

inaugural Statesman boat express from Waterloo to Southampton in connection with the sailing of the liner *United States*. Another regular job around this time was to work the Hampton Court branch morning goods before taking up normal duties on the main line expresses out of London, but there were occasions when this locomotive was used for special traffic; in April 1961 it was noticed being serviced on Willesden shed having worked through to Wembley, while two years later it hauled an excursion throughout from Southampton to Bristol. No 34007's last re-allocation came in August 1964 when it moved to Salisbury, again for main line passenger and freight work but in December it was chosen to haul an enthusiasts' brakevan special from Exeter to Meldon Quarry.

Intended for use on the Plym Valley Railway in Devon, *Wadebridge* was delivered to the private sidings of Bass-Charrington at Plymouth during May 1981 for initial storage before going on to Marsh Mills at the end of the following year.

With its air-smoothed casing removed, *Wadebridge* reveals some of its internal plumbing while awaiting restoration at Marsh Mills in May 1987. (*Jeff Nicholson*)

128th: GWR 0-6-0PT No 9629

BUILT: December 1945
WITHDRAWN: September 1964

ARRIVED BARRY: March 1965
DEPARTED BARRY: May 1981

The Great Western Railway was always a very large user of tank engines, and the 5700 series pannier tanks built from 1929 onwards were the successors to a long line of similar if smaller locomotives which were scrapped as they became life-expired. Though officially classed as shunting and light freight locomotives, many of them were regularly used on passenger trains and speeds in excess of 60mph were sometimes recorded.

No 9629 was built at Swindon in December 1945 and entered service in South Wales at Cardiff (Canton) shed. Included amongst its passenger duties here were the services up the Rhondda Valley, while during the peak morning and evening periods it was also sometimes employed on the commuter trains to Barry. Like most pannier tanks it was frequently put to use on short-distance freight duties, but No 9629 also spent a lot of time shunting in the many yards and sidings in the Cardiff area such as those at Pengam, while the considerable amount of coal and other mineral traffic dealt with at the Docks always kept it gainfully employed there. In June 1953 it was transferred to Exeter, and appeared on the local services

over the Exe Valley line to Tiverton and Dulverton as well as those over the Teign Valley line to Heathfield on the Moretonhampstead branch, but when not on these trains it would shunt the yard at Exeter Riverside. After this period in Devon, No 9629 went on to Oswestry in May 1960 and saw service on the Llanfyllin branch together with the usual shunting and pilot duties until moved back to Cardiff in November 1962, this time at East Dock shed. By now virtually all the pannier tanks' duties had been dieselised, so it remained on the more humdrum sort of work until transferred to Pontypool Road in April 1964, being withdrawn from there five months later.

Having arrived at Steamtown, Carnforth in May 1981, No 9629 was cosmetically restored for display at the Holiday Inn, Cardiff and took up its place in the car park there during March 1986.

Never to steam again, No 9629 stands on its short length of track outside the Holiday Inn at Cardiff in May 1987. (*Louise Philips*)

129th: WR 4-6-0 No 7903 *Foremarke Hall*

BUILT:	April 1949	ARRIVED BARRY:	August 1964
WITHDRAWN:	June 1964	DEPARTED BARRY:	June 1981

The Halls were mostly named after the stately homes of England, although a few such as *Queen's Hall* and *Albert Hall* were exceptions. With such a numerous class as this, finding names must have been something of a problem for Swindon, and so many of these locomotives were built that the list of country residences in Great Western territory became completely exhausted. As a result many of the later locomotives had names taken from places in the Lake District, Yorkshire and even East Anglia!

No 7903 *Foremarke Hall*, turned out from Swindon in April 1949, is a perfect illustration of this problem for it was named after a large Georgian Hall near Repton in Derbyshire. For the greater proportion of its time in service with BR this locomotive was allocated to Old Oak Common from where it worked to most areas of the Western Region's network. Apart from the rush-hour trains to and from Henley, Reading and Oxford it also dealt with long-distance passenger and freight work as far away as Plymouth or even Birkenhead. However, some of the Old Oak rosters were quite complex. As an example it is worth quoting one of

No 7903's regular turns during 1953: this took it to Reading with an evening commuter train which was followed by a Reading to Bordesley (Birmingham) freight, then a Langley Green to Banbury goods and finally a quick run back to London with a fast freight, the whole duty taking nearly two days! However, such a versatile class as this could be found on almost any sort of working, and in August 1958, *Foremarke Hall* was recorded double-heading with another Hall on the Cornish Riviera Express. Prestigious workings such as this were fairly unusual, and when services were gradually taken over by the new diesel-hydraulics, No 7903 was transferred to Cardiff East Dock in October 1963 from where it worked its last eight months in service.

Leaving Barry in June 1981 for the Swindon and Cricklade Railway, No 7903 was temporarily displayed at a Swindon Works Open Day before continuing its journey to Blunsdon for overhaul.

The fireman picks his way carefully over the fully loaded tender of *Foremarke Hall* during a stop for water at Kingham in 1961. (*M. Mensing*)

130th: GWR 2-8-0 No 2807

BUILT: October 1905
WITHDRAWN: March 1963

ARRIVED BARRY: November 1963
DEPARTED BARRY: June 1981

After the 1903-built prototype of this class had been running for a couple of years, general production was commenced at Swindon and the first batch of 20 locomotives was turned out from there between September and December 1905. This design became the standard Great Western heavy freight locomotive and ultimately no fewer than 167 were built, their simple and robust construction ensuring that many were to lead very long lives.

As one of this initial batch, No 2807 was completed in October 1905 and appears to have passed most of the time up to the 1923 Grouping based at Pontypool Road, Chester, and Bristol sheds. During this early period it was mainly confined to coal traffic but when transferred to Tyseley in September 1924 it soon began to work more general heavy freight up to London. The remainder of its days under GWR ownership were spent at Newton Abbot, Llanelly and Cardiff. Shortly before Nationalisation No 2807 was sent to Hereford and for a while was the only representative of the class to be based there, but within a few years it had moved on to Worcester where once again there were only a small number allocated. This period of

relative isolation from its sister locomotives ended in September 1957 when it was moved around between several depots until coming to rest at Newton Abbot towards the end of 1958. The 2-8-0s there normally found work on heavy mineral trains including, of course, the china clay traffic from Cornwall. No 2807 was frequently seen on the main line with such workings, although at this late stage of its career it was just as commonly used on intermediate freights or even pick-up goods. Final move came in May 1960 to Severn Tunnel Junction and it remained there until condemned just under three years later.

As the oldest locomotive to enter Barry scrapyard, No 2807 was a prime candidate for preservation and accordingly in June 1981 it was moved to Toddington on the Gloucestershire Warwickshire Railway. The long task of rebuilding is now underway and has already included extensive repairs to the main frames.

Three months after withdrawal, No 2807 stands silently among the weeds outside Severn Tunnel Junction shed in June 1963. (*Peter Cookson*)

131st: GWR 0-6-2T No 6634

BUILT: August 1928   ARRIVED BARRY: August 1964
WITHDRAWN: April 1964   DEPARTED BARRY: June 1981

Collett's design of 0-6-2 tank engine for the Welsh valleys could be easily identified by the front over-hang of the smokebox, which tended to give an un-balanced appearance. From 1957 onwards a start was made on replacing the dull BR plain black livery with fully lined-out green and this, together with the traditional copper cap to the chimney, produced an extremely smart locomotive.

No 6634 was built at Swindon in August 1928 and after a period of testing at Cardiff (Cathays) was allocated to the shed at Barry a few weeks later. There it performed on the normal tasks for which these 0-6-2Ts were so well suited but in November 1931 it was unusually transferred to Slough. This class was always a rare sight in the London Division but No 6634 found use on some local freight and passenger jobs until sent to Swindon for overhaul in early 1934. On completion it returned to South Wales, this time based at Pontypool Road and apart from brief spells on loan to Newport, Aberbeeg and Cardiff (Radyr) at various times between 1937 and 1951, it was destined to remain at this one shed until withdrawal. The range of duties at Pontypool Road was quite extensive and passenger work

included the early-morning workmen's trains to Blaenavon and Griffithstown, local services to Aberdare, Neath and Cardiff, as well as some of the excursion traffic, No 6634 often being recorded at Porthcawl on these once-popular trains. Freight work took it to a diversity of locations such as Ebbw Vale, Merthyr, Porth, Abertillery and Severn Tunnel Junction but at other times it was used as a banking engine at Abergavenny or Pontypool (East Jct), or even as station pilot at Pontypool Road. However, after an active life of around thirty-six years, No 6634 was finally declared surplus in April 1964 and sold for scrap.

Purchased privately in early 1981, No 6634 was taken to the Torr Works of Foster Yeoman quarries for some initial mechanical attention before being towed up the freight-only Cranmore branch to its new home on the East Somerset Railway.

No 6634 passes through Street on its way from Barry to Merehead Quarry in June 1981. (*Steve Marcks*)

200

132nd: WR 4-6-0 No 7821 *Ditcheat Manor*

BUILT: November 1950
WITHDRAWN: November 1965

ARRIVED BARRY: May 1966
DEPARTED BARRY: June 1981

The route availability of the Manors was such that they were able to operate over several hundred route miles from which the Grange Class was barred. Initial allocations saw many of the earlier locomotives working through trains from the North East to South Wales over the restricted route between Banbury and Cheltenham, but it is for their work on the lines of the former Cambrian system and as pilot on the Devon banks that the Manors will long be remembered.

Built at Swindon in November 1950, No 7821 *Ditcheat Manor* entered service from Oswestry shed and found employment chiefly on the Whitchurch–Welshpool–Aberystwyth trains for around three years until transferred to Shrewsbury during 1953. The stay there was a short one, for in December of that year it was re-allocated to Tyseley to handle an assortment of duties which included some of the freight workings from Oxley through to Pontypool Road, although rather unexpectedly it was also recorded on Paddington to Reading and Didcot trains for a week in January 1955! During the summer of 1959, No 7821 moved on to Newton Abbot where it joined one or two others of the class

for pilot duties over the steep banks at Rattery, Hemerdon and Dainton, the respective gradients being 1 in 46, 1 in 42 and 1 in 36. It can be imagined what an impressive sight this locomotive must have made when helping a King or a Castle with a heavy holiday express! In September 1961, *Ditcheat Manor* went on to Croes Newydd and regularly appeared on the local services from there across to Barmouth until transferred to Machynlleth for Cambrian line duties in March 1963. For most of the time there it was actually sub-shedded at Aberystwyth but by November of the following year had been sent to Oxley, near Wolverhampton, for a 12 months spell before coming back to Shrewsbury a few weeks before withdrawal in November 1965.

Leaving Barry for the Gloucestershire Warwickshire Railway at Toddington during June 1981, No 7821 is now awaiting the outcome of negotiations which may see it move to the Llangollen Railway.

Ditcheat Manor enters Wrexham with a Barmouth to Chester train in the late summer of 1961. (*Peter Cookson*)

133rd: WR 4-6-0 No 7828 *Odney Manor*

BUILT: December 1950   ARRIVED BARRY: May 1966
WITHDRAWN: October 1965   DEPARTED BARRY: June 1981

It was originally intended to build 100 examples of each of the Grange and Manor Classes to replace the 43XX Moguls on passenger work. However, on the outbreak of World War II the order was suspended with only 20 Manors having been built, and apart from a further 10 constructed in 1950, the total order was never completed; illustrative of this fact is that the great majority of the allotted names were in the first half of the alphabet.

No 7828 *Odney Manor* was completed at Swindon in December 1950 and after the usual period of running-in was surprisingly placed in store at the beginning of 1951. Just over one month later it re-entered service at Neath for use on secondary duties in the Swansea area, but in October 1952 was transferred away to commence its phase of operation on the lines of the former Cambrian Railway. This began at Shrewsbury from where No 7828 became a frequent choice for the Cambrian Coast Express as well as the local services across to Aberystwyth, but apart from this regular work on the Cambrian it also worked goods traffic out of Shrewsbury and accordingly travelled over the Severn Valley route many times. Re-allocated

to Croes Newydd in May 1961, *Odney Manor* was soon put to use on the workings from Wrexham to Barmouth and Pwllheli, but a chance to stretch its legs came on one occasion when it was rostered to head a freight down to Stratford-upon-Avon. Although transferred to Machynlleth in March 1963, this locomotive was actually sub-shedded at Aberystwyth to handle the traffic from there to Carmarthen, Shrewsbury and Oswestry, but as a change from this routine it double-headed with No 7827 on the first leg of the Royal Train's journey between Aberdovey and Barmouth in August 1963. Moving back to Shrewsbury at the beginning of 1965, No 7828 remained there until working its last train in October of that year.

Purchased at the same time as *Ditcheat Manor*, No 7828 went to Toddington three months later and was successfully test steamed during the summer of 1987. It is now likely that following a period on loan to another private steam railway, *Odney Manor* will go to work on the Llangollen Railway.

Odney Manor prepares to leave Shrewsbury with one of its regular workings, the Cambrian Coast Express, in 1963. (Alan Warren collection)

134th: LMS 4-6-0 No 45491

BUILT: December 1943
WITHDRAWN: July 1965

ARRIVED BARRY: January 1966
DEPARTED BARRY: July 1981

W. A. Stanier's extremely popular Class 5 mixed-traffic locomotives were equally at home on express passenger or heavy freight trains, and regularly achieved in excess of 150,000 miles between general repairs. These 'Black Fives' were so nicknamed because their standard finish as originally turned out was black all over with only a certain amount of red lining on locomotive and tender.

Built at Derby Works in December 1943 at a cost of £9,332, LMS No 5491 was sent to Corkerhill depot on the western outskirts of Glasgow to assist with the essential wartime freight traffic. This meant that the locomotive travelled to almost anywhere on the system, often spending many days away from its home shed, but on the cessation of hostilities it settled into a more regular pattern of freight and passenger work until transferred to Carlisle (Kingmoor) in July 1952. Now renumbered 45491, its main source of work there was on the numerous fitted freights which traversed the West Coast main line, and which also included ascents of the notorious gradients at Shap and Beattock, while other freight work took it over the Settle & Carlisle route to Leeds. Passenger work

also featured prominently amongst No 45491's duties and it was often used on expresses between Crewe and Glasgow or on the local stopping trains from Carlisle to Hellifield, Skipton and Leeds. On many occasions it would be 'borrowed' by other sheds for some of their jobs, and as an example it was noted on a Blackpool to Wakefield (Kirkgate) scheduled service in the summer of 1959. 'Black Fives' were also a popular choice for excursion or other holiday traffic and No 45491 regularly appeared on this work, being recorded on the Saturdays-only Heads of Ayr (Butlins) to Leeds in June 1961. Withdrawn in July 1965 it made the long, ignominious, journey down to Barry just a few months later.

After purchase from Barry in 1981 No 45491 underwent initial restoration at ICI's Thornton Works near Blackpool where excellent progress was soon made. It is now based at the Fleetwood Locomotive Centre for this work to be completed.

The smokebox numberplate of No 45491 has still to be painted as it gets ready to leave Carstairs with an express in the early 1950s. (*L. R. Peters*)

135th: LMS 2-8-0 No 48624

BUILT: December 1943

WITHDRAWN: July 1965

ARRIVED BARRY: October 1965

DEPARTED BARRY: July 1981

The Stanier 2-8-0 was introduced during 1935 and eventually 852 were built for service at home and overseas, making it the fourth largest class of British locomotive. Although primarily a goods locomotive, the Class 8F had a good turn of speed which was sometimes shown when they were pressed into passenger service, but otherwise they performed their day to day duties without fuss, and like the 'Black Fives' survived until the very end of standard-gauge BR steam.

As a result of the serious shortage of freight locomotives in the early years of the war, the Ministry of Transport decided that the Stanier Class 8F should become the standard heavy freight locomotive because of proven soundness and good route availability. Built to Railway Executive Committee order at the Southern Railway Ashford Works in December 1943, LMS No 8624 spent all its working life based at just one shed, Willesden, in North London. This was the main freight depot for the area and the 2-8-0s there worked extensively over the Western Division lines to the Crewe, Liverpool and Manchester districts, but they were also very common on Midland metals via Rugby and Leicester, one of their duties on this latter route being the Toton to Brent coal trains which they shared in the late 1950s with the BR Standard Class 9F 2-10-0s. Renumbered 48624 in November 1948, this locomotive was also used on other Willesden rosters such as the inter-regional freights across London, these turns often taking it into Southern territory at Feltham, Norwood Junction or even as far as Three Bridges. Another job that No 48624 was used on from time to time was the empty coaching stock trains from Euston up the 1 in 70 of Camden Bank to the carriage sidings – although normally carried out by smaller engines, the 8Fs were frequently employed on this duty when available. In July 1965, after 22 years at Willesden, No 48624 was withdrawn just a few weeks before the depot itself was finally closed.

These 2-8-0s were always a regular sight on the line between Matlock and Buxton so it is appropriate that No 48624 has been purchased for use on the Peak Railway, arriving at Buxton in 1981.

Before it was dismantled for restoration No 48624 sits in the sun at Buxton in April 1982. (*Alan Warren*)

136th: GWR 4-6-0 No 5952 *Cogan Hall*

BUILT: December 1935
WITHDRAWN: June 1964

ARRIVED BARRY: November 1964
DEPARTED BARRY: September 1981

The success of the 1924 prototype *Saint Martin* prefaced the construction of a further 329 Hall Class locomotives to the same basic design from 1928 onwards. By the end of 1961 only 12 had been withdrawn, but the diesel 'invasion' soon reduced numbers drastically, with the result that not a single example remained in service at the beginning of 1966.

Turned out from Swindon in December 1935, No 5952 *Cogan Hall* spent the first six years in the West of England allocated to a number of sheds including Penzance, Plymouth (Laira), Truro and St Blazey. For the majority of this time it dealt with both passenger and freight trains over the main line, and was often seen on the Cornish expresses which it worked to and from Plymouth, while the busy seasonal broccoli and potato traffic kept it occupied for certain periods each year. Throughout most of the War, No 5952 was based at Cardiff and Bristol (Bath Road) but in February 1945 it went to the London Division for the first time, going initially to Old Oak Common and then to Southall from September 1950 onwards. During this time in the capital its mixed-traffic capabilities were put to

good use over an extremely wide area, but at the beginning of 1955 it went back to the West Country for a nine-month period at Penzance and Plymouth before moving on to Worcester shed in September. Its work there was once again most varied, and included the semi-fast and stopping trains to Leamington Spa, Oxford and Paddington amongst others, and when transferred the short distance to Hereford in August 1959 it remained on the equivalent services, although during 1960 it was recorded leaving Shrewsbury with a train for Craven Arms and Swansea over the Central Wales route. From November 1963 onwards *Cogan Hall* spent its remaining days operating from Cardiff East Dock and when withdrawn the following summer was stored there.

After an initial period on the Gloucestershire Warwickshire Railway, No 5952 is now likely to move to the Llangollen Railway when negotiations have been completed.

Cogan Hall sets off from Evesham on the Oxford to Worcester line in May 1958. (*C. L. Caddy collection*)

137th: GWR 2-8-2T No 7200

BUILT: August 1934
WITHDRAWN: July 1963

ARRIVED BARRY: September 1963
DEPARTED BARRY: September 1981

To widen their sphere of operation, C. B. Collett took 20 surplus 2-8-0Ts in 1934 and rebuilt them as 2-8-2Ts, the end result proving to be the longest and heaviest of all GWR tank locomotives. Classified 8F, the 72XX class replaced the ageing Aberdare 2-6-0s on the longer-distance heavy goods workings and eventually 54 were converted between 1934 and 1939, with the first withdrawals not taking place until the early 1960s.

Originally built as 2-8-0T No 5275 in 1930, No 7200 was the first locomotive to undergo rebuilding into this new form at Swindon, in August 1934. Initial allocation was to Llanelly where it soon became established on the main line coal trains from South Wales to London and the South West, but it was by no means confined to this work and could also be seen on other more general freight traffic. Shortly after the War, in February 1947, No 7200 was sent to Newton Abbot along with two others of the class for use on quite a variety of duties; these included banking from Aller Junction up to Dainton tunnel, working the Stoneycombe ballast trains and the monthly coal train up the Kingswear branch, while at times of extreme loco-

motive shortage on summer Saturdays they were even known to have worked holiday trains from Paignton as far as Newton Abbot with no trouble at all! In February 1950, No 7200 moved down to St Blazey to help out with the considerable china clay traffic, which it did until transferred to Landore (Swansea) in October the same year. Although its longer-distance duties had now been taken over by tender locomotives, the growth of the petroleum industry together with an increased traffic in iron-ore and other goods provided the locomotive with plenty of medium-distance work to handle, and No 7200 remained on these sort of jobs when re-allocated to Duffryn Yard (Port Talbot) in June 1960 and finally back to Llanelly four months later.

As the first of the class to be built, No 7200 just had to be preserved but it took until October 1981 before the locomotive was saved and taken to the Buckinghamshire Railway Centre for restoration.

No 7200 patiently waits its turn for restoration on an isolated section of track at Quainton Road in May 1987. (*Alan Warren*)

138th: LMS 0-6-0 No 44123

BUILT: June 1925
WITHDRAWN: June 1965

ARRIVED BARRY: August 1965
DEPARTED BARRY: December 1981

This very large class of 0-6-0s was built by Derby, Crewe, St Rollox, Horwich, and private contractors between 1911 and 1941. Unfortunately the design contained several weaknesses, in particular the front end layout and the undersized axlebox bearings, so it is perhaps surprising that so many were built without any modifications.

Built at Crewe in June 1925, LMS No 4123 spent its early years at Willesden trundling up and down the main line with sometimes lengthy loose-coupled goods trains. This was followed from February 1928 onwards by a period operating in the Liverpool area, based at both Sutton Oak and Edge Hill depots in the nine years up to November 1937, after which it returned briefly to Willesden before being transferred again, this time to Toton in October 1938. Its work now consisted of dealing with the considerable quantity of freight that passed through the yards there and the Class 4Fs sometimes appeared on the coal workings down to Brent, despite really being unsuited for this type of work. The 1940s were spent at Westhouses, Tilbury, Coalville and Leicester sheds but in September 1950, No 44123 moved on to Gloucester (Barn-

wood) where it was used on both goods and occasional passenger workings over the former Midland route between Bristol and Birmingham as well as on freight over the Sharpness and Nailsworth branches. There are also several recorded instances when it strayed from this area – for example, in the summer of 1952 it was noted piloting trains on the Somerset & Dorset line between Evercreech Junction and Bath, while in August 1953 it worked as far as Kettering and back with an excursion from Birmingham New Street to Clacton. Residing at Gloucester (Barnwood) until April 1964, No 44123 was transferred to the other shed in that city at Horton Road where it stayed until withdrawal the following year.

Saved from the cutter's torch by the Fowler 4F Society, No 44123 was taken to the Mid-Hants Railway in 1981 but just under five years later, in May 1986, moved on to the Avon Valley Railway at Bitton in company with Jinty No 47324.

With withdrawal only a few months away, No 44123 stands on the coaling road at Gloucester Horton Road depot in April 1965. (*Peter J. C. Skelton*)

207

139th: BR 4-6-0 No 75079

BUILT: January 1956
WITHDRAWN: November 1966

ARRIVED BARRY: April 1967
DEPARTED BARRY: March 1982

In their original form the Standard Class 4 4-6-0s were quite capable of producing enough steam to cope with the semi-fast and local trains for which they were designed. However, after draughting tests had been carried out at Swindon, it was found that their already good performance could be improved by the fitting of a double chimney; seven of the class based on the Western Region and all those on the Southern were so fitted from 1957.

Although numerically the final number of the class, No 75079 was not actually the last one to be built, for several others were turned out by Swindon Works right up to June 1957. Entering service from the shed at Exmouth Junction it spent six months there before being transferred to Basingstoke in the summer of 1956 where it was soon put to use on the semi-fasts to Waterloo and Salisbury. Obviously such a versatile mixed-traffic design as this was also employed on other secondary duties as required, and as an example it was seen double-heading with Schools class No 30905 *Tonbridge* on an evening train from Eastleigh to Reading in April 1959. After almost seven years at Basingstoke, during which time it acquired its

handsome double chimney, No 75079 moved to Eastleigh in March 1963 and found occasional employment on the boat trains from Southampton up to Waterloo together with the local services between Portsmouth and Reading, while at various times it also appeared on the stopping trains from Southampton (Terminus) to Wimborne. Other duties included the through services from the North to the South Coast which it would have worked between Basingstoke and Bournemouth, but by now the days of steam were numbered and following withdrawal in November 1966, No 75079 spent some months in store at both Guildford and Eastleigh.

With the help of a cash grant from Plymouth City Council lottery funds, No 75079 was brought to the Plym Valley Railway's Marsh Mills site in March 1982, where it will ultimately be named *City of Plymouth* in recognition of the council's generosity.

Mike Lawrence's low-loader delivers another Barry resident to its new home, on this occasion No 75079 to the Plym Valley Railway in March 1982. (*Jeff Nicholson*)

208

140th: SR 4-6-2 No 34010 *Sidmouth*

BUILT: September 1945
WITHDRAWN: March 1965

ARRIVED BARRY: September 1965
DEPARTED BARRY: November 1982

The West Country light Pacifics introduced in 1945 were a few inches shorter and several tons lighter than the earlier Merchant Navies, but the two classes were so alike that if the nameplates and numbers were removed it would take an expert to tell them apart. The term 'lightweight' is also slightly misleading, for with a tractive effort of 31,000lb, only the Merchant Navy and Lord Nelson classes were more powerful on the Southern Railway.

21C110 *Sidmouth* emerged from Brighton Works in September 1945 to undergo the normal period of trials and testing on local duties in the Brighton area. For most of November 1945 it was observed working two return trips a day over the Redhill to Reading line in place of the more usual Maunsell 2-6-0s. By December, it had taken up its first allocation proper at Exmouth Junction for duties in North Devon and Cornwall as well as over the main line, normally as far as Salisbury. Of the 70 light Pacifics that carried the unique Bulleid system of numbering, *Sidmouth* was the last to be given its new BR number, 34010, during January 1950. In June the following year it was transferred to Nine

Elms for service over the routes to Southampton, Bournemouth and Exeter, and in April 1953 was chosen to head an Ian Allan *Trains Illustrated* 'high-speed' special from Waterloo to Exeter and back. No 34010 remained at Nine Elms following re-building in February 1959 and a few months later was rostered for special duty again, this time taking the Shah of Iran's train from Gatwick to Victoria. Generally it continued on the more normal routine of main line workings out of Waterloo, yet in March 1964 was noted on a Newhaven relief express, despite steam working over the Central Section having officially finished three months earlier. Transferred to Eastleigh in September 1964, *Sidmouth* was kept busy on top-link duties until withdrawn in March 1965.

Purchased privately by a member of the North Yorkshire Moors Railway, No 34010 was taken on the long journey north in November 1982 and is now in store at Grosmont while parts are acquired for its restoration.

Sidmouth passes Poole with the Waterloo-bound Channel Islands Boat Express in August 1962. (*C. L. Caddy collection*)

141st: WR 0-6-0PT No 9682

BUILT:	May 1949	ARRIVED BARRY:	October 1965
WITHDRAWN:	July 1965	DEPARTED BARRY:	November 1982

The vast majority of Great Western locomotives built after the Grouping were products of the famous works at Swindon, but in 1929–31 200 of the 57XX 0-6-0 pannier tanks were ordered from outside contractors under a Government scheme to relieve the effects of the trade depression. As a result, examples of this class were produced at such diverse locations as Stoke-on-Trent, Stafford, Gorton, Newcastle, Sheffield and even Glasgow.

Built at Swindon under BR auspices in May 1949, No 9682 was among the last dozen or so of these pannier tanks to be constructed. Initial allocation was to Tyseley, where it was employed on the customary range of duties in that part of the West Midlands, although within a few months of arrival it was recorded leaving Birmingham (Snow Hill) as pilot to a 43XX Mogul on a Weymouth to Wolverhampton passenger train. No 9682's principal source of work was either shunting in the yards at Bordesley Junction, Hockley and Handsworth, dealing with occasional trip freights up to the large marshalling yard at Oxley, or other local goods duties. From time to time it would also appear on some of the shorter-distance suburban

passenger trains, and although not having the 41XX 2-6-2T's turn of speed it still coped admirably well with six or seven coaches. Transferred to the very different environment of Aberbeeg in South Wales during June 1960, No 9682 busied itself on the lines from Newport up to Ebbw Vale and Brynmawr, but when the local passenger services were withdrawn at the end of April 1962 it concentrated more on the freight side of things together with shunting at the various collieries in the area. In November 1964 it moved down to Cardiff (Radyr) but when this shed closed its doors in July of the following year, No 9682 was declared redundant and sold for scrap to Woodhams.

As all the other pannier tanks at Barry were taken away one by one for preservation, No 9682 alone silently awaited its fate on the scrap lines. Rescue was close at hand, for in November 1982 it was bought by the GWR Preservation Group and moved to the Railway Centre at Southall.

Just six months after arrival at Barry, No 9682 is still in basically as withdrawn condition; the cannibalisation of later years is still to come . . . (Murray Brown)

210

142nd: SR 4-6-2 No 35027 *Port Line*

BUILT: December 1948
WITHDRAWN: September 1966

ARRIVED BARRY: March 1967
DEPARTED BARRY: December 1982

Various proposals had been put forward as to suitable names for these new Southern Pacifics and initial suggestions included British land, sea and air victories of World War II or capital cities of the UK and Commonwealth. The theme finally chosen was the names of those shipping companies which called at Southampton; an interesting side note is that both left- and right-hand nameplates were provided to make sure that the companies' house flags flew correctly when the locomotives were running forwards.

No 35027 *Port Line* was completed at Eastleigh Works in December 1948 and entered service from Bournemouth on the express services to Waterloo. At the beginning of 1950 it moved on to Stewarts Lane, Battersea, where it took over many of the boat trains to Dover and Folkestone as well as several of the Victoria to Ramsgate workings. Perhaps the most famous of the Continental services were the Night Ferry and the Golden Arrow, and No 35027 regularly headed the latter train for many years, until transferred back to Bournemouth in May 1955. Here the Merchant Navies were almost exclusively rostered to the

Weymouth and Waterloo services, and after rebuilding in May 1957 *Port Line* was often photographed on the route's most distinguished train, the Bournemouth Belle. In April 1959 it achieved even greater distinction when chosen to haul the Royal Train from Windsor on part of the outward journey to Weymouth, as well as on the entire return working from Southampton. From 1963 onwards, when the Pines Express had been rerouted away from the Somerset & Dorset, No 35027 began working frequently on this train between Bournemouth and Oxford, but in March 1966 it travelled even further afield with a Southampton football special which it took right through to Wolverhampton. Withdrawn at Weymouth shed in September 1966, this locomotive then spent six months in store at Eastleigh.

Taken to the Swindon & Cricklade Railway in December 1982 *Port Line*'s restoration progressed much quicker than expected and in 1988 it will move to a permanent home on the Swanage Railway.

Port Line and the stock of the Bournemouth Belle pass through Bournemouth Central in July 1961. (*Port Line Loco Project Collection*)

143rd: BR 2-6-0 No 76084

BUILT:	April 1957	ARRIVED BARRY:	September 1968
WITHDRAWN:	December 1967	DEPARTED BARRY:	January 1983

Designed and largely built at Doncaster, the Standard Class 4 2-6-0s were based very closely on the Ivatt Moguls of 1947 (Nos 43000–43161) but with various modifications to their external appearance and draughting arrangements. The final locomotive of the BR class, No 76114, was the very last steam locomotive to be built at Doncaster Works in 1957, but all the preserved ones come from the 45 built at Horwich.

Completed at Horwich in April 1957, No 76084 appropriately began its career at the former Lancashire & Yorkshire Railway shed at Lower Darwen, a few miles south of Blackburn. In September of the following year it moved on to Midland metals for a few months, allocated to both Lancaster (Green Ayre) and Skipton sheds before returning to Lower Darwen in March 1959. There it was employed on local freight work throughout this part of Lancashire to Liverpool, Manchester, Preston and Blackpool among other places, while it also saw use on one or two passenger duties which included pilot work on some of the main line expresses. No 76084 remained there until March 1965 when it was transferred to Sutton Oak. By this time the rosters

at this shed were very much freight orientated and so a few of the Mogul's more regular turns took it down to Mold Junction with the North Wales coal workings or on the sand trains to Pilkington's glass works at St Helens. When Sutton Oak closed in June 1967 it moved for the last time to Wigan (Springs Branch) to deal with the substantial amount of coal trains that were generated in the area, but by then the days of the steam locomotive were numbered and when this shed closed its doors to steam in December 1967, No 76084 had achieved the dubious distinction of being the last member of its class to remain in service.

At some time during its period in residence at Barry, this locomotive was treated to a coat of red oxide by a would-be purchaser, but obviously the scheme fell through and it was not until January 1983 that No 76084 left for a private location in Lincolnshire.

In a condition typical of steam in its latter years, No 76084 passes through Lower Darwen with a sand train in September 1964. (*H. L. Holland*)

144th: SR 4-6-2 No 35006 *Peninsular & Oriental S.N. Co.*

BUILT: December 1941
WITHDRAWN: August 1964

ARRIVED BARRY: December 1964
DEPARTED BARRY: March 1983

During the final years of steam on the Southern Region, the Merchant Navies continued to put in some outstanding performances on the main line, particularly with the two-hour expresses from Waterloo to Bournemouth. There are many stories of speeds in excess of 100mph being recorded in the last few months, mainly with the 17.30 up Weymouth train, as the Southern footplate crews made a final attempt to demonstrate the capabilities of steam power.

Turned out from Eastleigh as SR No 21C6, the lengthily-named *Peninsular & Oriental S.N. Co.* was based at Salisbury depot throughout its entire 23 years of service. However, the troubles experienced with the initial members of the class meant that it spent most of the War years on main line goods trains, and it was while working one of these in December 1942 that part of the chain drive came adrift spreading oil everywhere. This oil soon ignited and set the boiler cladding and lineside bushes on fire – the unfortunate crew had to wait for the local fire brigade to arrive and put the blaze out! Nevertheless it was not long before 21C6 was rostered to top-link passenger duties, its main area

of operation being over the main line between Waterloo and Exeter, although because of weight restrictions it never worked west of that city. Its duties took in such well-known trains as the Devon Belle and Atlantic Coast Express, but one of Salisbury's regular turns in the 1950s was to work the morning stopping train down to Exeter followed by the 2.30pm Exeter–Waterloo express and then returning home with a late night fitted freight from Nine Elms. No 35006 was the last Merchant Navy to undergo rebuilding in October 1959, after which it returned to Salisbury and continued on the Southern Region's more important trains until August 1964, when the decision not to carry out any further general repairs to the class led to its withdrawal.

Purchased from Barry in the summer of 1982 by the P & O Locomotive Society, No 35006 should make an interesting and welcome addition to the collection of stock at Toddington on the Gloucestershire Warwickshire Railway.

No 35006 is pictured just south of Clapham Junction with the down 13.00 West Country express in July 1964. (*P. H. Groom*)

213

145th: BR 2-6-0 No 78059

BUILT:	September 1956	ARRIVED BARRY:	June 1967
WITHDRAWN:	November 1966	DEPARTED BARRY:	May 1983

The 65 Class 78000 Moguls were the smallest tender locomotives in the BR Standard range and were so similar to the excellent Ivatt Class 2 design that there seemed little real need for this new class at all. Darlington Works was responsible for their construction and turned them out in batches between 1952 and 1956; when withdrawals began in 1963 the class was widely distributed, but became extinct four years later when the last examples ended their days as station pilots at Preston.

Completed at Darlington in September 1956, No 78059 and four other newly-built members of the class were sent initially to the former Cheshire Lines Committee depot at Chester (Northgate) and there they replaced the ageing Great Central 4-4-0s on the services between there and Manchester (Central). After a few years on this work No 78059 was transferred away to Llandudno Junction in April 1959 and then spent the next six years operating in the North Wales area based subsequently at Bangor and Holyhead sheds. Its duties throughout this period were quite varied and included some of the lighter stopping and semi-fast trains over the coastal line between Holyhead and

Crewe, while during the holiday season it also frequently dealt with excursion traffic down to Portmadoc (via Afonwen), taking over from the larger locomotives at Bangor. This Mogul also had one or two regular freight workings, the most usual of these being the evening Menai Bridge to Mold Junction goods, a duty on which it was photographed several times. In June 1965, No 78059 moved on to Willesden where it was mainly used on empty coaching stock and pilot work at Euston until the depot finally closed its doors to steam in September of that year. There then followed short spells at Nuneaton and Stoke before making the last move to Crewe South in October 1966 – quite obviously there was very little for the locomotive to do and it was withdrawn as surplus to requirements just a few weeks later.

As the last member of the class to survive at Barry, No 78059 was saved from destruction following purchase by a group of Bluebell Railway members at the beginning of 1983.

During its six year period based in North Wales, No 78059 poses on Holyhead shed in 1964. (D. K. Jones collection)

214

146th: SR 4-6-2 No 34070 *Manston*

BUILT: November 1947
WITHDRAWN: August 1964

ARRIVED BARRY: December 1964
DEPARTED BARRY: June 1983

The thin sheet-metal casing that made the Bulleid Pacifics so distinctive was officially referred to as 'air-smoothed' rather than streamlining; when these locomotives first appeared it was rumoured that they were so designed for putting through a carriage washing plant, although one must wonder how it was proposed to keep the water out of the various working parts!

As the last light Pacific to receive the unusual Bulleid system of numbering, 21C170 *Manston* emerged from Brighton Works during November 1947 and thus also achieved the notability of being the last locomotive to be built for the Southern Railway before Nationalisation. Its first allocation was to Ramsgate for duty on the main line services up to London, and on 31 May 1948 it worked the inaugural Thanet Belle all-Pullman express in both directions between Ramsgate and Victoria. By 1950, the renumbered 34070 was operating from Stewarts Lane on the more important Eastern Section trains together with a few of the Central Section services down to Brighton, but in early 1955 it moved on to Dover to give a helping hand with the busy Continental boat trains, including

the Night Ferry, this latter train being so heavy that it was often piloted by one of the former SECR L1 4-4-0s. Completion of the Kent Coast electrification in May 1961 meant that there was no longer any work for *Manston* to do at Dover, so it was sent to Ashford where once again few suitable duties could be found and it therefore spent most of its time there back on loan to Stewarts Lane. Within a few months No 34070 was transferred for the last time to Exmouth Junction and like the other unrebuilt Bulleid Pacifics based here regularly appeared on the 'Withered Arm' (the enthusiasts' name for the Southern lines west of Exeter) while at other times it could be seen on the stopping trains from Exeter to Yeovil and Salisbury, work on which it remained until withdrawal in August 1964.

After an enforced exile of 18 years in Wales, No 34070 was purchased by the Manston Locomotive Preservation Society and moved to CEGB sidings at Richborough.

The excellent progress made on *Manston's* restoration is clearly evident in this summer 1987 view at Richborough. (*Tony Laming*)

147th: LMS 0-6-0T No 47406

BUILT: December 1926
WITHDRAWN: December 1966

ARRIVED BARRY: June 1967
DEPARTED BARRY: June 1983

Of the nine 'Jinties' that have survived into the 1980s, seven were once residents of the famous 'scrapyard by the sea'. Of the two exceptions, one was purchased direct from BR by the Severn Valley Railway while the other, No 47445, was acquired by the National Coal Board for use at one of its collieries and painted in a curious orange livery with red side rods – it is now owned by Derby Corporation and undergoing restoration at Butterley.

Built by the Vulcan Foundry, Newton-Le-Willows, at a cost of £3,330, LMS No 16489 spent its first week on test from the nearby Warrington depot before taking up duty from Crewe South. There it was mainly employed on shunting work at the carriage stock shed or at Basford Hall Yard and occasionally dealt with the transfer freights across to the GWR yard at Gresty Lane. In October 1928 this 0-6-0T was transferred to Carnforth in Lancashire and spent the greater part of its working life based there, during which time it was also renumbered twice, eventually carrying its BR number 47406 from May 1950 onwards. Duties included shunting in the local goods yard together with trip freights down to Morecambe and Heysham, while from time to time it also acted as station pilot at Lancaster. After almost 32 years allocated to Carnforth No 47406 moved south to Warrington (Dallam) in March 1960 where there were a large number of 'Jinties' for shunting the numerous works and sidings in that district, but just over two years later it was transferred away and spent brief periods at Workington, Bank Hall and Gorton sheds before coming to rest at Liverpool (Edge Hill) in January 1965. That depot's allocation of 0-6-0Ts were a common sight in the local yards, but probably most enthusiasts remember them fussing about Lime Street station on pilot duty, and No 47406 regularly performed this work until condemned in December 1966.

Although stripped of most parts to provide spares for the other 0-6-0Ts which had previously left Barry, No 47406 was itself acquired by the Rowsley Locomotive Trust in 1983 for the Peak Railway.

Sheltered from the weather for the first time in 16 years, No 47406 stands in its shed at Buxton shortly after delivery in June 1983. (*D. and S. E. Barratt*)

148th: LSWR 4-6-0 No 30499

BUILT: May 1920
WITHDRAWN: January 1964

ARRIVED BARRY: June 1964
DEPARTED BARRY: November 1983

Design work for the Urie S15 mixed-traffic 4-6-0s had been completed during the latter part of 1917, but the effects of the steel shortage following World War I meant that the first of the class was not turned out from Eastleigh until early 1920. The twenty locomotives eventually built were destined to lead very long lives and the last to be withdrawn in April 1964, No 30512, was actually sold to Woodham's at Barry although, ironically, it was cut-up almost straight away.

Built at Eastleigh Works in May 1920 as LSWR No 499, this locomotive entered traffic at Nine Elms shed in London and soon settled into its principal task of dealing with the heavier freight workings over the main line, although at peak periods it was regularly used on passenger trains. During 1940, No 499 was transferred to Feltham, but in December of the following year was loaned to the Great Western Railway along with three others of the class and based at Old Oak Common, where it was apparently used on freight work around London as well as on some passenger work in the Wiltshire area; when LMS 2-8-0s and similar USA locomotives arrived on the scene in mid-1943

it returned to more normal duty at Feltham. Following Nationalisation the S15s here remained the mainstay of Western Section heavy goods turns which mainly took No 30499 to Southampton and Eastleigh goods yards, while there were also a number of duties to Bournemouth and over the West of England main line, these latter trains normally being worked as far as Basingstoke or Salisbury. Several of Feltham's rosters included secondary passenger services over these same routes, while the busy holiday periods also provided additional passenger work. However, by the early 1960s the quantity of traffic dealt with at Feltham was steadily declining; this, together with dieselisation, were the major factors leading to No 30499's withdrawal in January 1964.

Having already successfully acquired one locomotive from Barry, the Urie S15 Preservation Group purchased No 30499 in early 1980 and moved it to the Mid-Hants Railway in November 1983.

Following withdrawal in January 1964, No 30499 spent six months stored in the open at Feltham and is seen here in April of that year with tender still fully coaled. (*P. H. Groom*)

217

149th: GWR 2-8-0 No 3803

BUILT: January 1939
WITHDRAWN: July 1963

ARRIVED BARRY: November 1963
DEPARTED BARRY: November 1983

When first introduced in 1903 the 28XX class was a completely new design and apart from the addition of superheating from March 1909 onwards they remained fundamentally unaltered throughout their long careers. With a tractive effort of more than 35,000lb they carried out the task they were designed for with great ease, making themselves very popular with their footplate crews in the process.

Completed at Swindon Works in January 1939, No 3803 spent its early years based in the Wolverhampton Division, working variously from Leamington, Tyseley and Banbury sheds. Six months after Nationalisation of the railways No 3803 was transferred to Old Oak Common to take part in the famous 1948 Locomotive Exchanges. During these trials it was tested over the East Coast main line between Ferme Park and Peterborough, over Southern and Western metals between Eastleigh and Bristol (via Salisbury), as well as over more familiar ground between Acton and Severn Tunnel Junction. Although the results of the trials should be looked at objectively No 3803 acquitted itself well on all three routes, having been pitted

against representatives from the LMS and LNER as well as an Austerity 2-8-0 and 2-10-0. On completion of the tests it returned to normal traffic at Old Oak Common before moving a short distance down the line to Southall in February 1949. Just over three years later it was transferred to Cardiff Canton where it remained until August 1958; there then followed brief periods at Llanelly and Gloucester before settling down at Severn Tunnel Junction from June 1960 onwards. From here it was used on the familiar pattern of heavy freight duties up to withdrawal in July 1963.

Following purchase by the Dumbleton Hall Preservation Society this much travelled locomotive is now undergoing restoration in Devon at Buckfastleigh on the Dart Valley Railway. When this is complete No 3803 will be transferred to the Paignton and Dartmouth Steam Railway where it should make an interesting addition to their motive power fleet.

Seen here soon after arrival at Buckfastleigh in November 1983, No 3803 will keep its new owners, the Dumbleton Hall Preservation Society, busy for many years to come. (*Roger Penny*)

150th: GWR 4-6-0 No 4953 *Pitchford Hall*

BUILT:	August 1929	ARRIVED BARRY:	November 1963
WITHDRAWN:	April 1963	DEPARTED BARRY:	February 1984

The Great Western Halls earned for themselves a reputation of being extremely fast runners having regard to their 6′ 0″ wheel diameter. Indeed on the not infrequent occasions when they stepped in to substitute for a failed Castle or King they did not seem to have too much trouble in keeping to schedule, providing of course the locomotive was in good condition and the fireman had plenty of energy!

Pitchford Hall was completed at Swindon in August 1929 and after an initial period at Bristol Bath Road spent the years leading up to World War II working from quite a variety of sheds including Weymouth, Old Oak Common, Westbury, Taunton, Penzance and Truro. By May 1941 it was based at Pontypool Road yet just over 5 years later moved again, this time to the busy depot at Cardiff Canton. The Halls allocated here had a tremendous mixture of work to keep them occupied; passenger duties included the Cardiff to Birmingham trains via Hereford and Gloucester as well as the cross-country services down to Portsmouth via Bristol which they worked as far as Salisbury. In fact Canton's rosters were quite complicated and No

4953 would have been seen at most locations on the Western region with main line passenger or freight work, particularly on busy weekends during the summer when all available motive power was pressed into service on relief and excursion trains. In April 1956 *Pitchford Hall* was transferred to Swindon and appeared regularly on that depot's wide range of mixed traffic duties until July 1960 when it moved to Bristol St Philips Marsh. Within two years No 4953 had returned to Cardiff Canton but when this shed was closed for conversion to handle diesel power at the end of August 1962 it moved the short distance to Cardiff East Dock, only to be withdrawn in April of the following year.

After its long exile in Woodham's yard at Barry, *Pitchford Hall* is now undergoing restoration at the Norchard base of the Dean Forest Railway in Gloucestershire.

A reminder of Great Western steam in its heyday as *Pitchford Hall* poses for the camera at an unknown location. (*Real Photographs Co*)

151st: GWR 2-8-0 No 3850

BUILT: June 1942
WITHDRAWN: August 1965

ARRIVED BARRY: October 1965
DEPARTED BARRY: March 1984

In GWR days the livery carried by the 28XX class was green on the boiler, cab and tender tank with the remainder painted black. Following Nationalisation the standard livery became unlined black throughout, a colour which seemed to suit this particular class well. However, like most freight engines they received little attention from the cleaners at their home sheds and it could often be anybody's guess as to what colour actually lurked beneath the layers of dirt and grime!

Built at Swindon Works during the middle years of the Second World War, No 3850 commenced its career working from Bristol St Philips Marsh depot which was then followed by a short spell at Westbury in the period up to March 1948. In that month it was transferred to Severn Tunnel Junction and for the next eleven years was kept busy on the usual coal and mixed freight trains that were synonymous with the Churchward and Collett 2-8-0s. Nevertheless No 3850 did manage on at least two occasions to enliven its otherwise dull existence; in December 1952 it was recorded as having worked a Fishguard to Paddington parcels and mail train right through to the London

terminus, while in August 1957 it presented an even more unusual sight for spectators when it proudly steamed into Exeter with the down Devonian! From February 1959 onwards No 3850 was based at both Aberdare and Banbury sheds prior to moving on to Oswestry in October 1964 where, with sister locomotive No 3852, it was employed on the heavy ballast trains from Llynclys to destinations on the Western and London Midland regions. The final move to Croes Newydd took place in January 1965 and, although taken out of service in August that same year, it was observed at Brymbo steelworks with an iron-ore train during the following month!

Purchased in 1984 at a cost of £8,625 (excluding tender), No 3850 was delivered initially to Bishops Lydeard on the West Somerset Railway before being towed up the line to Minehead where restoration is now taking place.

Steaming well, No 3850 approaches Bentley Heath with a train of empties in 1964. (*M. Mensing*)

220

152nd: LMS 4-6-0 No 45337

BUILT: March 1937
WITHDRAWN: February 1965

ARRIVED BARRY: January 1966
DEPARTED BARRY: May 1984

When Stanier joined the LMS in 1932 the locomotive position was still far from satisfactory, particularly with regard to the provision of a suitable mixed-traffic engine. Accordingly the first Black Five emerged in 1934 and no less than 842 were subsequently built at Horwich, Crewe, Derby and by outside contractors. It could perhaps be said that the design continued into BR days for the Standard Class 5 4-6-0 bore a clear resemblance to its LMS predecessor.

Built at a cost of £6,244, including tender, No 5337 left Armstrong Whitworth's works at Newcastle in March 1937 and travelled across country to take up duty from Blackpool. However, within a few months it had moved on to Manchester Newton Heath followed by further moves to Bank Hall (Liverpool) in December 1940, Low Moor (Bradford) in October 1943 and Agecroft in October 1947. Its work here took it over most of the former Lancashire & Yorkshire lines radiating from Manchester and it was frequently seen in the Bolton, Preston and Blackpool areas with both passenger and freight traffic. Another source of work was provided by the considerable number of

excursions that ran at Bank Holidays and throughout the summer to various coastal destinations, and in the early 1950s No 45337 is recorded as having made several trips across to Scarborough with these popular trains, while in April 1955 it even travelled up the East Coast main line between York and Newcastle with a relief passenger working from Manchester. After 16 years based at Agecroft No 45337 was transferred to Southport in the summer of 1963 and continued on the normal range of mixed traffic duties dealt with by the class until November 1964, when it joined the increasing number of Black Fives allocated to Carlisle Kingmoor. Nevertheless this association with such a well known shed was to be brief for withdrawal followed just three months later.

Despite its long exile in South Wales No 45337 returned to familiar territory in May 1984 when it was taken by road to the East Lancashire Railway at Bury where restoration is now underway.

No 45337 speeds away from its Rochdale stop in September 1959 with the 14.02 York to Liverpool express. (*R. Greenwood*)

221

153rd: SR 4-6-2 No 34053 *Sir Keith Park*

BUILT:	January 1947	ARRIVED BARRY:	March 1966
WITHDRAWN:	October 1965	DEPARTED BARRY:	June 1984

Prior to World War II the most powerful locomotives permitted to run west of Exeter on the SR routes were the U1 and N Class 2-6-0s. Because of the operating problems this produced, Bulleid brought out a scaled-down version of his Merchant Navy Class which was capable of travelling over practically all the secondary routes, save only the minor branch lines. Appropriately the first locomotive was named *Exeter* and several of the class carried scroll nameplates incorporating the coats of arms of West Country towns.

Southern Railway No 21C153 came out of Brighton Works at the beginning of 1947 and was named *Sir Keith Park* shortly afterwards. Initially allocated to Salisbury, it appears to have spent a period on loan to Stewarts Lane in September 1948 during which time it was recorded on several of the heavy Continental boat expresses, including the Golden Arrow. There then followed brief spells at Nine Elms and Exmouth Junction sheds before returning to Salisbury in June 1951 for express work over the main line between London and Exeter, although some of its other duties saw it working the Portsmouth to Plymouth through

service together with the occasional fast freight turn. Following rebuilding in November 1958, No 34053 went back to Salisbury for just over another year prior to its final transfer to Bournemouth in February 1960. There its main source of work was on the expresses to Weymouth and Waterloo, while from time to time it would also be seen on the Swanage branch with the through trains to and from the capital. After the Pines Express had been re-routed away from the Somerset & Dorset in September 1962, the Oxford to Bournemouth section of this famous train became a regular working for the light Pacifics from Bournemouth and *Sir Keith Park* was photographed on this train many times before its withdrawal in October 1965 after clocking-up over 825,000 miles.

Following several years rusting away in company with the large number of other Bulleid Pacifics that found their way to Barry, No 34053 was eventually purchased for preservation and taken to Hull Dairycotes for rebuilding.

With a Great Western pannier tank in the adjacent platform, *Sir Keith Park* gets ready to leave Waterloo with a Bournemouth train in the early 1960s. (*Andrew C. Ingram collection*)

154th: GWR 2-8-0 No 3802

BUILT: December 1938
WITHDRAWN: August 1965

ARRIVED BARRY: October 1965
DEPARTED BARRY: September 1984

All 167 of the 28XX class survived to become the property of British Railways following Nationalisation in January 1948. From this large total 16 engines were acquired for scrap by Woodhams of Barry and all but one have been purchased for further use by preservation groups or private individuals. The unfortunate locomotive concerned was No 3817 which, after having stood at Barry for almost eight years, finally succumbed to the cutter's torch in March 1973.

Turned out from Swindon Works at the end of 1938 No 3802 entered traffic from Leamington shed but by May of 1941 could be found working from Banbury. During the difficult years of the Second World War it would have been called upon to play its part in handling the vastly increased amount of freight traffic generated at this time, particularly the important iron-ore trains that ran from here to feed the furnaces of the South Wales steelworks. In April 1952, No 3802 was transferred to Oxley on the outskirts of Wolverhampton and was regularly seen on that depot's freight duties especially on the main line to London, across to Shrewsbury and northwards to Chester. However, on one busy summer Saturday during August 1959 an acute shortage of motive power led to its working a Newquay to Cardiff passenger train from Plymouth right through to its destination, certainly a change from the normal daily routine! In October 1962 this 2-8-0 moved the short distance to Tyseley where it stayed until March 1963 but for the last few years of its time in BR ownership No 3802 was to lead a transient life, going first to Severn Tunnel Junction, then to Taunton and finally to Bristol (Barrow Road) from October 1964 onwards. Inevitably the onset of dieselisation meant there was less work for this locomotive to do and so during August 1965 it was withdrawn, only having just failed to survive to the official end of Western region steam.

Following a fairly active life No 3802 can now look forward to a welcome retirement on the formative Plym Valley Railway in Devon.

No 3802 has received some cosmetic attention before the long task of restoration gets underway at Marsh Mills in May 1987. (*Jeff Nicholson*)

155th: BR 2-6-4T No 80104

BUILT: March 1955
WITHDRAWN: July 1965

ARRIVED BARRY: January 1966
DEPARTED BARRY: September 1984

One of the earliest BR Standard types to be built was this group of attractive 2-6-4 tanks, yet owing to the rapid progress made in the modernisation of suburban services most of them had comparatively short careers, the last survivors congregating on the Southern Region.

No 80104 was built at Brighton Works in March 1955 and like most locomotives constructed there was run-in for a week or so on local services around the Brighton area. First allocation proper was to Plaistow in East London where it joined the fleet of other Standard tanks, eventually numbering 28, on the busy London, Tilbury & Southend commuter trains in and out of Fenchurch Street. These heavy workings were its main employment for several years together with the more leisurely service between Upminster and Grays, but as a change it was recorded in April 1958 heading through York, en route to Darlington Works for overhaul, with former Great Central Class A5 No 69805 in tow. No 80104 remained on LT&S services, latterly working from Tilbury shed, right up to electrification of the line in the summer of 1962, when it was then placed in store at Old Oak Common while a decision was

made as to its future. This came shortly afterwards when it was transferred to Croes Newydd depot for duty on the Cambrian lines and on the route up to Chester (Northgate) but only a few months later, in March 1963, it moved on to Machynlleth and the sub-shed at Aberystwyth. In these last years No 80104 was chiefly noted on the stopping passenger services to Barmouth and Pwllheli, while at other times it could be seen on the pick-up freights from those two places across to Shrewsbury, work on which it was to remain until withdrawal.

Purchased by the Southern Steam Trust in 1981, No 80104 remained at Barry while sufficient funds could be raised for transporting it to the Swanage Railway to join sister locomotive No 80078 acquired seven years earlier. It is now on static display at Swanage while awaiting its turn for rebuilding.

Awaiting its turn for rebuilding, No 80104 has received a coat of black paint and lining-out to enhance its appearance while on display at Swanage. (*Mike Frackiewicz*)

156th: GWR 2-8-2T No 7229

BUILT: August 1935
WITHDRAWN: August 1964

ARRIVED BARRY: November 1964
DEPARTED BARRY: October 1984

Following on from the successful conversion of several surplus 2-8-0Ts to 2-8-2Ts during 1934, a further two batches were dealt with in the years up to 1939. The middle series of twenty locomotives appeared in 1935–6 and became known as the '7220' class because they retained the old straight platforms above the cylinders of the original 2-8-0Ts. The class as a whole was highly regarded for use on the heaviest freight turns, while one was even tried as a banking engine on the Lickey Incline in 1958!

First completed as 2-8-0T No 5264 in March 1926, this particular locomotive was converted to 2-8-2T No 7229 at Swindon Works in the summer of 1935. Entering traffic from Severn Tunnel Junction shed it was chiefly employed on main line intermediate freight working from South Wales as far as London or Exeter, although the longer-distance duties were soon taken over by the increasing number of tender engines available for this work. After no less than 19 years based at Severn Tunnel Junction, No 7229 was transferred to Newport (Ebbw Junction) in March 1954 where it continued to be used on the familiar heavy coal and

steel trains over the South Wales main line, although by this time it could just as frequently be seen on any sort of mixed freight duties. During February 1962 it moved on to the former Port Talbot Railway shed at Duffryn Yard but when this closed down in March 1964 following the opening of the new depot at Margam, most of the steam allocation was transferred the short distance to Neath. This proved to be a temporary arrangement, however, for just three months later, No 7229 finally went back to Newport (Ebbw Junction) only to be withdrawn that same August during the mass extinction of Great Western steam power.

Consigned to Barry along with several other redundant locomotives from the South Wales area, No 7229 had to wait almost 20 years for its turn to be removed from Woodham's scrap lines and subsequent journey to a new home at Marsh Mills on the Plym Valley Railway.

After almost 20 years at Barry, No 7229 is seen here in May 1987 safely tucked away at Marsh Mills awaiting restoration. (*Jeff Nicholson*)

157th: BR 2-6-4T No 80098

BUILT: December 1954
WITHDRAWN: July 1965

ARRIVED BARRY: January 1966
DEPARTED BARRY: November 1984

The day to day performance of the Standard 2-6-4 tanks has rarely been published in the form of tabulated logs, yet their work on the hectic commuter services in and out of large cities such as London and Glasgow was frequently demanding and brought the best out of these locomotives, considered by many to be the best of the BR Standard designs.

No 80098 first saw the light of day at Brighton Works just before Christmas in 1954, and soon after entered traffic from Plaistow shed for duty on the suburban services out of Fenchurch Street to Tilbury, Southend and Shoeburyness. However, when this depot closed its doors just under five years later the Standard tanks moved *en masse* to Tilbury where they continued on the same workings until electrification of the route in the summer of 1962 put them all out of work. Several of these redundant locomotives subsequently spent a brief period in store at Old Oak Common before finding a more permanent allocation elsewhere on the Western Region, No 80098 in turn going to Shrewsbury. Just a short while later, in November 1962, it moved on to Croes Newydd and saw

service on the route north to Chester as well as on one or two duties over the lines of the former Cambrian Railway. During March of the following year No 80098 was transferred to Machynlleth and thus began the final phase of its career back on the Cambrian system, an area in which these tanks were extremely successful and popular. Initially it was based at the sub-shed of Aberystwyth and, in addition to the more normal duties for the class there, also appeared on the ex-GWR line down to Carmarthen with holiday and other local traffic. When operating from the parent depot at Machynlleth No 80098 was regularly recorded on both passenger and goods workings to Barmouth and Pwllheli right up to withdrawal in July 1965.

Many years exposure to the salt-laden sea air at Barry left No 80098 in far from pristine condition but in November 1984 it was delivered to the Midland Railway Centre at Butterley to provide long-term spares for sister locomotive No 80080.

No 80098 calls at Porthmadog to pick up a reasonable complement of passengers with the 1.20 p m Machynlleth to Pwllheli in August 1964. (*Midland Railway Trust Ltd*)

158th: SR 4-6-2 No 34072 *257 Squadron*

BUILT: April 1948
WITHDRAWN: October 1964

ARRIVED BARRY: March 1965
DEPARTED BARRY: November 1984

Withdrawals of Bulleid's West Country and Battle of Britain Pacifics began in 1963 and continued right up to the end of Southern steam in July 1967. The vast majority of the class were broken up in South Wales scrapyards and although 20 of these were sold to Woodhams, two of them were cut up shortly after arrival and thus did not survive to become part of the Barry 'miracle'.

On completion at Brighton Works in April 1948, *257 Squadron* was allocated to Dover to work the heavy Continental expresses up to London and for long spells it appears to have consistently headed the Night Ferry. When not on boat train duty No 34072 made several trips on the local services from Margate to Charing Cross but in March 1950, owing to failure of the rostered Schools class locomotive, it worked the through Birkenhead train in both directions between Dover and Redhill, thought to be the first occasion a light Pacific worked over the Tonbridge to Redhill line. Impending electrification saw *257 Squadron* move away to Exmouth Junction at the beginning of 1958 and within a short time it was soon handling that shed's main line and local services which included

a regular run down to Plymouth Friary with a goods train. No 34072 was also frequently photographed on the Ilfracombe portion of the Atlantic Coast Express as well as on the Plymouth to Brighton through trains which by this date had become an Exmouth Junction duty; during its layover period at Brighton it was often used on a fill-in freight turn up to Norwood Junction returning on a London Bridge to Brighton parcels train prior to working back to the West Country. In July 1964 *257 Squadron* was transferred for the last time to Eastleigh and although withdrawn in October of the same year was resteamed in December to work an enthusiasts excursion between Fareham and Southampton Docks.

Purchased by the owners of Merchant Navy No 35027, *257 Squadron* joined *Port Line* at Blunsdon in November 1984 but will eventually be restored to full working order on the Swanage Railway in Dorset.

An unusual shot of *257 Squadron* spending the night in a lay-by during its journey from Barry to Blunsdon in November 1984. (*A. Scott*)

159th: GWR 4-6-0 No 6023 *King Edward II*

BUILT: June 1930
WITHDRAWN: June 1962

ARRIVED BARRY: December 1962
DEPARTED BARRY: December 1984

Throughout their careers the King Class 4-6-0s put in some really outstanding performances, particularly after the improved draughting and fitting of a double chimney in the mid-1950s, and three-figure speeds were quite regularly recorded on both the Bristol and Birmingham main lines. It is also ironic to consider that while all the Kings had working lives in excess of 30 years, many of the diesel-hydraulics that replaced them were to last less than a third of this time before becoming obsolete.

No 6023 *King Edward II* was completed at Swindon in June 1930 and spent the whole of its time in GWR ownership based at Newton Abbot, where it was used almost exclusively on top-link duties over the main line between Plymouth and Paddington, including of course that most famous of titled trains, the Cornish Riviera Express. It remained on these same workings when transferred to Plymouth (Laira) in January 1950, although by then it was wearing the standard light blue livery which was fortunately short-lived and soon replaced by the familiar Brunswick green, a colour that suited the Kings' elegant lines much better. In June 1956 No 6023 moved up to Old Oak

Common, and in addition to the usual West of England expresses it also appeared on the London to Bristol and London to Wolverhampton trains (via Bicester). By September 1960 the Plymouth services had virtually been taken over by the new diesel-hydraulics. Thus *King Edward II* and several other Kings were soon transferred to Cardiff (Canton) where they were principally used on that depot's regular London turns, together with the three Cardiff to Shrewsbury duties. Other work sometimes included the Swindon and Kensington milk trains or services down to Bristol, and when finally condemned in June 1962, No 6023 had covered just over 1½ million miles in its 32 years of main line work.

With its driving wheels cut in half many people thought the restoration of No 6023 to be an impossible task but in 1984 it was purchased for the Brunel Trust by the wine merchants Harveys. Rebuilding is now taking place in the old fish dock at Bristol Temple Meads.

King Edward II attacks the gradient near Bayston Hill, south of Shrewsbury, with the 12.15 p m Manchester to Plymouth in September 1960. (M. Mensing)

160th: SR 4-6-2 No 35010 *Blue Star*

BUILT: July 1942
WITHDRAWN: September 1966

ARRIVED BARRY: March 1967
DEPARTED BARRY: January 1985

When withdrawals of the Merchant Navies began in 1964 these locomotives were far from life-expired and many had given as little as seven or eight years' revenue-earning service since rebuilding. The first two to be condemned were scrapped at the attractively named Slag Reduction Co at Rotherham, and apart from three others that were dismantled at Eastleigh, all the remaining locomotives were dispatched to South Wales scrapyard.

Built at Eastleigh in July 1942, locomotive No 21C10 *Blue Star* began work for the Southern Railway based at Salisbury, but in December of that year returned to Eastleigh where it was used for six months as a mobile testbed in an attempt to cure the problem of drifting smoke which frequently obscured the driver's view forward to a dangerous extent. Resuming normal work at Salisbury it appeared on the West of England main line services which of course included the distinguished named trains that traversed this route. By 1950 *Blue Star* had moved up to Nine Elms where its activities were more widespread and took in the Southampton and Bournemouth trains as well. After rebuilding in January 1957, during which time the main

frames were renewed ahead of the cylinders, it was allocated to Bournemouth running shed and for several years became a regular sight on the Bournemouth Belle and the other faster timed trains between there and London. In February 1960 No 35010 was transferred to Exmouth Junction and its time there was almost entirely spent on the Exeter to Waterloo express services, although a photograph does exist of it shunting goods wagons in the yard at Axminster station. During the autumn of 1964 it returned to Bournemouth for the usual main line duties but at this late stage of its career, *Blue Star* also worked some of the slower stopping services up to London before being withdrawn at Weymouth shed in September 1966 following accident damage to its right-hand cylinder.

With its move from Barry sponsored by Tate and Lyle, No 35010 was taken to a private site at Custom House where it will remain until facilities are available for its restoration at the nearby North Woolwich Station Museum.

The prediction written on the tender of No 35010 was never to come true, with Blue Star having to wait another 10 years for rescue by a private buyer. (*Steve Worrall*)

161st: GWR 2-8-0T No 4247

BUILT:	March 1916	ARRIVED BARRY:	August 1964
WITHDRAWN:	April 1964	DEPARTED BARRY:	April 1985

When the prototype locomotive of this class took to the tracks in December 1910, it was destined to be the forerunner of the first and only 2-8-0 Tank type ever constructed for a British railway. General production of the class commenced just over fourteen months later and although the coal and water capacity was somewhat limited, their strength and good adhesion capabilities made them ideal engines for the heavy short-haul freight turns so typical of the South Wales area.

No 4247 was turned out by Swindon during the middle years of the First World War in March 1916 and went straight into traffic from Newport (Dock Street). Following closure of the shed just over thirteen years later, this 2-8-0T moved on to the former Alexandra Docks Railway depot at Newport (Pill) which was especially extended to receive the influx of locomotives from Dock Street. Nevertheless, by October 1930 No 4247 had been transferred again, this time to the shed at Newport (Ebbw Junction) and apart from a short spell at Aberbeeg between March 1935 and November 1938, was destined to remain here until the end of 1952. Its work included the usual pattern of short distance

main line heavy freight trains together with a reasonable amount of more general goods traffic. However, in November 1952 it was transferred to the unfamiliar surroundings of St Blazey in Cornwall. Although the class is generally associated with South Wales, St Blazey usually had a pair of these powerful engines for dealing with the heavy china clay trains down to the docks at Fowey and several photographs exist of No 4247 on these workings. However, in January 1958, it returned to Ebbw Junction for a few years before going to Aberbeeg and then finally Tondu in June 1962. When this shed was closed in February 1964, No 4247 spent a short time out of use until officially withdrawn that same April.

After spending more than two decades in the salt laden sea air of Barry scrapyard, this 72 year old veteran was saved for further use on the Cholsey and Wallingford Railway following a whirlwind fund raising campaign which achieved the £7,500 purchase price in just 12 weeks.

The last few remaining flakes of paint peel off from No 4247's platework at Barry in May 1983. (*D. Short*)

162nd: BR 2-6-4T No 80097

BUILT: December 1954
WITHDRAWN: July 1965

ARRIVED BARRY: January 1966
DEPARTED BARRY: May 1985

Although many consider the Standard Class 4 2-6-4 Tanks to have been among the most successful of all the BR designs it is perhaps surprising that one of them, No 80103, achieved the dubious distinction in September 1962 of being the very first Standard locomotive to be withdrawn, receiving the coup de grace at Stratford Works a few weeks later.

Brighton Works released No 80097 for traffic in December 1954 and within a short time it was seen operating side by side with the large number of other 2-6-4Ts that monopolised the busy commuter trains from Fenchurch Street out to Southend and Shoeburyness. To work these services it was initially based at Plaistow but on that shed's closure in November 1959 moved to Tilbury, remaining there until made redundant by electrification of the line in June 1962. No 80097 was then transferred to Stratford, being noted several times on cross-London parcels workings until August when the decision was made to send it down to Swansea East Dock to help out with the services to Craven Arms and Shrewsbury over the Central Wales line; the members of the class based at Swansea were well received by the shed staff, their smart acceleration

giving them little problem in maintaining the comparatively slow Central Wales schedules. In July 1963 No 80097 was transferred to the Cambrian section of the Western region, being based first at Oswestry and then Machynlleth from June 1964 onwards. Its workings included the all-stations locals between Oswestry and Aberystwyth together with those up the coastal line from Dovey Junction to Pwllheli; at other times it could be seen working down to Carmarthen over the former GWR line from Aberystwyth, part of which is now being reopened by the Gwili Railway at Bronwydd Arms. Following withdrawal in July 1965 it was dumped at the back of Machynlleth shed until making the final journey down to South Wales.

After having patiently waited at Barry for so long No 80097's turn for rescue came in May 1985 when it was put on a low-loader and taken to the East Lancashire Railway's headquarters at Bury.

Bunker first, No 80097 approaches Southend Central with a train from London in July 1959. (*Frank Church*)

163rd: BR 2-10-0 No 92219

BUILT: January 1960
WITHDRAWN: August 1965

ARRIVED BARRY: October 1965
DEPARTED BARRY: May 1985

With a tractive effort approaching 40,000lbs the Standard 9Fs were extremely powerful locomotives and nearly always masters of their task. Perhaps the most exacting duty of all was undertaken by those ten members of the class based at Tyne Dock to work the iron-ore trains to Consett, a load of almost 800 tons having to be hauled up gradients as steep as 1 in 35 in places.

Of all the ex-Barry locomotives No 92219 holds a unique position in having been the last but one steam engine ever built for British Railways, emerging from Swindon Works in January 1960. Its first allocation was to Bristol St Philips Marsh but within a month it had been transferred to Cardiff Canton. The freight traffic dealt with here was quite considerable but generally the 9F 2-10-0s replaced the 28XX and WD 2-8-0s on the longer distance turns to London, Woodford, Oxley, Honeybourne, Hackney and Saltney, while the Banbury iron-ore trains also became their preserve from 1959 onwards. This latter duty was shared with the 9Fs based at Banbury and together they ended the long association that Churchward's 2-8-0s had with these heavy workings. Just occa-

sionally No 92219 was also seen on Canton's more local freight work to Newport, Severn Tunnel Junction and Swansea, together with the odd passenger duty when there was a shortage of other suitable motive power, but generally it continued on the fast fitted heavy freight work for which it was so well suited until Canton was closed to steam in August 1962 to be rebuilt as a new diesel depot. Accordingly No 92219 moved the short distance to Cardiff East Dock that summer and continued on very much the same sort of duties until withdrawn three years later. Built at a cost of £35,000 in January 1960, this locomotive had depreciated almost £7,000 per year while in BR service, hardly an economic use of such a fine machine.

Obviously other people felt the same way and although in far from its original pristine condition No 92219 has now joined sister locomotive No 92214 on the Peak Railway at Buxton.

With a full head of steam, No 92219 makes an impressive sight near Solihull with its train of hopper wagons in 1965. (*M. Mensing*)

164th: BR 4-6-0 No 73096

BUILT: December 1955
WITHDRAWN: November 1967

ARRIVED BARRY: February 1968
DEPARTED BARRY: July 1985

The British Railways Standard Class 5 4-6-0s were built under the direction of R. A. Riddles and the first locomotive appeared from Derby in the spring of 1951. Their design owed a lot to the excellent Stanier Black Fives of the LMS and the boilers were almost identical save for the substitution of BR fittings.

No 73096 was turned out from Derby Works at the end of 1955 and working from Patricroft shed in Manchester was soon to be seen living up to its mixed-traffic pedigree by travelling throughout the North West on both passenger and fast goods trains. In August 1958 it moved down to Shrewsbury with several other Standard 4-6-0s and while here was recorded at such varied locations as Euston, Pontypool Road, Taunton, and following general repairs at Doncaster in March 1961 also spent three days running-in on light duties over the East Coast main line. No 73096 was subsequently transferred to Gloucester Barnwood in July 1962 and following closure of that shed in April 1964 moved across to Horton Road depot in the same city. There then followed brief periods at Oxley, Nuneaton and Croes Newydd sheds before it finally

returned to Patricroft from July 1965 onwards. At first it had a regular working over the North Wales coastal line with the semi-fast trains between Manchester Victoria and Holyhead yet No 73096's career took a strange turn in April 1966 when it arrived at Cowlairs Works in Scotland for overhaul. Initially it was marked for cutting up and spent three months lying derelict on Eastfield shed before eventually entering the Works for repair and then finally returning south in September with a Glasgow to Carlisle parcels train. After this lucky escape No 73096 resumed working from Patricroft, making many appearances on passenger workings over the Manchester to Leeds line, although during its last week before withdrawal in November 1967 it was kept occupied on banking duties at Manchester Exchange.

No 73096's luck was to continue when it was purchased for scrap by Woodhams of Barry rather than one of the many other yards closer to home and it is now undergoing restoration at Ropley on the Mid-Hants Railway.

With only memories of its days at Patricroft to keep it company, No 73096 stands at Barry in the late 1970s. (*Steve Worrall*)

233

165th: GWR 2-6-2T No 5199

BUILT: November 1934
WITHDRAWN: March 1963

ARRIVED BARRY: November 1963
DEPARTED BARRY: July 1985

These impressive looking 2-6-2Ts must have become a very familiar sight to the countless thousands of commuters who daily used the railways to travel into London Paddington or into the large towns and cities of the West Midlands. Their aptitude for smart acceleration and a quick turn of speed meant that despite any delays time could normally be made up and thereby ensure that everyone would arrive for work on time!

No 5199 was a product of Swindon Works in November 1934 and it soon joined the very large stud of these 2-6-2 Tanks which operated out of Tyseley shed. Their work here normally consisted of handling the suburban passenger services from Birmingham up to Wolverhampton and Wellington and out to Leamington, Stratford-upon-Avon and Kidderminster while on occasions they were also used on short-distance freight work, principally between the large marshalling yards in the area. In October 1949 No 5199 was transferred the short distance to Stourbridge where it could still be seen on the area's commuter trains from Stourbridge Junction to Birmingham Snow Hill and Wolverhampton Low Level. After spending 16 years

working from here it was re-allocated to Wolverhampton (Stafford Road) in September 1961; at this late date diesel multiple-units were increasingly taking over its traditional duties and as a consequence it was more commonly observed on parcels or general goods work although from time to time a diesel failure would give it a chance to show that the potential for passenger duty was still there. In February 1963 No 5199 left the Wolverhampton Division for the first time in its career and moved on to Gloucester but this was to prove an extremely brief departure because once again diesel locomotives ensured that there was little useful work for it to do and withdrawal inevitably followed within just a few weeks.

After almost a quarter of a century of inactivity at Barry No 5199 was delivered to the Toddington base of the Gloucestershire Warwickshire Railway in the summer of 1985, but could move to the Llangollen Railway if negotiations to that end prove successful.

In between its normal round of suburban passenger duties No 5199 stands at Stourbridge Junction with a short parcels train in June 1960. (*Michael Hale*)

234

166th: GWR 2-6-2T No 5526

BUILT: May 1928
WITHDRAWN: June 1962

ARRIVED BARRY: November 1962
DEPARTED BARRY: July 1985

The long line of Prairie tanks on the GWR dates back to 1904 when the 44XX 2-6-2Ts entered traffic. Excellent engines though they were, their small 4' 1½″ driving wheels handicapped them in respect of speed and it was not surprising when in 1906 Churchward introduced a revised version, numbered in the 4500 series, with 4' 7½″ wheels, this extra six inches increasing their overall suitability for general branch line work.

Emerging from Swindon Works in May 1928, No 5526's first shed was at St Blazey in Cornwall although it does also seem to have spent a few months outstationed at the sub-shed of Bodmin for use on the line to Wadebridge. In November 1929 this locomotive was transferred to Exeter for a two year spell before embarking on a grand tour of sheds in the West Country which took it for brief periods to Plymouth (Millbay and Laira), Moorswater, Launceston and Newton Abbot before finally ending up at Truro from June 1935 onwards. There was always a reasonable sized complement of these 2-6-2Ts based here to handle the branch services to Falmouth and Newquay (via Chacewater) while they also had a regular duty down the

short goods-only branch to Newham Quay. During the mid 1950s in particular No 5526 became a common sight on the Par to Newquay line, a heavily graded route that passed through some spectacularly scenic countryside, but in 1959 it joined the mass departure of the class from the West Country branches caused by the arrival of diesel multiple-units and was accordingly transferred away to Westbury in March of that year. Here it was used on local passenger and freight work to Bristol (via Radstock) and occasionally up the main line to Swindon but fate eventually caught up with No 5526 and withdrawal came during the early summer of 1962.

During its 23 years at Barry this locomotive had been heavily stripped of parts to provide spares for other preserved 45XX engines but in due course left the yard itself in July 1985 to a new home at Toddington on the Gloucestershire Warwickshire Railway. Towards the end of 1987 it was put up for sale and discussions have subsequently been held with interested purchasers.

A small crowd looks on as No 5526 is safely lowered back on to the rails at Toddington in July 1985. (*Quentin McGuinness*)

167th: GWR 2-8-0T No 4270

BUILT:	December 1919	ARRIVED BARRY:	August 1963
WITHDRAWN:	September 1962	DEPARTED BARRY:	July 1985

The 42XX tanks were introduced in 1910 especially for the South Wales mineral traffic and they had long and successful careers right up to the time when diesels inevitably took over this work. Their design was based on the larger 28XX 2-8-0s, 195 examples being built between 1910 and 1930, while an additional 10 were turned out in 1940 as replacements for those which had been converted to 2-8-2Ts during the depression of the mid-1930s.

Built at Swindon in December 1919, No 4270 spent almost the whole of its time under GWR ownership based at Newport (Ebbw Junction), principally for working the short-haul heavy coal trains from the pits to the steelworks and docks. The only period employed away from Newport was between September 1937 and December 1944 when it stayed for short spells at both Tondu and Aberbeeg sheds, while perhaps even more unusual was an allocation of four months to Slough during the latter part of 1945, this class rarely being found east of the Severn. In January 1948, No 4270 returned to Aberbeeg but in October of the following year made its final move on to Cardiff Canton. Here it was still mainly employed on the numerous

heavy mineral workings, but it could also frequently be seen on mixed freight duties over the main line and to various locations within the Valleys. It should be noted that the route availability of the 42XX tanks was somewhat restricted on account of their relatively high axleloads and they were therefore rated as 'Red' category locomotives. Even so, this did not stop No 4270 from turning up in some unexpected places – for example in September 1959 it arrived at Reading with an up morning goods, presumably with numerous stops for liquid refreshment en route! Essentially however, it remained on the short-distance work for which it was designed, until withdrawn from service when Canton was closed to steam in September 1962.

Purchased by Swansea City Council No 4270 was delivered to the Swansea Vale Railway in July 1985 for eventual use on the Six Pit to Upper Bank line.

All spruced up and awaiting the low-loader, No 4270 is given a sheen by the steady drizzle on 28 July 1985. (*Deryck Lewis*)

168th: LMS 2-8-0 No 48305

BUILT: November 1943
WITHDRAWN: January 1968

ARRIVED BARRY: September 1968
DEPARTED BARRY: November 1985

The first Stanier 2-8-0s emerged from Crewe in 1935 equipped with a domeless boiler and were classified 7F. An improved boiler with a dome and separate top feed was soon introduced and all subsequent locomotives so fitted were uprated to Class 8F. As such the design was a great success and fortunately no less than seven of these fine engines still survive at various preservation sites in the UK.

LMS No 8305 was completed at Crewe in November 1943 and after an initial allocation to Leeds was transferred to the former Midland Railway shed at Wellingborough towards the end of 1944. Here it dealt with the bulk of the heavy freight traffic that passed over the Midland main line, in particular handling many of the coal trains that ran between Toton and Brent but just occasionally the Stanier 8Fs also appeared on passenger duty and No 48305 was no exception to this as in March 1955 it was observed arriving at Bedford with a Leicester to Cambridge local working! By April 1957 this 2-8-0 had moved to Northampton and apart from its normal duties over the main line north and south of that city it also had a regular

goods working that took it across to Doncaster via Newark. The next move took place in November 1962 with a re-allocation to Crewe South; this was principally a freight depot and although its rosters took it over a remarkably large area No 48305 still rather surprisingly managed to earn a dubious place in the record books by working the last goods train over the Holmfirth branch from Huddersfield on 28 April 1965 in place of the expected Hillhouses WD 2-8-0. Transferred to Northwich in July 1965 and finally to Speke Junction in September of the same year, No 48305 remained in service until January 1968 and was thus among the last 300 or so locomotives to work into this final year of steam power on British Railways.

8Fs were no strangers to the Great Central main line in its latter years and No 48305 can now continue this association following its delivery to Loughborough at the end of 1985.

Soon after arrival from Barry in November 1985, No 48305 receives some preliminary attention at Loughborough on the GCR. (*Graham Wignall*)

169th: SR 4-6-2 No 35025 *Brocklebank Line*

BUILT: November 1948
WITHDRAWN: September 1964

ARRIVED BARRY: December 1964
DEPARTED BARRY: February 1986

Although great trouble was taken in keeping the weight of the Merchant Navies down they were still limited in their route availability. The majority of their work took place between Waterloo and Exeter, Waterloo and Weymouth and on the main lines to the Kent coast; despite this they gave excellent service to their owners and went out in a blaze of glory with the completion of the electrification to Bournemouth in June 1967.

No 35025 was built at Eastleigh in November 1948 and named *Brocklebank Line* by the Chairman of that company at a special ceremony held at Waterloo in September of the following year. When transferred from Bournemouth to Stewarts Lane in February 1950 its main source of work was on the Victoria to Dover and Folkestone services including the Night Ferry and other boat train expresses. During March 1952 it moved to Exmouth Junction and just a few months later was chosen to haul the Royal Train conveying the Queen from Gillingham in Dorset up to Waterloo. While based at Exmouth Junction No 35025 also became a consistent performer on the Atlantic Coast Express yet by May 1954 had been re-allocated again, this time to Nine

Elms. Within two years it had moved back to Bournemouth and after being rebuilt at Eastleigh during December 1956 was subsequently sent to Swindon Works in August of the following year to undergo trials on the stationary testing plant there; on completion of these tests *Brocklebank Line* resumed normal working over the busy route between Weymouth and Waterloo. In February 1960 it was transferred for the last time back to Exmouth Junction and once again became a common sight on the ACE although from time to time it also performed more humble work, being recorded in one instance on a Southampton to Milford Haven tanker train which it took as far as Westbury. Despite being among the earlier Merchant Navy withdrawals, No 35025 achieved a total of 884,000 miles when condemned in September 1964.

Although having been next in line for scrapping when Woodhams resumed cutting up in 1980, *Brocklebank Line* managed to survive at Barry until February 1986 when it was delivered to the Great Central Railway.

Brocklebank Line speeds through Wimbledon with a Waterloo to Exeter train in 1964. (*D. A. Buckett*)

170th: SR 4-6-2 No 35022 *Holland – America Line*

BUILT:	October 1948
WITHDRAWN:	May 1966

ARRIVED BARRY:	October 1966
DEPARTED BARRY:	March 1986

The first Merchant Navy Pacific to be preserved, No 35028 *Clan Line* was acquired direct from British Rail in 1967. Since that date it has worked numerous enthusiast specials over BR's approved steam routes, and in its immaculately restored condition should act as inspiration to all those societies and individuals who have purchased one of these impressive locomotives from Woodham Brothers at Barry.

Completed at Eastleigh Works in October 1948, No 35022 *Holland–America Line* spent the early years of its most varied career working Exeter–London services based at Exmouth Junction, but in March 1952 it was sent to Rugby for trials on the testing plant there as well as for road tests with the LMR dynamometer car. These took place in October and November on the Midland main line between Durranhill, Carlisle and Skipton but unfortunately on one of these runs it slipped so violently that the coupling rods buckled. Further experiments were carried out on this locomotive at Rugby on two additional occasions in 1953 but eventually it settled down to more normal Southern main line service based at Bournemouth from May

1954 onwards. After rebuilding in June 1956, No 35022 became a regular performer on the Bournemouth Belle while in the following year it was frequently seen on the recently accelerated Bournemouth Central to Waterloo two-hour expresses. In February 1960, *Holland–America Line* returned to Exmouth Junction for a four-year spell before going on to Nine Elms in the early part of 1964. On 5 September that year it was specially cleaned to work the last down steam-hauled Atlantic Coast Express and then a few days later was re-allocated for the last time to Weymouth shed. Apart from the usual main line duties dealt with from here, it was also frequently seen on special workings, perhaps the most unusual of these being one from Waterloo to Crewe in November 1965.

No 35022 left the scraplines at Barry in March 1986 to travel to the Swanage Railway, a line on which the Merchant Navies were not permitted during BR days.

Saved! Holland America Line is pulled onto its low loader at Barry prior to leaving for the Swanage Railway in March 1986. *(Deryck Lewis)*

171st: SR 4-6-2 No 34028 *Eddystone*

BUILT: April 1946
WITHDRAWN: May 1964

ARRIVED BARRY: November 1964
DEPARTED BARRY: April 1986

In anticipation of the Bournemouth electrification and the introduction of main line diesels it was officially decided that no further general repairs were to be carried out on the Bulleid Pacifics from 1964 onwards. Thus when a fault developed and a trip to works became necessary the locomotive was withdrawn instead, a particularly wasteful decision when applied to the rebuilt members of the class that could have still given many years of revenue earning service.

No 21C128 *Eddystone* was outshopped from Brighton Works in April 1946 and went straight into traffic from Ramsgate where it took up regular duty on the Kent Coast services up to Victoria and Cannon Street. In its first few months under British Railways ownership No 34028 was re-allocated to Exmouth Junction and soon appeared on that depot's top-link duties such as the Atlantic Coast Express and Devon Belle which it worked as far as Salisbury. Shortly after rebuilding in August 1958 it was transferred to Bournemouth and with several other members of the class worked the services over the main line between Weymouth and Waterloo, but every year it also joined the ranks of

Bournemouth light Pacifics that helped out on the summer Saturday trains over the Somerset and Dorset route up to Bath. During this period of its career *Eddystone* was often photographed on that doyen of S & D trains, the Pines Express, although it was just as frequently seen on the numerous holiday reliefs that ran this way between the South Coast and the Midlands. At the end of the summer service in September 1962, No 34028 moved for the last time to Eastleigh and in April of the following year notably worked a Southampton FA Cup special right through to Birmingham Snow Hill via Reading, Oxford and Leamington Spa. When withdrawn in May 1964 *Eddystone* had the dubious honour of being the first rebuilt Bulleid light Pacific to be condemned.

This was not to be the end of the line for No 34028, however, for it was purchased by the Southern Pacific Rescue Group and moved to the Sellindge base of the Ashford Railway Trust almost exactly 40 years after leaving Brighton Works.

Eddystone stands outside an empty-looking Nine Elms shed in May 1964, the month this engine was withdrawn from service. (*Andrew C. Ingram collection*)

240

172nd: GWR 2-8-0T No 4248

BUILT: April 1916
WITHDRAWN: May 1963

ARRIVED BARRY: November 1963
DEPARTED BARRY: May 1986

Apart from those examples withdrawn for rebuilding as 2-8-2 Tanks during the mid-1930s this entire class of 2-8-0 Tanks survived to enter BR service in 1948. Withdrawals did not commence in earnest until 1959 while the last locomotive lasted until September 1965. Although most of them were disposed of at Swindon Works or in one of the numerous South Wales scrapyards, one was actually towed all the way to East Anglia to be cut up!

A product of Swindon Works in April 1916, No 4248 entered traffic from Newport (Dock Street) and, apart from a few weeks on loan to Gloucester in the summer of 1921, remained here until the end of 1923. This was then followed by brief periods at Neath and Swansea East Dock before it left South Wales to take up duty at St Blazey in Cornwall. Its work here principally consisted of taking the heavy china clay trains down to Fowey Docks although on occasions it also worked up the main line to Plymouth with other general mixed freight. As the effects of the trade and economic depression of the early 1930s began to bite into railway business throughout the country, No 4248 was placed into store at Swindon in January 1932 where it remained

for three years. As the situation began to improve it returned to traffic in January 1935 and resumed normal working from Newport (Ebbw Junction), the shed where it was to stay for the next 25 years. Along with the large number of other 2-8-0Ts based here it handled a considerable proportion of that depot's short-distance coal and mineral duties both east and west of Newport. This long association with the same shed eventually ended in August 1961 when No 4248 was transferred away to Llanelly yet within a few months it moved again to Bristol St Philips Marsh, followed quickly by a final move to Severn Tunnel Junction. When withdrawn in May 1963, No 4248 had given no less than 47 years of faithful service to its owners.

Having been privately purchased from Barry during 1986 this veteran locomotive was moved to the workshops of Shipyard Services at Brightlingsea in Essex for an extensive rebuild to take place.

As if ashamed of its condition, No 4248 hides among the undergrowth at Barry in March 1986. (*Deryck Lewis*)

173rd: GWR 2-8-0T No 4277

BUILT: April 1920
WITHDRAWN: June 1964

ARRIVED BARRY: August 1964
DEPARTED BARRY: June 1986

Despite being the first and only tank locomotive to run in Britain utilising the 2-8-0 wheel arrangement, the 42XX class can generally be considered to have been a very successful design indeed. Although their weight of approximately 82 tons gave them good adhesion capabilities it did mean that the consequently high axle-loading restricted their route availability somewhat, the entire class being rated as 'Red' category engines.

No 4277 was completed at Swindon in April 1920 and following an initial two-year allocation to Aberbeeg was to spend the years up to Nationalisation working variously from Newport, Swansea East Dock, Llanelly and Duffryn Yard sheds. In the summer of 1948 it was transferred to Severn Tunnel Junction where, in addition to the normal routine of freight work, it was also regularly used on banking duties through the tunnel itself. Relief from this strenuous work came in July 1953 when No 4277 was moved to Newport (Ebbw Junction) for employment on the heavy iron-ore trains that ran from Newport Docks to the Ebbw Vale steelworks in addition to the oil tanker trains to and from the refineries. By April 1955 this 2-8-0T had

returned to Aberbeeg, a medium sized four-road shed situated on the line from Newport which always maintained a number of these strong locomotives for their coal and other mineral duties. In June 1963 No 4277 returned to Severn Tunnel Junction for a few months before it was re-allocated for the last time back to Aberbeeg, the shed where its working career had begun some 44 years previously. After having spent its entire life based in South Wales this seasoned locomotive was finally retired in June 1964.

Although purchased in the summer of 1985, No 4277 had to wait for more than a year before it could be removed from the confines of Barry scrapyard. Part of the delay was caused by the necessity to move a Bulleid Pacific out of the way onto an adjacent siding so that the 2-8-0T could be winched onto its low-loader for transporting to the Gloucestershire Warwickshire Railway. Initially it will only be cosmetically restored for display until resources permit complete rebuilding.

Photographed in September 1987, No 4277 has obviously received a lot of attention to prepare it for display at Toddington. (*G. Tavener*)

174th: GWR 2-6-2T No 5552

BUILT: November 1928
WITHDRAWN: October 1960

ARRIVED BARRY: May 1961
DEPARTED BARRY: June 1986

During their time in GWR ownership the 45XX series of tanks were painted unlined green but following Nationalisation their livery became plain black as intended for all the less important classes, although a few were nevertheless lined-out in red, cream and grey. From 1958 onwards fully lined-out green became standard and many of these locomotives were kept in sparkling condition by shed staff right up to withdrawal.

Completed at Swindon Works in November 1928 No 5552 entered traffic from Tyseley and initially helped out with the Birmingham area local passenger services along with a few other members of the class based here. However, the arrival of the larger prairie tanks soon displaced No 5552 from this work and in July 1931 it was transferred away to Bath Road depot in the city of Bristol. During its time here this 2-6-2T did spend brief periods operating from the sub-sheds at Weston-Super-Mare, Yatton and Wells but could more normally be seen on the Bristol to Frome workings as well as on the Portishead and Avonmouth branches. In January 1937 No 5552 was re-allocated to Newton Abbot and this marked the beginning of a long

association between this locomotive and the Kingsbridge branch which ran for 12½ miles from Brent on the Exeter to Plymouth main line. Although a regular performer on this branch it was also frequently observed on Newton Abbot's other local duties including those over the Teign Valley line to Exeter St Davids, but following the drafting in of five BR Standard Class 3 2-6-2Ts (in the 82000 series) during February 1955, No 5552 was ousted from its normal work and transferred to Plymouth (Laira). A few months later it made its last move to Truro and passed the time up to withdrawal in October 1960 principally working over both the Falmouth and Newquay lines.

Delivered to Bodmin General station during the summer of 1986 No 5552 will be initially restored as a static exhibit prior to the commencement of rebuilding but it could be many years before the familiar bark of a 45XX is heard again on the Bodmin branch.

The classic Great Western branch line scene. No 5552 stands at Kingsbridge before setting off for Brent on the main line in August 1952. (*Frank Church*)

175th: SR 4-6-2 No 34058 *Sir Frederick Pile*

BUILT: March 1947
WITHDRAWN: October 1964

ARRIVED BARRY: April 1965
DEPARTED BARRY: July 1986

Bulleid's light Pacifics were extremely impressive locomotives to watch in action especially when hauling a lengthy train right up to the weight limit for the class. In their last few months in service enthusiasts travelled from all over the country to take a ride behind one of these fine machines and often the footplate crew responded by putting on a thrilling display to show exactly what they were capable of.

Emerging from Brighton Works in March 1947 as No 21C158, *Sir Frederick Pile* initially went to Nine Elms with 5 other light Pacifics to take over from the ageing ex-LBSCR N15X 4-6-0s but after a short spell on the Waterloo to Salisbury semi-fasts it was soon put to work on Nine Elms top-link duties including the numerous boat trains through to Southampton Docks and the more famous Bournemouth Belle express. By mid-1951 it was working from Exmouth Junction on a broad scope of both passenger and freight duties and it was while heading a Plymouth Friary to Exeter goods in April 1955 that the oil-soaked insulation behind No 34058's boiler cladding caught fire at North Tawton and the local fire brigade has to be summoned to

put it out! Despite this minor inconvenience *Sir Frederick Pile* soon returned to normal duty and was frequently seen on the Ilfracombe to Exeter local services as well as those down to Plymouth over both the former SR and GWR main lines, while on one occasion in March 1956 it managed to work all the way up to Twickenham with a Rugby Union excursion from the West Country. No 34058 remained at Exmouth Junction after rebuilding in November 1960 and continued on very much the same sort of work until transferred to Eastleigh in October 1963. When withdrawn from here just one year later it had managed to amass a final mileage in excess of 812,000 miles.

Thanks to the existence of Barry scrapyard and the efforts of countless enthusiasts, Bulleid's Pacifics can now be seen at many preservation sites throughout England, No 34058 *Sir Frederick Pile* making its way to the Avon Valley Railway near Bristol during 1986.

After more than 21 years at Barry, *Sir Frederick Pile* presents a formidable challenge for its team of restorers at the Avon Valley Railway in July 1987. (*Steve Worrall*)

244

176th: GWR 2-8-0 No 3814

BUILT: March 1940
WITHDRAWN: December 1964

ARRIVED BARRY: February 1965
DEPARTED BARRY: July 1986

When compared with the BR Standard class 9F 2-10-0s that were to eventually replace them on many of their traditional duties, the Churchward and Collett 2-8-0s led extremely long lives. The first withdrawal took place in April 1958 while the last member of the class soldiered on until November 1965. Apart from those dealt with at Swindon Works the vast majority of the class went to South Wales for breaking up although a few ended their days in scrapyards in Sheffield and Wigan!

Following completion at Swindon Works during March 1940 No 3814 had a brief spell running-in at Newport (Ebbw Junction) before taking up duty from Cardiff Canton. Its work here principally consisted of hauling the considerable quantity of heavy coal trains out of South Wales to a wide variety of destinations throughout the region, the good adhesion qualities of the class being particularly useful when working these trains through the Severn Tunnel. By July 1955 No 3814 had moved to the London Division, being initially based at Didcot and Southall before spending a six-year period, between March 1958 and April 1964, at the busy shed at Oxford. Here it dealt with that depot's

main line goods work, regularly travelling to London and Banbury or making longer journeys down to Hackney Yard at Newton Abbot. Traffic handled included the usual coal and other heavy mixed freight trains while on occasions it could be seen at the head of a train of car parts from the nearby Morris Cowley works. In April 1964, No 3814 was transferred back to South Wales, this time operating from Neath shed but just seven months later was re-allocated for the last time to Didcot. Obviously there was not a lot of work to keep it busy here for within a few weeks No 3814 was condemned and consigned to Woodhams early the following year.

After several groups had shown interest in the locomotive, No 3814 was eventually purchased for use on the North Yorkshire Moors Railway. As a result of the larger Great Western loading gauge minor alterations will have to be made to certain lineside structures before it can enter service on this railway.

Some of the large lumps of coal in the tender will need attention from the fireman as No 3814 rests on shed at Old Oak Common in June 1960. (*P. H. Groom*)

177th: BR 4-6-0 No 73156

BUILT: December 1956
WITHDRAWN: November 1967

ARRIVED BARRY: February 1968
DEPARTED BARRY: October 1986

In traffic, the Standard Class 5s proved to be sure-footed and reliable locomotives often capable of putting up performances more in keeping with the larger Standard Pacifics. Unfortunately they were destined to lead short uneconomic lives with the first examples being withdrawn in 1964; of the 172 built only five managed to evade the cutter's torch.

No 73156 was released from Doncaster Works just before Christmas 1956 and then travelled south light engine during the first week of 1957 to commence work from Neasden where it soon settled down on the Great Central services out of Marylebone, in particular making several trips at the head of the Master Cutler between London and Sheffield. By April 1958 it had been transferred to Sheffield itself, initially operating from Millhouses but subsequently moving across to Grimesthorpe shed in that same city. While here it worked many of the north-south expresses that passed through Sheffield and was often seen in the Gloucester area on these specific workings although it was also reported as having visited Southport, Cardiff and even Peterborough during the same period. After a few weeks at Derby in September 1960, No 73156

returned to its former GCR haunts being variously based at Neasden, Leicester and Woodford Halse in the period leading up to May 1963. At this date it was re-allocated to Cricklewood shed and frequently worked fitted freights and local passenger services over the Midland main line. In October 1964 No 73156 and two other Standard 5s were sent to Leamington to take over from ex-GWR Granges on the stone and cement traffic from Greaves Siding at Harbury but it appears they were not in very good condition and spent most of their time under repair at Bescot and Saltley! Obviously the situation eventually improved and following a short interval at Tyseley between June 1965 and April 1966 No 73156 was finally allocated to Bolton, working out its last year or so principally on local freight work in that part of the North West.

Almost 30 years after it was built No 73156 has now returned to the North West, leaving Barry in October 1986 for a new future on the East Lancashire Railway at Bury.

No 73156 and No 45612 *Jamaica* double-head the 8.05 a m Birmingham to Newcastle near Pontefract in August 1960. (*Peter Cookson*)

178th: GWR 4-6-0 No 6984 *Owsden Hall*

BUILT: February 1948
WITHDRAWN: December 1965

ARRIVED BARRY: February 1966
DEPARTED BARRY: October 1986

The Halls could be seen on most parts of the GWR system over which their 'Red' route availability permitted them to run, the London and Wolverhampton divisions in particular always maintaining a large allocation of the class. A sure sign of their general popularity was that like several other GW classes they were built in large numbers, a total of 330 being constructed over a 26-year period.

No 6984 was among the first batch of Halls to be turned out from Swindon during the early months of Nationalisation and it went straight into traffic from Hereford shed, soon settling down on the local stopping and semi-fast trains dealt with here. At times it also took turns on longer-distance duties and is known to have made several appearances on the Cardiff to Birmingham through trains, while in July 1955 it even arrived at Exeter with a Newport to Paignton holiday express, this latter working illustrating the fact that the Halls were very much common user engines and could be borrowed at any time by a troubled shedmaster to overcome his motive power shortage on summer weekends. In June 1958 *Owsden Hall* was transferred to Worcester and although handling that depot's wide

range of mixed-traffic duties it seems to have become almost a daily performer (alternating with sister locomotive No 6989) on the up Cambrian Coast Express between Shrewsbury and Wolverhampton during the latter part of 1959. In February 1963 No 6984 commenced a period of operation in South Wales, being based at Neyland, Cardiff East Dock, Neath and Severn Tunnel Junction sheds in the months up to April 1965 when a final transfer to Bristol Barrow Road took place. Even at this late date it was kept fairly busy and managed to survive until December 1965 when all the remaining Halls were withdrawn en masse at the 'official' end of Great Western steam.

Having spent longer at Barry than it had in BR service *Owsden Hall* was purchased for preservation and moved to a private site at Bicester in Oxfordshire for restoration to commence.

Owsden Hall runs into Banbury (General) with an up parcels train in May 1960. (*M. Mensing*)

247

179th: GWR 4-6-0 No 4979 *Wootton Hall*

BUILT: February 1930
WITHDRAWN: December 1963

ARRIVED BARRY: June 1964
DEPARTED BARRY: October 1986

The Hall class 4-6-0s were the standard mixed-traffic locomotives of the GWR and worked over most of that company's system. During British Railways' days in particular there were many occasions when the class regularly appeared on other regions and they could be seen at such diverse locations as Chester, Crewe, Bournemouth, Weymouth and also on the former Great Central line to Leicester.

Turned out from Swindon at the beginning of 1930, *Wootton Hall* entered service from Plymouth (Laira) and in the period up to July 1934 remained in the West Country, being stationed additionally at Penzance. There then followed a six-year spell working out of Tyseley shed but by March 1940 it had been transferred to Severn Tunnel Junction to help out with that depot's increased wartime workload. From December 1947 onwards No 4979 was allocated to Cardiff Canton but in early 1953 it moved to the London Division, being based initially at Southall before going on to Didcot, Reading and finally Oxford in July 1958. The rosters for the Halls based at Oxford were fairly complex but took them as far north as Wolverhampton, as far south

as Bournemouth, as far west as Gloucester, and up to Paddington on express and local passenger workings, while there was also a goods duty across to Pontypool Road via Worcester that kept them away from their home shed for three days. In between all this quite feverish activity, *Wootton Hall* did have less hectic moments such as when it was acting as Oxford station pilot but even this could result in a sprint down the main line when called upon to stand in for a locomotive failure. However, towards the end of 1963 there was obviously little for it to do and withdrawal followed in December.

In 1979 No 4979 was purchased privately to join the other exhibits at the Buckinghamshire Railway Centre but because terms could not be agreed between the owner and the museum it was re-sold to Woodhams without having actually left the yard! Salvation finally came in 1986 when it was sold for the second time to the 45491 Preservation Society and moved to the Fleetwood Locomotive Centre.

With many parts missing, *Wootton Hall* waits its turn for restoration at Fleetwood in September 1987. (*L. E. Taylor*)

248

180th: BR 2-10-0 No 92207

BUILT: May 1959
WITHDRAWN: December 1964

ARRIVED BARRY: March 1965
DEPARTED BARRY: October 1986

Most famous of all the Standard engines was without doubt No 92220 *Evening Star*, the very last steam locomotive to be built for BR, completed at Swindon in March 1960. While all the other 9Fs were painted plain black, No 92220 was turned out in lined passenger green livery with copper capped chimney, the name *Evening Star* having been chosen as a result of a competition among Western region staff.

No 92207 emerged from Swindon Works 'A' shop during the last week in May 1959 and entered revenue-earning service early the next month based at St Philips Marsh depot in the city of Bristol. Although allocated here primarily to help out with that shed's freight duties, within a very short time it was pressed into passenger service on a Swansea to Brockenhurst semi-fast which it took as far as Salisbury, while over the following months it was also noted passing through Wrexham with a Bristol to Blackpool excursion and a few weeks later left Paddington with the 12.05 for Plymouth! In February 1960 No 92207 was transferred to Southall and soon began appearing on fast fitted freights over the main line but once again wandered

off its normal course at the beginning of 1961 when put in charge of a Salisbury to Portsmouth parcels train which it worked through to Southampton Terminus. More usually, however, it passed most of its time at Southall on the less glamorous but vitally important heavy freight traffic from London out to a wide variety of destinations, No 92207 in particular seeming to have spent a lot of time in the Oxford area. In November 1964 it was moved down to Newport (Ebbw Junction) for the heavy iron-ore traffic dealt with there but just 4 weeks later was condemned, a mere 5½ years after having left Swindon Works.

In October 1986 No 92207 was removed from the scraplines at Barry and travelled north to its new home on the East Lancashire Railway at Bury. Purchased privately from Woodhams, the new owner of this 9F had spent 12 months working abroad to raise sufficient funds to enable him to acquire the locomotive!

No 92207 steams through Aller Junction with a Bristol to Plymouth fast goods and parcels train in 1959. (Real Photographs Co)

181st: SR 4-6-0 No 30825

BUILT: April 1927
WITHDRAWN: January 1964

ARRIVED BARRY: June 1964
DEPARTED BARRY: November 1986

The Maunsell S15s are considered to have been excellent general-purpose locomotives and with a tractive effort of almost 30,000lbs were classified 6F by British Railways. Economical and light on maintenance they gave excellent service for over 35 years and although the last members of the class were withdrawn in 1965, No 30837 was retained in store until 1966 to work an enthusiasts special.

Completed at Eastleigh Works in April 1927, No 30825 was immediately put to work on the Western section of the Southern Railway operating out of Exmouth Junction. The major part of its work comprised taking the considerable quantity of West Country heavy goods traffic up the main line to Salisbury, the Exmouth Junction-based members of the class rarely travelling all the way to London. This situation gradually changed after Nationalisation and in May 1950 No 30825 is recorded as having worked the down milk empties throughout from Waterloo to Exeter, this being the first appearance of a type other than Bulleid Pacifics on this particular working. A few months later this locomotive was also observed leaving Exeter with the Torrington portion of the Atlantic Coast Express,

this apparently being due to a shortage of suitable motive power at Exmouth Junction! In June 1951 No 30825 was transferred to Salisbury where it joined several other S15s which together handled a mixture of freight and stopping passenger services east and west of that city. On occasions it could also be seen at the head of a main line relief holiday express or, in complete contrast, shunting in some wayside station yard on a local pick-up goods but eventually No 30825's turn for withdrawal came and it was condemned at the beginning of 1964.

No 30825 is unique among the ex-Barry locomotives in that it left Woodhams in two separate parts over a five-year period. The boiler was taken to the Mid-Hants Railway in 1981 and fitted to Urie S15 No 30506 while the frames and wheels were taken to the workshops of Shipyard Services in Essex during 1986 where it is intended to fabricate a new all-welded boiler.

Pictured at Barry in 1968, another 18 years will pass before the remains of No 30825 finally leave Woodhams Yard.
(*Graham Wignall*)

250

182nd: LMS 4-6-0 No 45293

BUILT:	December 1936	ARRIVED BARRY:	January 1966
WITHDRAWN:	August 1965	DEPARTED BARRY:	December 1986

From 1947 onwards a number of Black Fives were turned out with experimental modifications and although some critics see this as an indictment of the class it was in truth a way of testing some aspect of steam locomotive design on an already proven successful engine. Modifications tried out included the fitting of roller bearings, the adoption of Caprotti valve gear and one sole example was given outside Stephenson link motion and double chimney.

Turned out by Armstrong Whitworth of Newcastle at the end of 1936, No 5293 went new to the former LNWR shed at Shrewsbury where it was chiefly employed on freight and passenger turns down to Swansea, although the 8F 2-8-0s that arrived at Shrewsbury the following year gradually took over most of the goods duties. In September 1938 this Black Five was transferred to Carnforth and there then followed an unsettled period when for varying lengths of time it also operated from the sheds at Patricroft, Mold Junction, Chester, Longsight and Shrewsbury again! However, in April 1942 it was re-allocated to Carlisle Upperby and as a contrast to its previous existence was destined to

spend the next 21 years at this one shed. Initially of course its main source of work would have been found in the vastly increased wartime traffic but following Nationalisation it settled down on more normal mixed-traffic duties and could be seen working over most of the lines that radiated from Carlisle. In 1963 the commissioning of the large marshalling yard at Kingmoor caused the transfer of all freight workings to the nearby motive power depot and accordingly in June No 45293 was moved across from Upperby. During these last years of its BR career it was recorded many times on both the Waverley route to Edinburgh and the now famous Settle and Carlisle line to Leeds, while just a few months before withdrawal it managed one final fling when working as far as Crewe with a Blackpool to Euston express.

Purchased by the British Enginemen Steam Preservation Society, No 45293 now awaits its turn for rebuilding at the North Woolwich Station Museum.

With its cab structure removed, No 45293 presents an unusual sight in the former goods yard at North Woolwich station in early 1987. (*Jim Arkell*)

183rd: LMS 2-6-0 No 42859

BUILT: March 1930
WITHDRAWN: December 1966

ARRIVED BARRY: June 1967
DEPARTED BARRY: December 1986

Turned out from both Horwich and Crewe Works between 1926 and 1932, the 245 Hughes/Fowler 2-6-0s were essentially designed for freight working although it soon became clear that they were equally suited for mixed-traffic duties despite a low boiler pressure and wheel diameter of only 5ft 6in. The class nickname of 'Crab' was earned as a result of their angled cylinders which led to a somewhat ungainly 'pincer-like' action while in motion!

LMS No 13159 was completed at Crewe in March 1930 and during the early years of its career was allocated for varying lengths of time to the sheds at Manchester (Longsight), Edge Hill, Carlisle, Crewe and Shrewsbury; while at this latter depot it is also known to have made a rare appearance on the Central Wales line with a passenger train from Shrewsbury to Swansea (Victoria). During the war years it operated from Abergavenny, Birkenhead and Longsight again before settling down at Stockport from April 1946 onwards. In the 13 years that this Mogul spent there, it mainly dealt with the local coal and mixed freight traffic but from time to time also worked out of the area with holiday excursions or other similar special

trains. In February 1959, No 42859 was transferred to Willesden and as a break from its more normal duties at this shed, was unusually recorded passing through Cambridge in October 1961 with a freight bound for Whitemoor Yard. By March of the following year it had moved on to Nuneaton but just a few months later was re-allocated for the last time to Birkenhead – the 'Crabs' here became the final representatives of the class to remain in service and one of their regular workings towards the end of steam was to head the Birkenhead–Paddington trains to and from Chester, a duty on which 42859 was frequently seen until withdrawn.

During its long stay at Barry No 42859 was reserved several times but possible firebox faults deterred would-be purchasers. Nevertheless in early 1983 it was eventually acquired privately and taken just over three years later to Hull Dairycotes for rebuilding.

Freshly outshopped from Horwich Works, No 42859 stands outside the paintshop with a group of members of the Roch Valley Railway Society in February 1962. (*R. Greenwood*)

184th: LMS 4-6-0 No 45163

BUILT: July 1935   ARRIVED BARRY: January 1966
WITHDRAWN: May 1965   DEPARTED BARRY: January 1987

The Stanier Class 5 4-6-0s combined the best of both GWR and LMS practice, proving to be a remarkable engine capable of working heavy and fast passenger trains on almost equal terms with the more powerful Royal Scots. Used over all the LMS system they remained in service right up to the very end of steam traction on British Railways in August 1968.

Armstrong Whitworth of Newcastle built more than 300 Black Fives for the LMS and No 5163 was among the first batch of these, having been completed in July 1935. An initial allocation to Crewe was quickly followed by a move north to Perth and apart from a few months on loan to Inverness in the summer of 1936 it was to remain here for the next 15 years. The arrival of the Black Fives at Perth in the 1930s soon displaced the Crab 2-6-0s and the older Highland Railway engines from most express passenger and fast goods trains over the main line, but as their true potential was realised they were used on almost every conceivable type of train over an extremely wide area. In April 1950 the renumbered No 45163 was transferred to Corkerhill where it shared that depot's duties with other Class 5 and Class 6 locomotives, particularly over the route to Stranraer, but in May 1954 it made a move to the large shed at Carlisle Kingmoor. Once again its work was most varied and could take it well away from home for many days, especially when 'borrowed' by some foreign shed such as in August 1956 when it appeared at Bristol Temple Meads with a parcels train from Derby! No 45163 was also frequently seen on excursion trains although on one of these in the summer of 1963 it failed at Gateshead and spent the rest of the week on shed there awaiting a spare part. Generally, however, it gave good service right up to withdrawal in May 1965.

Leaving Barry in January 1987 No 45163 ran into heavy snow on its road journey north to Hull and had to be abandoned in a service area on the M6. The journey eventually continued and the locomotive is now undergoing restoration in the shed at Dairycotes on behalf of a London-based record company.

After its adventurous journey north, No 45163 is pictured safely at Hull Dairycotes in February 1987. (*Jim Arkell*)

185th: GWR 2-6-2T No 5538

BUILT: July 1928
WITHDRAWN: October 1961

ARRIVED BARRY: March 1962
DEPARTED BARRY: January 1987

The 2-6-2 wheel arrangement had proved to be very popular in America but it was not until the beginning of this century that Churchward developed it for use on the GWR. In this formation the driving wheels were 'led' by a pony truck in each direction and when adopted for the 45XX series of tanks gave a locomotive capable of working chimney or bunker first with equal flexibility, together with an excellent balanced ride quality.

Completed at Swindon in the summer of 1928, No 5538 was destined to pass the first 32 years of its working life based at just three sheds in the Worcester Division, namely Cheltenham (Malvern Road), Kidderminster and Gloucester. Throughout this period it moved between all three of them at frequent intervals although on balance the majority of the time was spent at Cheltenham. Amongst its duties here were the branch trains across to Kingham, the local stopping service to Honeybourne and general mixed traffic down to Gloucester. While based at Horton Road depot in this latter city, it tended to work the same sort of trains although on occasions it would have also travelled over the Ledbury branch when the auto-train or railcar that normally worked this service was under repair. However, the 'star turn' of the 45XXs based at Horton Road was without doubt the working of the Cheltenham portions of through expresses from Paddington onwards from Gloucester, a job which gave them every opportunity to show their speed capability. By comparison with the other two sheds Kidderminster was quite small but normally had a couple of 2-6-2Ts on its books to handle local services over the Severn Valley line to Shrewsbury as well as those down to Worcester. No 5538 left the area for the first time in January 1960 when it was transferred to Truro but by June 1961 had been re-allocated to the former Cambrian shed at Machynlleth. However, within a few weeks it was moved to Shrewsbury and finally withdrawn from there in October 1961.

Within a very short time of a rescue fund being launched the necessary amount was raised and accordingly No 5538 was delivered to the Llangollen Railway in January 1987.

Obviously in need of a lot of care and attention, No 5538 bides its time at Llangollen in June 1987. (*Steve Worrall*)

186th: BR 2-6-0 No 76077

BUILT: December 1956
WITHDRAWN: December 1967

ARRIVED BARRY: September 1968
DEPARTED BARRY: May 1987

Designed at Doncaster the Standard Class 4 2-6-0s were largely developed from Ivatt's design for the LMS but with the usual BR modifications. They were simple two-cylinder machines with Walschaerts valve gear developing a tractive effort of just over 24,000lbs, and apart from the Western region were to be seen at work in most parts of the country at various times throughout their relatively short careers.

Built at Horwich in December 1956, No 76077 was among five brand-new Standard Moguls which entered traffic from Sutton Oak. This shed was situated on the line between St Helens and Widnes and although dealing mainly with freight work did have the occasional passenger turn on its books to add interest. Thus No 76077 passed the greater proportion of its time in the Liverpool and Manchester areas, frequently being seen on the line from Rainford Junction with sand trains for the Pilkington glass works at St Helens. From time to time it travelled further afield, being recorded on a Crofton to Mytholmroyd pick-up goods and a Middleton to Manvers freight on two separate occasions in 1961, while it also had a regular North

Wales-bound coal working which it would have normally taken as far as Mold Junction near Chester. In early 1964 No 76077 journeyed south to undergo a general overhaul at Eastleigh Works following which it was run-in on local passenger trains up to Waterloo before returning to more mundane duties at Sutton Oak. When the shed eventually closed in June 1967 No 76077 was transferred to Springs Branch depot in Wigan and in August of the same year hauled an LCGB brake van special on a tour of the lines in the Warrington and Widnes area prior to withdrawal in December. Following purchase by Woodhams it left Wigan during April 1968 and in convoy with three other Standard 2-6-0s made the journey down to South Wales spending four months stored in Cadoxton goods yard before entering Barry in September.

After several previous preservation attempts had failed No 76077 eventually left Woodhams in 1987, being delivered to the Gloucestershire Warwickshire Railway during May.

Although it will be many years before No 76077, seen here at Toddington in June 1987, receives attention, at least it has been saved from the cutter's torch at Barry. (*G. Tavener*)

187th: GWR 4-6-0 No 5967 *Bickmarsh Hall*

BUILT: March 1937
WITHDRAWN: June 1964

ARRIVED BARRY: July 1964
DEPARTED BARRY: August 1987

On Nationalisation the standard livery adopted for the Hall Class 4-6-0s was BR mixed-traffic lined-black, a choice which no doubt upset many a true GWR enthusiast. However, the examples painted this colour did look extremely smart (when clean) but by the summer of 1955 the decision was made to revert to lined-green.

Turned out from Swindon during March 1937, No 5967 *Bickmarsh Hall* began work for the GWR in the Wolverhampton Division, allocated to Chester, Oxley and Banbury, the longest period being spent at this latter shed where it was based almost continuously between July 1941 and January 1955. No 5967 then found itself transferred to Newton Abbot where the Halls were in great demand each summer to assist with the numerous holiday expresses and reliefs that passed through on their way to and from the popular resorts in Devon and Cornwall; when not on this work it would have been used on some of the local stopping passenger trains together with the usual parcels and freight traffic. In March 1960 *Bickmarsh Hall* was re-allocated to Westbury. There it appeared on local secondary services over the West of England main line, particularly those up to Reading, as well as on stopping trains between Newbury and Westbury, while from time to time it would also travel down to Yeovil and Weymouth. Just seven months later, No 5967 was transferred to Old Oak Common and joined several other members of the class on that depot's wide range of duties, but in July 1963 it finally returned to Westbury and worked out its last year in BR ownership from that shed. Even so, it still occasionally wandered away from there, and only one month before withdrawal it was noted leaving Woodford Halse with LMS 2-8-0 No 48396 on a southbound freight over the Great Central main line.

No 5967 *Bickmarsh Hall* was passed over many times by various preservation groups looking for a suitable locomotive but its turn eventually came in 1982 following acquisition by a private buyer. It will undergo rebuilding on the Pontypool and Blaenavon Railway at Big Pit.

Bickmarsh Hall hurries through Tilehurst station with a heavy express in September 1961. (*R. Greenwood*)

188th: GWR 2-8-0 No 3855

BUILT: October 1942
WITHDRAWN: August 1965

ARRIVED BARRY: October 1965
DEPARTED BARRY: August 1987

To meet the need for further heavy freight locomotives during the late 1930s, the Churchward 2-8-0 design was updated by C. B. Collett and an additional 83 locomotives were built between 1938 and 1942, almost doubling the previous class total. The introduction of the BR Standard Class 9F 2-10-0s eventually signalled the decline of their importance although they were only finally ousted by dieselisation in the 1960s, the last to go being No 3836 at the end of 1965.

No 3855 was one of a batch of seven 2-8-0s built at Swindon Works during October 1942 which all entered service from Southall shed. Here they were kept fully occupied dealing with the vastly increased quantity of freight brought about by wartime conditions, and this also meant that they worked to all parts of the GWR network, spending several days at a time away from their home depot. In March 1953 No 3855 was transferred to Pontypool Road and exactly five years later moved on again to Cardiff Canton. During this time in South Wales it was seen mainly on coal trains and other heavy goods duties, familiar work for this class. At the beginning of 1961 it was sent to Banbury; in

addition to taking freight over to the large Hinksey Yard at Oxford it also helped out with the numerous ironstone trains which ran between Banbury and South Wales, a duty shared with the BR Standard 2-10-0s. Perhaps the most unusual period of No 3855's career was in November 1963 when twice within the space of a week it was called upon to take over from failed diesel power on the Pines Express – on the first occasion it triumphantly entered Wolverhampton with the prototype Western diesel-hydraulic, D1000, in tow, and on the second it replaced an expired member of the same class at Wellington. In October 1964 this 2-8-0 was transferred to Oswestry but just over three months later went on to Croes Newydd, staying there until withdrawn in August 1965.

Several representatives of these Churchward and Collett locomotives survived at Barry into the 1980s and in 1982 No 3855 was acquired by the owner of No 2874 for rebuilding, a job which will be undertaken on the Pontypool and Blaenavon Railway.

No 3855 passes Pandy signal box with a South Wales-bound goods in the summer of 1956. (*Real Photographs Co*)

189th: GWR 0-6-2T No 5668

BUILT: June 1926
WITHDRAWN: September 1964

ARRIVED BARRY: November 1964
DEPARTED BARRY: August 1987

The 56XX tanks rendered faithful service throughout their long careers and although normally found in South Wales several were dispersed to other parts of the Western region following Nationalisation, particularly for general shunting duties. The class remained intact until 1962 but an intensive scrapping programme soon took a heavy toll and by 1966 the entire class had been condemned, the last two survivors being withdrawn from Croes Newydd in May.

No 5668 was released to traffic by Swindon Works in June 1926 and began working from the former Taff Vale shed at Cardiff Cathays. There then followed brief intervals at Barry, Cae Harris and Treherbert sheds before being re-allocated to Ferndale just before the outbreak of the Second World War. This was a small two-road shed on the line between Porth and Maerdy and apart from a few months on loan to Dowlais in the mid-1940s it was to remain here until July 1951 when a transfer to Treherbert took place. The 0-6-2Ts operating from here covered quite a large area and No 5668 was often seen on the passenger and goods services across to Neath and Swansea over the former

Rhondda and Swansea Bay Railway as well as on the local services down to Cardiff, a duty it shared with sister locomotives based in that latter city. From time to time it also helped out with the numerous specials that ran down to Barry Island from most parts of the system during the summer months – return excursions could be seen departing at about five-minute intervals at peak times, those from the valleys being dealt with by the 56XX tanks while the longer-distance trains were hauled by tender engines. In June 1961 No 5668 was re-allocated to Barry and after amassing a total in excess of 750,000 miles during its career was finally withdrawn in September 1964 and made the short journey to Barry Docks a few months later.

Having spent more than 60 years based in South Wales it is perhaps appropriate that No 5668 should have been taken to the Pontypool and Blaenavon Railway in Gwent for restoration to working order.

Newly arrived from Barry, No 5668 waits its turn for rebuilding at Blaenavon in October 1987. (*Deryck Lewis*)

190th: GWR 2-8-0T No 4253

BUILT: March 1917
WITHDRAWN: April 1963

ARRIVED BARRY: August 1963
DEPARTED BARRY: August 1987

In typical GWR fashion life began very cautiously for this class of 2-8-0 Tanks; the prototype was completed in 1910 and underwent meticulously analysed trials for well over a year before production proper commenced in January 1912. With a lengthy wheelbase and a necessity to traverse some relatively short radius curves during their working day in the South Wales coalfield, the coupling rods were fitted with special articulated joints that allowed a degree of both lateral and vertical movement.

No 4253 emerged from Swindon Works in March 1917 and entered traffic from Newport (Dock Street) where it was to stay for the next seven years. There then followed allocations to Pontypool Road, Newport (Ebbw and Pill), Cardiff and Llantrisant in the period up to October 1939. In that month it was transferred back to Newport (Pill) and remained at this one shed for the rest of its working life; Pill was a former Alexandra Docks Railway depot which had been extended in 1929 to make room for most of the engines sent across from the by then closed Newport (Dock Street). Despite this extension it was still a relatively small shed with a large allocation of both freight and shunting locomotives; on a Sunday when little goods activity was taking place almost the entire allocation would be on shed, standing in long lines both inside and outside waiting for Monday morning and a return to work. No 4253 was normally kept occupied on hauling the heavy coal trains between the pits, steelworks and docks, together with short-distance heavy freight east and west of Newport; very occasionally it would have travelled further afield to such locations as Caerphilly, Shrewsbury and Gloucester but limited water capacity precluded any regular long-distance runs. Generally No 4253 seems to have led an anonymous existence typical of most of the freight locomotives that worked in South Wales, with few photographs or recorded sightings appearing in the railway press prior to withdrawal in April 1963.

No 4253's purchase by Woodhams was to end this anonymity and after patiently waiting for 24 years it was eventually removed to the Pontypool and Blaenavon Railway for rebuilding.

No 4253 begins to take on a ghostly appearance as it receives a coat of primer at Blaenavon in October 1987. (*Deryck Lewis*)

191st: GWR 2-8-0 No 2874

BUILT:	November 1918	ARRIVED BARRY:	July 1963
WITHDRAWN:	May 1963	DEPARTED BARRY:	August 1987

One of Churchward's best designs was undoubtedly his heavy freight 2-8-0, 84 being built at Swindon during his term of office as Chief Mechanical Engineer of the GWR. They proved to be extremely long-lived machines and the first withdrawal did not come until 1958, with the prototype, No 2800, being cut up at Swindon during May after a working life of almost 55 years.

Assembled at Swindon Works towards the end of 1918, No 2874 was sent initially to Old Oak Common where it worked turn and turn about with the considerable number of 28XX locomotives based at South Wales sheds for the busy coal traffic between there and London. From August 1922 until the early years of Nationalisation No 2874 operated from a number of sheds in most divisions of the GWR, and these included Reading, Oxford, Leamington, Tyseley, Neath, Cardiff, Stourbridge and Banbury! In October 1955 it went to Newport (Ebbw Junction) for a few months before going on to Cardiff Canton, where the 2-8-0s were mainly employed on that depot's longer-distance freight duties to locations such as Oxley, Hackney, Saltney or Banbury. Although not to be regarded as a

normal working, it was relatively common in the hectic summer months of the late 1950s for a Canton 28XX to take a morning Cardiff to Portsmouth train as far as Salisbury and it is therefore quite likely that No 2874 made an appearance on this duty at some time. The arrival of further Class 9F 2-10-0s at Canton in early 1959 displaced No 2874 from many of its usual workings, particularly the Banbury iron-ore trains, and as a result it was transferred away to Aberdare in December of the following year. By November 1962 it had moved to its final shed at Neath, and during those last few months of service was used on the full range of freight work from heavy trains over the main line to the more humble pick-up goods.

Purchased privately from Barry in 1981, No 2874 is now ensured of a future away from its depressing scrapyard surroundings on the Pontypool and Blaenavon Railway at Big Pit in Gwent.

In need of some attention from the cleaners, No 2874 passes through Tyseley station on an up freight in August 1958. (M. Mensing)

192nd: SR 4-6-0 No 30830

BUILT:	August 1927	ARRIVED BARRY:	December 1964
WITHDRAWN:	July 1964	DEPARTED BARRY:	September 1987

Arguably the Maunsell S15 4-6-0s were particularly handsome mixed-traffic locomotives, with or without the smoke deflectors that were fitted to the class during the mid-1930s. Even in the latter stages of their careers they were regularly pressed into main line passenger service at peak holiday periods, frequently touching speeds of up to 75mph in the process.

Built at a cost of just over £10,000, SR No 830 left Eastleigh Works in August 1927 and was sent to Salisbury, the shed where it was destined to remain until withdrawal some 37 years later. The S15s here saw use in considerable numbers over the Salisbury to Exeter route in conjunction with their counterparts based at Exmouth Junction and as a whole they performed very well over the steep gradients on this line. However, No 30830 was by no means confined to this route and it also took some of the heavy freight turns up to London and down to Southampton Docks and Eastleigh yard, while every so often it is known to have worked the local goods over the Exmouth branch. Because of an ability to run fast when required it was additionally employed on the stopping and semi-fast passenger

workings from Salisbury to Basingstoke and Waterloo and in the opposite direction to Yeovil and Exeter Central. There are many recorded instances of No 30830 having worked into Western Region territory, perhaps its most common trip being up to Westbury with through freights to and from the South Coast but more unusually it was observed leaving Didcot in May 1964 with a heavy goods bound for Southampton. Right up to the time of its withdrawal in July 1964 this 4-6-0 was still handling the top-link freight duties over the SR main line and when finally retired that summer had achieved in excess of 1¼ million miles in revenue-earning service.

As the last ex-Southern engine to remain unpurchased at Barry, No 30830 was eventually acquired by the Maunsell Locomotive Society in the summer of 1987. Moved to the Bluebell Railway in September of that year it joined sister loco No 30847 which had been bought by the same society nine years previously.

No 30830 stands in Templecombe station with a ballast train in August 1963. (*Peter Cookson*)

193rd: GWR 2-8-0 No 2859

BUILT: May 1918
WITHDRAWN: December 1964

ARRIVED BARRY: March 1965
DEPARTED BARRY: October 1987

In their early years the 28XX class were principally to be seen on the important coal traffic emanating from South Wales but as time passed they began to operate regularly over a much wider area, performing more varied duties at the same time. In many ways they were typical Great Western engines – simple, hard working, well liked and with a surprising turn of speed when called upon to work the occasional parcel or passenger train.

No 2859 left Swindon Works in May 1918 and went straight into service for the London Division, staying for three years at Southall followed by another three at Old Oak Common. At the beginning of 1924 it was transferred to Swansea East Dock but was destined to become one of those locomotives that never really seemed to settle down and over the ensuing years also spent time operating from Newport (Ebbw Junction), Severn Tunnel Junction, Bristol, Reading and Cardiff. However, by November 1936 it was allocated to Bristol St Philips Marsh and remained employed on that depot's heavy freight rosters until April 1951 when it moved to Severn Tunnel Junction. From the summer of 1957 onwards No 2859 was working out of Cardiff Canton principally appearing on the long-distance freight duties dealt with there including the important iron-ore traffic to and from Banbury, but when the new Standard Class 9F 2-10-0s were allocated to Canton from 1959 onwards the 28XX locomotives found themselves virtually redundant and No 2859 was transferred in February of that year to Oxley, quickly followed by a further move to Pontypool Road in November. This 2-8-0 did earn one minor claim to fame in February 1964 when it became the last steam engine to be overhauled at Stafford Road Works, Wolverhampton but time was running out for No 2859 and after a few weeks at Cardiff East Dock it was finally condemned at Southall in December 1964, ironically the very shed where it had begun its career some 46 years earlier.

Having bought 2-6-2T No 5538 in early 1987, the Llangollen Railway went back to Barry to buy another locomotive and took possession of this 70 year old veteran in October of the same year.

With tender fully loaded, No 2859 stands ready for its next turn of duty at Gloucester Horton Road shed in August 1964.
(*Peter J. C. Skelton*)

GWR 2-8-0 No 2861

BUILT: June 1918
WITHDRAWN: March 1963

ARRIVED BARRY: November 1963
DEPARTED BARRY:

Shortly after the end of the Second World War the worsening coal supply situation in the country led to many railway companies experimenting with oil as an alternative fuel. On the GWR twelve of the 2800 class and eight of the 2884 class were converted between 1945 and 1947. Eventually problems with obtaining an adequate supply of oil led to the scheme being abandoned and the last locomotive was reconverted to coal firing at the beginning of 1950.

Turned out from Swindon Works during the summer of 1918, No 2861 commenced its career working from Pontypool Road shed in South Wales but within a very short time was transferred to the Wolverhampton Division being allocated variously to Chester, Stourbridge, Wolverhampton and Tyseley sheds in the period up to July 1928. In that month it was moved to Aberdare and while here achieved a singular distinction in being the locomotive selected by the GWR publicity department to be featured on one of their popular jigsaw puzzles entitled 'The Freight Train'! Remaining at Aberdare until December 1930 it then went back to Pontypool Road followed by additional allocations

to Severn Tunnel Junction and Neath prior to a move to the London Division at Oxford from December 1941 onwards. The wanderings of this engine were to continue after Nationalisation for in October 1948 No 2861 returned to Severn Tunnel Junction and assisted with the considerable quantity of goods traffic that passed out of South Wales to a large number of destinations throughout the Western region, in particular making several trips down the West of England main line to Newton Abbot and Plymouth. In June 1950 it was transferred again, this time to Newport (Ebbw Junction), a large shed that always maintained an allocation of these locomotives for its long-distance main line goods work but in December 1958 No 2861 was transferred for the third and last time to Severn Tunnel Junction, finally being withdrawn from there in March 1963.

Now in its seventieth year, No 2861 has a secure future as part of the collection of locomotives being assembled at the Wales Railway Centre in Cardiff.

In February 1959 No 2861 nears Acocks Green station, Birmingham with a down fitted freight. (*M. Mensing*)

GWR 2-8-0 No 2873

BUILT:	November 1918	ARRIVED BARRY:	February 1965
WITHDRAWN:	December 1964	DEPARTED BARRY:	

Being primarily freight locomotives, the Church-ward 28XX 2-8-0s were never much in the public eye, yet year after year they unobtrusively carried out their relatively unglamorous task on goods trains of sometimes quite incredible length. Only very rarely were they to be seen on passenger turns, a situation which will undoubtedly change now that so many examples have been saved for use on our private steam railways.

No 2873 was built at Swindon Works in November 1918 and commenced its career in the West Midlands based at Tyseley. By May 1927 it was working from Bristol St Philips Marsh and between then and February 1947 alternated between here, Salisbury and Swindon sheds for varying lengths of time. Bristol was an important focal point for freight traffic on the GWR with three large yards handling a remarkable range of general goods, mineral and perishable items, No 2873 travelling over a wide area with these frequently lengthy trains. At the beginning of 1947 it began a brief spell in the West Country working from both Exeter and Newton Abbot sheds but in Spring 1951 moved to South Wales with an initial allocation to

Severn Tunnel Junction. Its work here was primarily involved with the movement of coal, No 2873 regularly journeying up to London with trains of loco coal for Old Oak Common and other depots in the area. With subsequent allocations to Newport (Ebbw Junction), Cardiff Canton, Severn Tunnel Junction again and then Aberdare, No 2873 remained in South Wales until December 1962 when it was transferred to the London Division at Southall. Like most members of this class in these final years of steam traction, it could just as easily be seen on intermediate freights or even pick-up goods in addition to its more normal duties on heavy long-haul work. After a very respectable career of 46 years No 2873 was finally declared surplus to requirements in December 1964.

Sent to Barry early in 1965, No 2873 was to remain there for another 23 years while the other 28XX locomotives slowly left the yard one by one but now discussions have taken place for its own eventual purchase.

With fire iron resting against the cab side, No 2873 is prepared for its next turn of duty at Old Oak Common in the 1920s (*Real Photographs Co.*)

GWR 2-8-0 No 3845

BUILT:	April 1942	ARRIVED BARRY:	September 1964
WITHDRAWN:	June 1964	DEPARTED BARRY:	

Although the 2-8-0 'Consolidation' wheel arrangement had proved to be a success in many other countries only five of the independent British railway companies, namely the Great Western, Great Central, Great Northern, London & North Western and Somerset & Dorset used this type prior to the 1923 Grouping. However, one of the Churchward locomotives, No 2804, actually underwent trials on the North British Railway in Scotland during 1921 when it hauled a 590-ton train up the 1 in 75 Glenfarg incline.

No 3845 left Swindon Works in April 1942 and immediately took up duty from Reading, finding no shortage of work in these dark years of the Second World War. Although transferred away from Reading in September 1952 it remained based in the London Division, going to Southall and then Didcot in the period up to May 1955, keeping itself occupied on heavy coal trains as well as on fast fitted freights over the main line. Following a two-year spell at Oxley No 3845 was transferred to Cardiff Canton during 1957 where the stud of Churchward 2-8-0s worked most of that depot's longer-distance goods duties; by early 1959 the

drafting in of several brand-new Standard Class 9F 2-10-0s led to their sphere of operations being somewhat reduced, particularly on the clay ironstone workings to and from Banbury. Nevertheless No 3845 managed to hang on at Cardiff until October 1961 when it was re-allocated to Severn Tunnel Junction. This was followed by one month at Aberdare during the autumn of 1962 before a final allocation to Banbury in October of that same year. Its duties here often took it to the large Hinksey Yard at Oxford with general mixed freight, although for many months it also seems to have performed regularly on the numerous goods workings that ran between Banbury and Stoke Gifford near Bristol. Despite this, time was running out for No 3845 and it was one of many of the class withdrawn during the summer of 1964.

Although one or two fund raising schemes were instigated to save this locomotive, negotiations are finally in hand to secure a purchaser for No 3845.

Still in its original condition without side window cab, No 3845 stands on shed at Wolverhampton Oxley in the immediate post-war years. (*Real Photographs Co*)

265

GWR 2-8-0 No 3862

BUILT:	November 1942	ARRIVED BARRY:	July 1965
WITHDRAWN:	February 1965	DEPARTED BARRY:	

Following trials with locomotive No 2806 during 1906 the limit of loaded wagons that could be hauled single-handed by a member of this class was increased to no less than 100. It is said that the limit was set at 100 for reasons of safety and passing loop accommodation, not because of the locomotive's incapability; trying to stop and start loose-coupled trains of this length must have called for a high degree of skill from the crew.

Turned out from Swindon Works in November 1942, No 3862 went new to Oxford shed where it was immediately pressed into service on the vital movement of wartime goods and supplies. Remaining here until October 1947 this 2-8-0 then moved to Pontypool Road for a six-year period before going on to Plymouth (Laira) at the end of 1953. No 3862 soon settled down on the usual pattern of heavy freight duties up and down the West of England main line although, according to a comment in a leading railway magazine of the mid-1950s, it spent so much time west of Plymouth during 1956 that it would have been easier to base the locomotive at Penzance! Although freight traffic was normally No 3862's main source of employ-

ment there is at least one recorded instance of it on passenger duty when in September 1958 it worked a Penzance to Swansea train from Plymouth onwards right through to its destination. On another occasion in 1961 it headed a parcels train from Bristol into Plymouth, while it is also known to have regularly helped out with the seasonal broccoli traffic from Cornwall, taking some of these as far north as Saltney near Chester. Transferred to Cardiff Canton in July 1962 and then Cardiff East Dock just one month later, No 3862 was finally allocated to Croes Newydd in September 1963, being withdrawn from there at the beginning of 1965.

During 1987 No 3862 was purchased by the LNWR Preservation Society with the view to restoring the locomotive at a site in the London area.

Photographed here just one year after arriving at Barry, No 3862 will have to wait another 20 years before being purchased in a heavily cannibalised state for preservation. (*Murray Brown*)

GWR 2-6-2T No 4115

BUILT: October 1936
WITHDRAWN: June 1965

ARRIVED BARRY: August 1965
DEPARTED BARRY:

In the late 1920s there was a need for a locomotive that could cope with the increasingly tightly timed multi-stop GWR suburban services. The 51XX and subsequent series of large prairie tanks were Collett's response to this demand and although diesel multiple-units were to eventually oust them from this work a few survived to the very end of Great Western steam in December 1965.

No 4115 was built at Swindon Works in October 1936 and like so many other members of the class went to the Wolverhampton Division to perform on the intensive suburban passenger services in the Birmingham area, being allocated to Wolverhampton (Stafford Road) and Stourbridge in the period up to October 1939. After a brief interlude at Banbury it then returned to these services in May 1940 operating from Wellington shed, although for a few weeks in the summer of 1941 it was loaned to Crewe Gresty Lane, a GWR outpost in the heart of LMS territory. Going back to Stafford Road in May 1942 No 4115 was not only observed on the Snow Hill commuter trains as before but also had a spell on banking duty at Hatton, taking over from Saint 4-6-0 No 2933 at the end of 1952. Six months later

this 2-6-2T moved to Chester and worked the local trains between Birkenhead, Wrexham and Shrewsbury until July 1958 when it was transferred to Newton Abbot; the work here comprised banking at Dainton, local passenger services to Exeter and Taunton together with those over the Kingswear and Moretonhampstead branches. At the end of 1958 No 4115 was re-allocated to Hereford for the services to Gloucester and Cheltenham but finished its days from January 1963 onwards at Severn Tunnel Junction; apart from the exhausting banking work through the tunnel itself No 4115 also worked the Pilning to Severn Tunnel Junction car ferry train. When the Severn road bridge was opened in June 1965 this service was suspended and No 4115 withdrawn.

As the last member of the class to remain at Barry, No 4115's patience was rewarded now that it is among the group of engines being put together at the Wales Railway Centre in Cardiff.

Having a well deserved day off No 4115 rests on Severn Tunnel Junction shed in August 1964. (*D. K. Jones collection*)

GWR 2-8-0T No 5227

BUILT:	June 1924	ARRIVED BARRY:	November 1963
WITHDRAWN:	February 1963	DEPARTED BARRY:	

Having been primarily designed for short-haul freight work, these 2-8-0 Tanks rarely travelled far from their home sheds, a journey of any distance necessitating frequent stops for water and even coal. Nevertheless one member of the class did make a trip of considerable distance in 1925 when No 5225 took part in the Stockton and Darlington Centenary Exhibition at Faverdale Works, having also been lined-out in full GWR passenger livery for the occasion.

Turned out from Swindon in June 1924, No 5227 spent the early years of its career at Newport and Llantrisant but as a direct consequence of the economic recession of the early 1930s was placed in store at Swindon in January 1932. After three years of inactivity it was released from store at the beginning of 1935 and recommenced its working life with a two-year spell at Neath before settling down at Swansea East Dock from October 1936 onwards. Coal and other mineral traffic was the mainstay of No 5227's work during this period although throughout the Second World War it would have been employed on any working where its full tractive effort could be put to use. In

September 1954 No 5227 was transferred to Newport (Ebbw Junction) and carried on with its usual short-haul freight work around the area until one memorable occasion in July 1957 when it proudly steamed into Cardiff with the 11-coach 12.20pm York to Swansea, having been hastily removed from its own goods train at Llanwern to replace the failed main line engine; such duties were obviously a rarity for the locomotive but fortunately a photographer was on hand to record this possibly unique event in No 5227's life for posterity. Despite this brief moment of glory it remained on the more down to earth goods workings until finally receiving its call to the scrapyard in February 1963 after almost 40 years of faithful service.

Although it looked at one time as if this loyal service was not to be rewarded, No 5227 is now destined for display at the proposed steam centre based around Cardiff Bute Road station.

Despite its long sojourn at Barry, No 5227 seems to have survived remarkably well in this March 1986 view. (*Deryck Lewis*)

GWR 2-6-2T No 5539

BUILT:	July 1928	ARRIVED BARRY:	September 1962
WITHDRAWN:	April 1962	DEPARTED BARRY:	

The 45XXs were primarily designed for branch line use and, at the time of their inception, provided a good modern machine capable of all the duties likely to be met on these and other secondary routes. The increased water capacity of the later 4575 series widened their sphere of operation while a tractive effort of 21,250lbs meant they were often employed on goods as well as passenger workings.

No 5539 was built at Swindon in July 1928 and sent new to Cheltenham (Malvern Road) where it regularly worked to the Kingham and Gloucester areas, staying for 5 months on loan to Horton Road depot in that latter city. During September 1931 it was transferred to the Neath Division and working variously from Neyland, Whitland and Pembroke Dock sheds passed most of its days on local services in this part of Wales including those over the branch up to Cardigan. At the beginning of 1938 No 5539 was transferred to Bristol Bath Road, spending a large proportion of its time here out-stationed at the sub-shed at Yatton for duty over the line to Cheddar and Witham as well as over the Clevedon branch. Other work included the services from Bristol to Radstock and Frome while just

occasionally it would also be seen at Bath, Avonmouth and Portishead. In June 1953 it was transferred to Newton Abbot and although there were several others of the class based here it stood out from the rest in still wearing GWR livery complete with 1930s style monogram! During the spring of 1955 No 5539 moved back to South Wales, operating from both Pontypool Road and Aberbeeg sheds on local freight duties together with a certain amount of pilot and banking work but in February 1958 it was re-allocated for the last time to St Blazey in Cornwall and worked out its final years on the Par to Newquay and Bodmin Road to Wadebridge branches.

Dispatched to Barry during September 1962 No 5539 has had to wait a long time for rescue but fortunately is now intended to be one of the exhibits at the embryonic Wales Railway Centre in Cardiff.

No 5539 gets ready to leave Moretonhampstead with the branch train for Newton Abbot in 1954. (*C. Whetmath collection*)

GWR 2-6-2T No 5553

BUILT: November 1928
WITHDRAWN: November 1961

ARRIVED BARRY: March 1962
DEPARTED BARRY:

This well-proportioned class of small prairie tanks must have been a familiar sight to the thousands of holidaymakers who visited Cornwall and South Devon each year. They had a virtual monopoly of the Great Western branch services within these two counties and looked very much at home at the head of a two- or three-coach train wending its often leisurely way through attractive countryside to the branch terminus.

Leaving Swindon Works in November 1928, No 5553 commenced working from Bristol Bath Road, a shed which always kept a large number of these locomotives for its branch and local passenger duties. Although having a three-year break at Westbury, No 5553 remained at Bath Road until January 1935 when it was transferred to Swindon, most of its time there being spent on the local services over the former M & SWJR line down to Savernake and Andover, and for many months it was outstationed at the small timber shed in that latter town. By September 1937 it had returned to Bristol and for the next 20 years worked a variety of services around the area, notably those between Yatton, Wells and Witham. On other occasions it is

known to have worked stopping passenger trains down the main line to Swindon as well as on less energetic duties such as station pilot at Temple Meads. Leaving Bristol in December 1958, No 5553 was sent to Machynlleth and saw frequent use on the Cambrian services to Barmouth and Pwllheli right up to the time of its transferral to St Blazey during November 1960. Its main source of work here was on the branch trains between Bodmin, Wadebridge and Padstow, although for a few months in late summer 1961 it was also based at Moorswater sub-shed on the Liskeard and Looe line prior to dieselisation of the branch services in September. No 5553 itself did not last much longer, being condemned in November 1961.

With Woodham's yard having brought the town of Barry to the attention of many thousands of people, it is perhaps appropriate that in November 1987 Dai Woodham donated this locomotive to the Barry Development Partnership for eventual display at a suitable location in the town itself.

No 5553 hurries through the Cornish countryside with a Wadebridge to Bodmin train in May 1961. (*Peter Cookson*)

GWR 0-6-2T No 6686

BUILT:	October 1928	ARRIVED BARRY:	August 1964
WITHDRAWN:	April 1964	DEPARTED BARRY:	

The most distinctive feature of Collett's design for the 56XX class was the extreme overhang of the smokebox in relation to the frame, so much so that the smokebox door was in line with the front buffer beam. It generally incorporated all the normal GWR fitments while in addition the forward parts of the side tanks were inclined forwards to enhance driver visibility, a feature which subsequently became popular on other tank locomotive designs of the GWR and LMS.

No 6686 was turned out from Armstrong Whitworth's works in Newcastle during October 1928 and shortly after made the long journey down from the North East to begin work from Landore depot in Swansea. After just over three years here it moved to the former Rhondda and Swansea Bay Railway shed at Danygraig for a few months before going on to Port Talbot (Duffryn Yard) in the summer of 1932. No 6686 remained at this shed for no less than 32 years during which it seems to have spent a lot of its time in the Maesteg area with coal trains bound for the docks, although it also made longer-distance forays along the main line as far as Cardiff, Newport and Severn Tunnel Junction with

mineral and other general freight traffic. Following Nationalisation No 6686 continued on very much the same sort of work and was also occasionally used on excursion trains, one such known working being in June 1962 when, double-headed with sister locomotive No 5604, it hauled a ten-coach special from Seven Sisters on the Neath and Brecon line through to Porthcawl, a popular destination for these trains. After this long stay at Duffryn Yard No 6686 was transferred to Merthyr at the beginning of 1964 but was withdrawn from there in April and then stood for a further four months dumped outside the shed before making a final journey down the valleys to Barry during August.

Having spent its entire life, both active and dormant, in South Wales it is very apt that No 6686 will one day be on show at the Cardiff based Wales Railway Centre.

There can be few parts left to remove from No 6686 as it stands among piles of cut rail at Woodhams in August 1987.
(*Deryck Lewis*)

WR 4-6-0 No 7927 *Willington Hall*

BUILT: October 1950
WITHDRAWN: December 1965

ARRIVED BARRY: February 1966
DEPARTED BARRY:

Hawksworth's Modified Halls were built with plate frames throughout and this overcame the weakness contained in the original Churchward design of having a bar frame extension in front of the combined cylinder and smokebox saddle to hold the buffer beam in place. 71 of these modified locomotives were built from 1944 onwards and they could be distinguished from the earlier design by their longer outside steampipes and plate frame at the front of the leading bogie.

No 7927 *Willington Hall* was among the very final batch of Halls to be constructed at Swindon Works, emerging from there in October 1950. Its first allocation was to Reading and the duties here mainly covered the stopping and semi-fast services up to Paddington and in the opposite direction to Didcot and Oxford. Other work included the North to South expresses that passed through Reading, No 7927 frequently appearing on the Margate to Birkenhead through train which it took as far as Chester. In common with other members of this successful mixed-traffic class *Willington Hall* was also kept busy on fitted freight duties over a remarkably wide area but could just as easily pass the

day in relative comfort while acting as Reading station pilot. In September 1958 No 7927 was transferred to Old Oak Common but following overhaul at Swindon Works almost exactly two years later was re-allocated to Cardiff Canton to assist with the varied rosters that the Halls dealt with there. Just prior to Canton's closure to steam power in September 1962 it was moved across to Cardiff East Dock which, after having lain abandoned and derelict for over four years, was specially reopened and refurbished to take the displaced Canton allocation. Remaining there until August 1965 *Willington Hall* then spent relatively short periods at Newport (Ebbw Junction) and Oxford sheds before succumbing to the inevitable and receiving its call to the scrapyard during December 1965.

With five years allocated to sheds in the Cardiff area No 7927 should feel at home when eventually exhibited to the public at the steam centre being established around the former Taff Vale Railway Bute Road station in Cardiff.

Willington Hall pulls away from Leamington Spa with an up freight in September 1956. (*M. Mensing*)

SR 4-6-2 No 34046 *Braunton*

BUILT: November 1946
WITHDRAWN: October 1965

ARRIVED BARRY: January 1966
DEPARTED BARRY:

In May 1957 the first rebuilt West Country took to the tracks minus its air smoothed casing and with Walschaerts valve gear in place of Bulleid's controversial chain-driven gear enclosed in an oil bath. A total of 75 were scheduled for reconstruction but, because of the short life expectancy of steam traction, this was later reduced to 60, the last being so treated during May 1961.

Completed at Brighton Works in November 1946, No 21C146 *Braunton* went initially to Exmouth Junction where its light axle-loading helped it to relieve the hard-working 2-6-0s on the lines west of Exeter although it was also employed on that shed's wide range of other main line duties. In June 1951 it was transferred to Brighton principally to work the through trains from there to the west, the 200 mile run to Plymouth being one of the longest continuous locomotive workings on the Southern region. *Braunton*'s turn for rebuilding came in February 1959 and on completion it returned to service from Bournemouth shed where it spent a good deal of its time travelling up and down the main line to London or over the Somerset and Dorset route to Bath with summer season

holiday expresses. However, throughout its life No 34046 earned a reputation for making regular appearances on special traffic, particularly on football excursions to Wembley. Other notable trips included one from Bournemouth right through to Walthamstow and one from Southampton to Birmingham Snow Hill via Oxford, Worcester and Kidderminster, but the proudest moment of all came in April 1959 when it hauled the Royal Train conveying the Queen and Prince of Wales on part of its journey back to London between Weymouth and Southampton. These special workings were obviously interspersed between the more normal revenue-earning trains up to Waterloo on which *Braunton* remained until withdrawn from Bournemouth in October 1965.

Heavily stripped of parts at Barry by owners of other Bullied Pacifics No 34046's restoration may prove to be a lengthy and expensive operation at the Brighton Locomotive Works, Preston Park.

As the last West Country to remain in Woodham's yard, *Braunton* presented a sorry sight for all Southern fans at Barry in July 1987. (*Deryck Lewis*)

SR 4-6-2 No 34073 *249 Squadron*

BUILT:	May 1948	ARRIVED BARRY:	April 1965
WITHDRAWN:	June 1964	DEPARTED BARRY:	

The Bulleid light Pacifics were capable of quite prodigious feats of haulage considering their overall size and tractive effort, a very high power-to-weight ratio helping in this respect. However, this did cause adhesion problems and it needed an understanding crew to appreciate the potential strength of their charge to avoid monumental bouts of slipping when starting off.

Having left Brighton Works in May 1948, *249 Squadron* was put to work initially from Ramsgate but within a few weeks had been re-allocated to Stewarts Lane, Battersea. Once again the stay here was to be brief for by mid-1949 No 34073 had moved to Dover to help out with the important Continental trains and other services to the coast, included among the latter being the Man of Kent business express from Charing Cross to Margate. As a break from this routine it was selected to take part in a series of haulage trials in March 1952 between Dover and Chislehurst to compare the performance of Battle of Britain, Merchant Navy and Britannia class Pacifics, while several times in the mid-1950s it also worked football specials through to Wembley before carrying on to Neasden shed for

servicing. However, completion of the Kent Coast electrification in 1961 meant there was little for *249 Squadron* to do at Dover and consequently it was sent across London to Nine Elms in May of that year. Although by this date there were plenty of rebuilt light Pacifics available, the unmodified engines were still employed on top-link work and No 34073 regularly assisted with the express workings over the Waterloo – Southampton – Weymouth route including, of course, the well-known Bournemouth Belle. In December 1963 it was transferred to Eastleigh and following withdrawal just over 6 months later was eventually towed down to Barry during April 1965 in a sad convoy of four other Bulleid Pacifics.

As the last Battle of Britain at Barry, *249 Squadron*'s condition had deteriorated somewhat over the two decades since it last turned a wheel in revenue earning service. Rebuilding will take place at the Brighton Locomotive Works.

A credit to the shed cleaners, No 34073 climbs out of Weymouth, near Radipole Halt, with a London-bound train in July 1962. (*C. L. Caddy collection*)

SR 4-6-2 No 35009 *Shaw Savill*

BUILT:	June 1942	ARRIVED BARRY:	December 1964
WITHDRAWN:	September 1964	DEPARTED BARRY:	

The final few years of steam on BR saw a profusion of enthusiasts' rail tours and the rebuilt Merchant Navies played their part in these sometimes interesting workings, which took them further afield than otherwise would have been the case. As a result representatives of the class travelled over the Settle & Carlisle, the Somerset & Dorset (despite being officially barred from this route) and also turned up at such unlikely places as Newcastle, Swindon and Nottingham (Victoria).

Completed at Eastleigh Works in June 1942, SR No 21C9 *Shaw Savill* began its career at Salisbury and like other early members of the class spent the first year or so on freight work while efforts were made to eradicate their initial teething problems. However, it soon began performing on the express passenger services east and west of that city, along with goods trains over the main line, in particular the 11.50pm Nine Elms to Exeter partly-fitted freight. This pattern of work at Salisbury continued throughout the 1950s until the renumbered 35009 entered the workshops at Eastleigh for rebuilding in March 1957. When completed it was re-allocated to Exmouth Junction and the first regular diagram

given to this locomotive saw it working up to Waterloo with the Atlantic Coast Express and then returning with an evening fast train for Exeter. *Shaw Savill* became a familiar sight on the ACE for most of the time that it was working from Exmouth Junction, although as a fill-in turn between these important express duties it was also commonly seen on some of the all-stations stopping services to Yeovil and Salisbury, super power indeed for such relatively lightweight trains! After a working life of 22 years, during which time it travelled some 1,127,452 miles (virtually all of which were over the West of England mainline), No 35009 was condemned in September 1964 and spent a few months in store at Exmouth Junction before being consigned to Woodhams.

Purchased in July 1982 *Shaw Savill* remained at Barry for many years waiting its turn to go to the Preston Park base of the Brighton Locomotive Works Association.

Shaw Savill pauses at Templecombe with an up express in the early 1960s. (*Andrew C. Ingram collection*)

SR 4-6-2 No 35011 *General Steam Navigation*

BUILT: December 1944
WITHDRAWN: February 1966

ARRIVED BARRY: June 1966
DEPARTED BARRY:

In the early years of Nationalisation BR decided to adopt standard colours for their rolling stock and as a result the top-link passenger locomotives, including the Merchant Navies, were painted a blue livery with black and white lining-out. Apparently this did not wear too well in service and the engines concerned were repainted in Brunswick Green as they passed through works, a colour which suited the strong lines of the rebuilt Bulleid Pacifics.

General Steam Navigation went to its first shed at Nine Elms in December 1944 and took up work on the Waterloo to Salisbury and Waterloo to Bournemouth services, often being seen on the named expresses that traversed these routes. By early 1950 through workings from London to Exeter were instituted, replacing the former practice of changing engines at Salisbury on all trains and No 35011 was soon rostered to these long-distance Nine Elms duties. In February 1954 it was transferred to Bournemouth and regularly appeared on the Royal Wessex and the 11.30am Weymouth to Waterloo, both these trains being too heavy for Bournemouth's light Pacifics to deal with on their own, but following the wholesale rediagramming of loco-

motive workings in May 1954 *General Steam Navigation* returned to Nine Elms. Three years later it was transferred again, this time to Exmouth Junction and in the summer of 1959 entered Eastleigh Works for rebuilding; on completion it resumed work from Exmouth Junction for a few months before going back to Bournemouth at the beginning of 1960. In these latter years of its career No 35011 continued to handle the Southern region main line services but did occasionally wander off normal territory for the class; in April 1964 it worked an excursion from Bournemouth through to Stratford-upon-Avon via Oxford and Honeybourne while just one month before withdrawal in February 1966 it headed an enthusiasts special over part of the Somerset and Dorset, despite the class being officially banned from this line!

Following its enforced absence in South Wales, No 35011 will undergo rebuilding back on Southern territory at the Brighton Locomotive Works, Preston Park.

Having received some attention from the cleaners, No 35011 is prepared for its next duty on Bournemouth shed in July 1964. (*Peter J. C. Skelton*)

276

LMS 4-6-0 No 44901

BUILT:	October 1945	ARRIVED BARRY:	January 1966
WITHDRAWN:	August 1965	DEPARTED BARRY:	

Withdrawal of the Stanier Black Fives did not begin until 1962 and, despite heavy inroads that were made into the class during the following years, around 150 were still at work in 1968, the last year of BR steam. Fortunately 18 examples survive in preservation and no doubt will give reliable and faithful service to their new owners, many of them having also been given names.

Completed at Crewe Works in October 1945, LMS No 4901 was destined to spend its entire career based at Kingmoor depot in Carlisle. Being just one Black Five among many at this shed it could have potentially led an anonymous existence but fortunately the activities of this particular locomotive have been well recorded and give an insight into the 'common user' policy often adopted with these 4-6-0s. Apart from its expected duties on passenger and freight trains up and down the West Coast main line, No 44901 also had regular work which took it to the West Riding of Yorkshire over the Settle and Carlisle route. Excursion traffic also featured prominently among its work and several trips were made to Morecambe and Blackpool on these sometimes heavy trains, while in May 1954

both it and No 44900 were turned out in pristine ex-works condition to head the Royal Train northwards from Carlisle. From time to time No 44901 was borrowed by other sheds to cover for a shortage of motive power – in March 1954 Holbeck used it on a diagram covering a Leeds City to Scarborough local and return via York while in October 1957 St Rollox appropriated it for a Glasgow to Kircaldy passenger working. Obviously being so close to the border it also made regular visits to Scotland appearing many times in Glasgow, Stranraer and Edinburgh, the latter city being reached via the now closed Waverley route. After a working life of just 20 years No 44901 was finally sold as scrap in August 1965.

Although having spent all its working life in the North of England and Scotland it is intended that No 44901 will go on display at the Wales Railway Centre to represent those other Stanier Black Fives that used to work into Wales during steam days.

What a sad demise for a locomotive that once hauled the Royal Train. No 44901 stands at Barry in October 1987. (*Deryck Lewis*)

LMS 2-8-0 No 48173

BUILT: June 1943
WITHDRAWN: July 1965

ARRIVED BARRY: October 1965
DEPARTED BARRY:

This excellent 2-8-0 design by Stanier formed the heavy freight equivalent of his earlier Black Five locomotives. Construction began in 1935 and continued right through to 1946 by which time around 850 engines were operating both at home and overseas, many of the latter giving excellent service in such diverse locations as Egypt, Palestine, Iraq, Persia and Turkey.

Costing £6,793 to build at Crewe Works in June 1943, LMS No 8173 entered traffic from Willesden shed and was principally kept employed on heavy goods work up to Toton together with interregional transfer freights via the West London line. In February 1948 it was re-allocated to Newton Heath in Manchester but during December of the following year moved to Rugby, receiving its BR number 48173 a few months later. Rugby shed had a wide range of duties apart from those up and down the West Coast main line and these took No 48173 across to Market Harborough, Northampton, Wellingborough and into the Eastern region via Peterborough, while there were several three or four day rosters that saw it travelling to Chester and Birkenhead with through freights and mineral

workings. Obviously such a prolific class as the Stanier 8Fs could be found on all manner of duties and in June 1957 No 48173 was unusually observed shunting in Dunstable goods yard prior to working back to Leighton Buzzard with a local freight, a job that was normally the preserve of the ex-LNWR 0-8-0s. Occasionally it would penetrate into Western region territory via Bletchley but in May 1963, after having worked a Banbury to Hinksey (Oxford) goods, it was sent light engine to Basingstoke to head the following morning's Basingstoke to Oxley sidings freight. In January 1965 No 48173 was transferred to Mold Junction (Chester) but this was to prove a brief move for withdrawal came just seven months later.

Ignored for many years by those groups and individuals seeking to own a Barry locomotive, No 48173 is now safe following its purchase in December 1987 by a group of Avon Valley Railway members.

Looking rather the worse for wear after its 22 years in South Wales, No 48173 waits its turn for rescue in July 1987. (*Deryck Lewis*)

LMS 2-8-0 No 48518

BUILT:	August 1944	ARRIVED BARRY:	October 1965
WITHDRAWN:	July 1965	DEPARTED BARRY:	

Just as the Black Fives dominated mixed-traffic services so the Stanier 8F 2-8-0s dominated heavy freight work on the LMS system, their light axle-loading of only 16 tons giving them a very wide route availability. Appropriately perhaps, both these fine designs remained in service right to the very end of steam on British Railways in August 1968.

Built to Railway Executive Committee order at Doncaster Works towards the end of August 1944, LMS No 8518 was retained by the LNER to carry out work from Heaton shed near Newcastle where it was used on the long-distance mineral and general freight turns up to Edinburgh and sometimes in the opposite direction to York, Hull or Leeds. In April 1947 it was handed back to the LMS and took up work from Wakefield shed, although according to this 8F's Engine Record Card, it seems to have spent more than a third of its time here stored out of use before being transferred to Swansea in February 1948 for duty over the Central Wales line to Shrewsbury. There then followed brief periods at Bescot and Newton Heath prior to its allocation to Willesden at the end of 1950; here No 48518

worked extensively over the Western Division, principally to Toton and Colwick as well as on the heavy cross-London freight traffic. Just occasionally it would appear at Euston on empty coaching stock duties, normally removing the heavy over-night sleeper trains from the terminus up the steeply graded Camden Bank to the carriage sidings for servicing. In November 1964 No 48518 was transferred to Croes Newydd, Wrexham, where it replaced the ex-GWR 28XX 2-8-0s on the Brymbo branch and on heavy freights to the West Midlands but within three months it had returned to Willesden, remaining there until condemned in the summer of 1965.

Although the collection of locomotives being assembled at the Wales Railway Centre are primarily of GWR origin, No 48518 can serve a dual purpose in representing not only the LMS but also the LNER who actually built it more than 40 years ago!

With chimney sheeted over as a token gesture, No 48518 waits for a potential buyer at Barry in the mid-1970s. (*Steve Worrall*)

279

BR 2-6-4T No 80072

BUILT: November 1953
WITHDRAWN: July 1965

ARRIVED BARRY: January 1966
DEPARTED BARRY:

Of the 15 Standard Class 4 2-6-4 Tanks now preserved only one, No 80002, was purchased direct from British Railways; the remainder have all been acquired from Barry, illustrating the importance of this scrapyard to the preservation movement.

No 80072 was completed at Brighton Works in November 1953 and following a week of running-in turns around the Brighton area travelled up to Plaistow to begin work on the intensive suburban commuter services out of Fenchurch Street over the former London Tilbury and Southend lines. Following the closure of Plaistow shed it moved down to Tilbury and continued on these workings until their electrification in June 1962. After a short period in store at Old Oak Common it was allocated to Swansea East Dock for use on the Central Wales line passenger services from Swansea Victoria up to Shrewsbury. In September 1963 No 80072 was transferred again this time to Leamington Spa, becoming the only Standard 2-6-4T ever to be based there; fortunately during this period its duties were well documented and initially included the morning shunt at Warwick Milverton followed by parcels trains to Stratford, Nuneaton or Birmingham. Before dieselisation of the service in September 1964 it also had a regular working, shared with GWR 2-6-0 No 6364, on the 17.38 10-coach Birmingham Snow Hill to Lapworth local. Freight work included a car transporter train from Knowle to Banbury marshalling yards and, more surprisingly perhaps, working back from Banbury with a heavy iron-ore train. Although having been sent to Crewe Works for overhaul in October 1964 No 80072 mysteriously spent five months stored out of use there before eventually having the repair work carried out and returning to work from Leamington. When this shed was closed in June 1965 it was re-allocated for the last time to Tyseley but they apparently had very little for it to do and withdrawal came early the next month.

Despite the rather forlorn appearance presented during its latter years at Barry, No 80072 can be considered secure now that discussions have taken place regarding its future home in preservation.

With the cab roof removed at some time during its stay in South Wales, No 80072 gives a new meaning to air conditioning at Barry in the 1970s. (*Steve Worrall*)

BR 2-6-4T No 80150

BUILT:	December 1956	ARRIVED BARRY:	January 1966
WITHDRAWN:	October 1965	DEPARTED BARRY:	

Throughout their careers the Standard 2-6-4Ts were always being made redundant by electrification or quite simply closure of the lines over which they worked. Nevertheless they were considered too good a locomotive to waste and often found themselves newly employed on long-distance cross-country routes far from their normal sphere of operation, such as the Somerset and Dorset and the Central Wales line.

On completion at Brighton Works in December 1956, No 80150 took up duty from the running shed at Brighton and was soon observed on the local services up to Tonbridge together with those to Horsham. Although the Bulleid Pacifics and Schools at Brighton dealt with the more prestigious turns these 2-6-4Ts did sterling work as well and were regularly used on middle-distance passenger workings, particularly those up to Victoria via Lewes and Eridge. Obviously such versatile locomotives could be seen on almost any sort of duty and No 80150 was also recorded on stopping trains between Redhill and Ashford, while every Christmas it seems to have been a constant choice on the busy parcels traffic both up to London and along

the coast to Eastbourne and Hastings. In August 1963 No 80150 was transferred to Eastleigh and continued its mixed-traffic duties around the Southampton area, which on one occasion included taking over from a failed diesel on the Cardiff to Portsmouth through train. By the spring of 1965 No 80150 appeared to have found a regular turn on the one-coach shuttle service between Bournemouth West and Bournemouth Central, the carriage being attached at that latter station to a London-bound train. Withdrawn in October 1965 this 2-6-4T did not manage to survive long enough to be among those members of the class that lasted to the very end of Southern Region steam in July 1967.

Compared with its sister locomotives that did survive until the end of SR steam, No 80150 has in the end been much more fortunate since it is intended to include this engine among the exhibits at the Wales Railway Centre in Cardiff.

No 80150 coasts into Redhill with a train from Tonbridge in August 1963. (*Andrew C. Ingram collection*)

281

BR 2-10-0 No 92245

BUILT: November 1958
WITHDRAWN: December 1964

ARRIVED BARRY: March 1965
DEPARTED BARRY:

The Standard Class 9 2-10-0s were distributed evenly throughout the Eastern, London Midland and Western regions with just a few on the Southern and none at all based in Scotland. However, to find a clean member of the class was extremely difficult, most of their working lives having been spent in the era when shed cleaners were scarce and little attention given to this seemingly unimportant aspect.

Turned out from Crewe in November 1958, No 92245 was among the last half dozen steam locomotives ever to be built at these famous Works before they were turned over completely to the construction of diesels. Entering traffic from Old Oak Common, No 92245 soon took charge of the fast-fitted freights from London up to Banbury and over the West of England main line to Plymouth, making several appearances on the important milk traffic which ran between the West Country and London. In October 1960 it was sent to Cardiff Canton to deal with that shed's more onerous freight rosters which up to that time had been the preserve of Churchward and WD 2-8-0s, particularly the heavy iron-ore traffic to and from Banbury.

In June 1962 No 92245 was transferred to Bath Green Park to help out with the summer services over the Somerset and Dorset line, and in company with several other 9Fs was employed on the through trains between Bournemouth and destinations in the Midlands and the North, regularly hauling these heavy trains single-handed over the notorious Mendip gradients. At the end of the 1962 summer season it was re-allocated to Oxford for just over one month before making a final move to Southall during October 1962. Working alongside the gradually diminishing number of 28XX 2-8-0s also based here, it was kept busy on the usual heavy freight duties up to the time of its premature withdrawal at the end of 1964.

Always considered to be impressive looking locomotives, 9F No 92245 is sure to be popular with the public when eventually put on display at the Wales Railway Centre.

The cabside number of No 92245 is hardly discernible through the grime as it waits its next turn of duty in Southall shed yard, April 1964. (*P. H. Groom*)

APPENDIX

Giving the order of departure of each locomotive from Barry together with its location and length of time spent in the yard.

Locomotive Number	Order of departure from Barry	Total time spent in scrapyard	Location
2807	130	17 years 7 months	Birmingham Railway Museum, Tyseley
2857	69	11 years 11 months	Severn Valley Railway, Shropshire
2859	193	22 years 7 months	Llangollen Railway, Clwyd
2861	200	24 years 3 months	Wales Railway Centre, Cardiff
2873	205	23 years 1 month	Birmingham Railway Museum, Tyseley
2874	191	24 years 1 month	Pontypool and Blaenavon Railway, Gwent
2885	123	17 years	Southall Railway Centre, West London
3612	98	13 years 9 months	Severn Valley Railway, Shropshire
3738	49	8 years 6 months	Didcot Railway Centre, Oxfordshire
3802	154	18 years 11 months	Plym Valley Railway, Devon
3803	149	20 years	Birmingham Railway Museum, Tyseley
3814	176	21 years 5 months	North Yorkshire Moors Railway
3822	80	11 years 10 months	Didcot Railway Centre, Oxfordshire
3845	212	25 years 2 months	Brighton Locomotive Works
3850	151	18 years 5 months	West Somerset Railway
3855	188	21 years 10 months	Pontypool and Blaenavon Railway, Gwent
3862	211	23 years 9 months	Northampton Steam Railway
4110	100	13 years 9 months	Southall Railway Centre, West London
4115	203	22 years 7 months	Wales Railway Centre, Cardiff
4121	120	15 years 6 months	Swindon Heritage Centre
4141	28	9 years 2 months	Swindon Heritage Centre
4144	50	8 years 8 months	Didcot Railway Centre, Oxfordshire
4150	57	8 years 9 months	Severn Valley Railway, Shropshire
4160	60	9 years	Plym Valley Railway, Devon
4247	161	20 years 8 months	Cholsey and Wallingford Railway, Oxfordshire
4248	172	22 years 6 months	Shipyard Services Ltd, Brightlingsea, Essex
4253	190	24 years	Pontypool and Blaenavon Railway, Gwent
4270	167	21 years 11 months	Swansea Vale Railway, West Glamorgan
4277	173	21 years 10 months	Gloucestershire Warwickshire Railway
4561	71	13 years	West Somerset Railway
4566	8	7 years 11 months	Severn Valley Railway, Shropshire
4588	11	7 years 11 months	Buckfastleigh and Totnes Steam Railway, Devon
4612	119	15 years 3 months	Swindon Heritage Centre (with boiler from 5775 ex L89)
4920	82	10 years 4 months	Buckfastleigh and Totnes Steam Railway, Devon
4930	29	8 years 8 months	Severn Valley Railway, Shropshire
4936	126	16 years 11 months	Gloucestershire Warwickshire Railway (see text)
4942	51	9 years 10 months	Didcot Railway Centre, Oxfordshire
4953	150	20 years 3 months	Dean Forest Railway, Gloucestershire

Locomotive Number	Order of departure from Barry	Total time spent in scrapyard	Location
4979	179	22 years 4 months	Fleetwood Locomotive Centre, Lancashire
4983	10	6 years 4 months	Birmingham Railway Museum, Tyseley
5029	81	12 years	Didcot Railway Centre, Oxfordshire
5043	43	9 years 2 months	Birmingham Railway Museum, Tyseley
5051	4	6 years 4 months	Didcot Railway Centre, Oxfordshire
5080	62	10 years 10 months	Birmingham Railway Museum, Tyseley
5164	30	9 years 2 months	Severn Valley Railway, Shropshire
5193	103	16 years 11 months	Steamport Transport Museum, Southport
5199	165	21 years 8 months	Llangollen Railway, Clwyd
5224	96	15 years 2 months	Great Central Railway, Leicestershire
5227	194	24 years 3 months	Wales Railway Centre, Cardiff
5239	42	9 years 7 months	Paignton and Dartmouth Steam Railway, Devon
5322	3	4 years 4 months	Didcot Railway Centre, Oxfordshire
5521	72	13 years	Dean Forest Railway, Gloucestershire
5526	166	22 years 8 months	Swindon Heritage Centre
5532	124	18 years 4 months	Llangollen Railway, Clwyd
5538	185	24 years 10 months	Dean Forest Railway, Gloucestershire
5539	204	25 years 5 months	Wales Railway Centre, Cardiff
5541	25	9 years 11 months	Dean Forest Railway, Gloucestershire
5542	73	13 years 6 months	Private premises in Taunton
5552	174	25 years 1 month	Bodmin and Wenford Railway, Cornwall
5553	213	27 years 8 months	Barry
5572	15	8 years 11 months	Didcot Railway Centre, Oxfordshire
5619	40	8 years 8 months	Telford Horsehay Steam Trust, Shropshire
5637	61	9 years 11 months	Swindon and Cricklade Railway, Wiltshire
5643	16	7 years 10 months	Steamtown Railway, Leisure Centre, Carnforth, Lancashire
5668	189	22 years 9 months	Pontypool and Blaenavon Railway, Gwent
5900	14	7 years	Didcot Railway Centre, Oxfordshire
5952	136	16 years 10 months	Llangollen Railway, Clwyd
5967	187	23 years 1 month	Pontypool and Blaenavon Railway, Gwent
5972	125	17 years	Private Premises in Wakefield, Yorkshire
6023	159	22 years	Bristol Temple Meads Station
6024	36	10 years 3 months	Buckinghamshire Railway Centre
6619	64	10 years 11 months	North Yorkshire Moors Railway
6634	131	16 years 10 months	East Somerset Railway
6686	197	23 years 6 months	Wales Railway Centre, Cardiff
6695	99	14 years 8 months	Swanage Railway, Dorset
6960	26	8 years 3 months	Severn Valley Railway, Shropshire
6984	178	20 years 8 months	Private Premises in Bicester, Oxfordshire
6989	88	13 years 5 months	Buckinghamshire Railway Centre
6990	76	9 years 9 months	Great Central Railway, Leicestershire
7027	23	8 years 3 months	Buckfast Steam Railway, Buckfastleigh, Devon
7200	137	18 years	Buckinghamshire Railway Centre
7202	52	9 years 9 months	Didcot Railway Centre, Oxfordshire
7229	156	19 years 11 months	Plym Valley Railway, Devon

Locomotive Number	Order of departure from Barry	Total time spent in scrapyard	Location
7802	109	13 years 4 months	Severn Valley Railway, Shropshire
7812	56	8 years	Severn Valley Railway, Shropshire
7819	31	6 years 8 months	Severn Valley Railway, Shropshire
7820	104	13 years 4 months	West Somerset Railway
7821	132	15 years 1 month	Llangollen Railway, Clwyd
7822	65	8 years 8 months	Llangollen Railway, Clwyd
7827	5	4 years 1 month	Paignton and Dartmouth Steam Railway, Devon
7828	133	15 years 1 month	Llangollen Railway, Clwyd
7903	129	16 years 10 months	Swindon and Cricklade Railway, Wiltshire
7927	201	22 years	Wales Railway Centre, Cardiff
9303	70	10 years 9 months	Severn Valley Railway, Shropshire
9466	74	10 years 10 months	Buckinghamshire Railway Centre
9629	128	16 years 2 months	Holiday Inn, Cardiff
9681	75	10 years 2 months	Dean Forest Railway, Gloucestershire
9682	141	17 years 1 month	Southall Railway Centre, West London
30499	148	19 years 5 months	Mid-Hants Railway
30506	79	11 years 6 months	Mid-Hants Railway
30541	54	9 years 3 months	Bluebell Railway, Sussex
30825	181	22 years 5 months	Shipyard Services Ltd, Brightlingsea, Essex (Frames and wheels only)
30828	122	16 years 9 months	BREL Eastleigh Works, Hampshire
30830	192	22 years 9 months	Bluebell Railway, Sussex
30841	24	8 years 3 months	North Yorkshire Moors Railway
30847	95	14 years 4 months	Bluebell Railway, Sussex
31618	2	4 years 7 months	Bluebell Railway, Sussex
31625	111	15 years 9 months	Mid-Hants Railway
31638	114	16 years 1 month	Bluebell Railway, Sussex
31806	85	12 years 4 months	Mid-Hants Railway
31874	48	9 years 9 months	Mid-Hants Railway
34007	127	15 years	Plym Valley Railway, Devon
34010	140	17 years 2 months	Cargo Fleet, Teeside
34016	22	7 years 8 months	Mid-Hants Railway
34027	112	15 years 4 months	Severn Valley Railway, Shropshire
34028	171	21 years 5 months	Ashford Railway Trust, Sellindge, Kent
34039	33	7 years 4 months	Great Central Railway, Leicestershire
34046	207	22 years 7 months	Brighton Locomotive Works
34053	153	18 years 3 months	Hull Dairycotes
34058	175	21 years 3 months	Avon Valley Railway, Bitton
34059	108	13 years	Bluebell Railway, Sussex
34067	118	15 years 9 months	Mid-Hants Railway
34070	146	18 years 6 months	CEGB Richborough near Ramsgate, Kent
34072	158	19 years 8 months	Swindon Works (for eventual use on Swanage Railway)
34073	199	22 years 10 months	Brighton Locomotive Works
34081	86	11 years 7 months	Nene Valley Railway, Cambridgeshire
34092	17	6 years 7 months	Keighley and Worth Valley Railway, Yorkshire

Locomotive Number	Order of departure from Barry	Total time spent in scrapyard	Location
34101	92	11 years 9 months	Private Premises in Derby
34105	90	13 years 1 month	Mid-Hants Railway
35005	38	7 years 2 months	Great Central Railway, Leicestershire
35006	144	18 years 3 months	Gloucestershire Warwickshire Railway
35009	209	24 years 2 months	Brighton Locomotive Works
35010	160	17 years 10 months	Private Premises at Custom House, East London
35011	210	22 years 9 months	Brighton Locomotive Works
35018	110	15 years 3 months	Mid-Hants Railway
35022	170	19 years 5 months	Swanage Railway, Dorset
35025	169	21 years 2 months	Great Central Railway, Leicestershire
35027	142	15 years 9 months	Bluebell Railway, Sussex
35029	47	6 years 10 months	National Railway Museum, York
41312	63	6 years 7 months	Caerphilly Railway Society, Caerphilly, Mid-Glamorgan
41313	68	9 years 5 months	Buckinghamshire Railway Centre
42765	91	10 years 10 months	Keighley and Worth Valley Railway, Yorkshire
42859	183	19 years 6 months	Hull Dairycotes
42968	45	6 years 6 months	Severn Valley Railway, Shropshire
43924	1	2 years 11 months	Keighley and Worth Valley Railway, Yorkshire
44123	138	16 years 4 months	Avon Valley Railway, Bitton
44422	87	11 years 8 months	North Staffordshire Railway
44901	202	22 years 1 month	Wales Railway Centre, Cardiff
45163	184	21 years	Hull Dairycotes
45293	182	20 years 11 months	North Woolwich Station Museum
45337	152	18 years 4 months	East Lancashire Railway, Bury
45379	55	8 years 7 months	Avon Valley Railway, Bitton
45491	134	15 years 6 months	Fleetwood Locomotive Centre, Lancashire
45690	18	7 years 10 months	Severn Valley Railway, Shropshire
45699	113	14 years 11 months	Severn Valley Railway, Shropshire
46428	106	12 years 1 month	East Lancashire Railway, Bury
46447	20	5 years	Buckinghamshire Railway Centre
46512	41	5 years 11 months	Strathspey Railway, Invernesshire
46521	12	4 years	Severn Valley Railway, Shropshire
47279	101	12 years 2 months	Keighley and Worth Valley Railway, Yorkshire
47298	58	7 years 1 month	East Lancashire Railway, Bury
47324	89	10 years 8 months	Avon Valley Railway, Bitton
47327	6	2 years 6 months	Midland Railway Centre, Butterley, Derbyshire
47357	7	2 years 8 months	Midland Railway Centre, Butterley, Derbyshire
47406	147	16 years	Peak Rail, Buxton, Derbyshire
47493	27	5 years 5 months	East Somerset Railway
48151	77	7 years 2 months	On temporary loan to Midland Railway Centre, Derbyshire
48173	208	22 years 11 months	Avon Valley Railway
48305	168	17 years 2 months	Great Central Railway, Leicestershire
48431	19	7 years 9 months	Keighley and Worth Valley Railway, Yorkshire
48518	198	22 years 10 months	Wales Railway Centre, Cardiff

Locomotive Number	Order of departure from Barry	Total time spent in scrapyard	Location
48624	135	15 years 9 months	Peak Rail, Buxton, Derbyshire
53808	9	6 years 4 months	West Somerset Railway
53809	78	11 years 4 months	Midland Railway Centre, Butterley, Derbyshire
61264	83	7 years 10 months	Great Central Railway, Leicestershire
71000	53	6 years 6 months	Didcot Railway Centre, Oxfordshire
73082	107	12 years 11 months	Bluebell Railway, Sussex
73096	164	17 years 5 months	Mid-Hants Railway
73129	32	4 years 11 months	Midland Railway Centre, Butterley, Derbyshire
73156	177	18 years 8 months	East Lancashire Railway, Bury
75014	121	13 years 4 months	North Yorkshire Moors Railway
75069	37	5 years 10 months	Severn Valley Railway, Shropshire
75078	21	5 years 7 months	Keighley and Worth Valley Railway, Yorkshire
75079	139	14 years 11 months	Plym Valley Railway, Devon
76017	46	8 years	Mid-Hants Railway
76077	186	18 years 8 months	Gloucestershire Warwickshire Railway
76079	59	5 years 10 months	East Lancashire Railway, Bury
76084	143	14 years 4 months	Private Premises in South Leverton, Lincolnshire
78018	97	11 years 4 months	Private Premises in Darlington, Co Durham
78019	35	5 years 9 months	Severn Valley Railway, Shropshire
78022	67	8 years 3 months	Keighley and Worth Valley Railway, Yorkshire
78059	145	15 years 11 months	Bluebell Railway, Sussex
80064	34	7 years 4 months	Bluebell Railway, Sussex
80072	206	22 years 6 months	Swindon Heritage Centre
80078	84	10 years 3 months	Swanage Railway, Dorset
80079	13	5 years 4 months	Severn Valley Railway, Shropshire
80080	115	14 years 10 months	Midland Railway Centre, Butterley, Derbyshire
80097	162	19 years 4 months	East Lancashire Railway, Bury
80098	157	18 years 10 months	Midland Railway Centre, Butterly, Derbyshire
80100	94	12 years 9 months	Bluebell Railway, Sussex
80104	155	18 years 8 months	Swindon Heritage Centre
80105	44	7 years 9 months	Bo'ness and Kinneil Railway
80135	39	7 years 3 months	North Yorkshire Moors Railway
80136	102	13 years 2 months	North Staffordshire Railway
80150	196	22 years 1 month	Wales Railway Centre, Cardiff
80151	66	7 years 5 months	East Anglian Railway Museum, Chappel and Wakes Colne, Essex
92134	116	13 years 6 months	Shipyard Services Ltd, Brightlingsea, Essex
92207	180	21 years 7 months	East Lancashire Railway, Bury
92212	105	11 years	Great Central Railway, Leicestershire
92214	117	15 years 2 months	Peak Rail, Buxton, Derbyshire
92219	163	19 years 7 months	Peak Rail, Buxton, Derbyshire
92240	93	13 years	Bluebell Railway, Sussex
92245	195	22 years 11 months	Wales Railway Centre, Cardiff

ACKNOWLEDGEMENTS

The preparation of a book of this sort would have been impossible without the help of so many people and organisations. In particular I should like to thank the officials of various railway societies who have taken great trouble in searching out photographs and other information for me, as well as the staff at both the Public Record Office, Kew, who provided the GWR allocation registers for my inspection, and at the National Railway Museum, York, for their patience while I sifted through the wealth of information contained in their archives.

Among the individuals who have given help I must single out Steve Worrall whose personal involvement with Barry and many of the locomotive owning groups has made the task of trying to collect around 250 photographs featuring every one of the Barry engines that much easier. Other friends and enthusiasts who gave help in various ways are Graham Wignall, Murray Brown, Peter Skelton, David Lovegrove, Bill Trite and David Fletcher, while I must not forget Jackie Leiser who gave up a lot of her spare time to decipher and type my manuscript.

Finally I must give extra special thanks to my family who, after having to endure long periods of silence at home while I wrote the book, must have wished that Dai Woodham had cut all the locomotives up a long time ago!

BIBLIOGRAPHY

The Locomotives of the Great Western Railway – various parts (RCTS)

Engines of the LMS 1923–1951, P. Rowledge (OPC, 1975)

What Happened to Steam – various volumes, P. Hands

BR Standard Steam Album, Alan Williams (Ian Allan, 1980)

Bulleid Locomotives, Brian Haresnape (Ian Allan, 1977)

Collett and Hawksworth Locomotives, Brian Haresnape (Ian Allan, 1978)

Maunsell Locomotives, Brian Haresnape (Ian Allan, 1977)

Fowler Locomotives, Brian Haresnape (Ian Allan, 1972)

⸱⸱t and Riddles Locomotives, Brian Haresnape ⸱llan, 1977)

⸱ Locomotives, Brian Haresnape and ⸱llan, 1976)

Passengers No More, G. Daniels and L. Dench (Ian Allan, 1980)

An Historical Survey of GW Engine Sheds, E. Lyons (OPC, 1974)

The Barry List – various editions, (Urie S15 Preservation Group)

The Barry Album, P. Nicholson (1981)

Pre-Grouping Atlas and Gazetteer (Ian Allan)

Periodicals:
   Trains Illustrated
   The Railway Magazine
   Railway World
   Steam World
   Steam Railway
   Locomotives Illustrated
Various house magazines of the numerous preservation societies concerned.